FROM A CULTURE OF VIOLENCE
TO A CULTURE OF PEACE

Also in the Peace and Conflict Issues Series

Peace and Conflict Issues after the Cold War
Non-military Aspects of International Security

From a culture of violence to a culture of peace

Peace and Conflict Issues Series
UNESCO Publishing

The authors are responsible for the choice and the presentation
of the facts contained in this book and for the opinions expressed therein,
which are not necessarily those of UNESCO and do not commit the
Organization. The designations employed and the presentation of material
throughout this book do not imply the expression of any opinion whatsoever
on the part of UNESCO concerning the legal status of any country,
territory, city or area or of its authorities, or concerning the delimitation
of its frontiers or boundaries.

Published in 1996 by the United Nations Educational,
Scientific and Cultural Organization,
7 place de Fontenoy, 75352 Paris 07 SP, France
Composed by Éditions du Mouflon, 94270 Le Kremlin-Bicêtre, France
Printed by Presses Universitaires de France, Vendôme

ISBN 92-3-103290-9

© UNESCO 1996

Printed in France

Preface

In keeping with its mandate to construct the defences of peace in the minds of men and women, UNESCO publishes biennially a volume in the series Peace and Conflict Issues, prepared in consultation with the Advisory Board for this series.

The present publication brings together the reflections of eminent peace researchers, philosophers and jurists on the multiple facets of a culture of peace. It elucidates its very concept and examines normative bases and universally recognized moral and ethical principles. It shows that a common system of values grouped around such key notions as justice, human rights, democracy, development, non-violence and peaceful resolution of conflicts, and behavioural patterns are the essence of a culture of peace.

Whilst recognizing that the construction of a culture of peace is a long-term process, this volume dwells on the ways, means and partners necessary for its implementation, notably education, the media, intercultural dialogue and cultural pluralism. The sustained efforts of the whole international community – states, governmental and non-governmental organizations as well as individuals and civil society – are indispensable for the achievement of a culture of peace.

It is hoped that this book will provoke further reflection on this subject which will, in turn, make yet another contribution to the promotion of a culture of peace.

Contents

Constructing a culture of peace: challenges and perspectives – an introductory note
Janusz Symonides and Kishore Singh — 9

Peace behaviours in various societies
Elise Boulding — 31

Normative instruments for a culture of peace
Emmanuel Decaux — 55

Cultural peace: some characteristics
Johan Galtung — 75

Social and cultural sources of violence
Santiago Genovés — 93

Creating global/local cultures of peace
Linda Groff and Paul Smoker — 103

Towards a planetary code of ethics: ethical foundations of a culture of peace
Hans Küng — 129

Understanding and dialogue between religions to promote the spirit of peace
Félix Marti — 145

Gandhi on the moral life and plurality of religions
Mrinal Miri — 163

An Agenda for Peace and a culture of peace
Nazli Moawad — 177

The teaching of Martin Luther King for a culture of peace
Solomon M. Nkiwane — 195

The role of education for a culture of peace
Keith D. Suter — 209

Towards a culture of peace based on human rights
Marek Thee — 229

UNESCO and a culture of peace: promoting a global movement
UNESCO's Culture of Peace Programme — 251

ANNEXES

I. Declaration on the Role of Religion in the Promotion
of a Culture of Peace — 269

II. Advisory Board for UNESCO's series on Peace
and Conflict Issues — 273

Constructing a culture of peace: challenges and perspectives – an introductory note

Janusz Symonides* and Kishore Singh**

A CULTURE OF PEACE: A NECESSITY FOR OUR TIME

At the end of the twentieth century humankind is still confronted with numerous armed conflicts, with the illegal use of military force and with various forms of violence. Permanent and lasting peace and security still remain as a goal to be achieved, as they were fifty years ago at the moment of the creation of the United Nations system.

An analysis of the present situation leads to the conclusion that the main objective formulated in UNESCO's Constitution half a century ago, namely the construction of the defence of peace in the minds of men and women, is more than ever valid. Indeed, 'a peace based exclusively upon the political and economic arrangements of governments would not be a peace which could secure the unanimous, lasting and sincere support of the peoples of the world . . . and peace must therefore be founded, if it is not to fail, upon the intellectual and moral solidarity of mankind'.

In a world where many regions suffer from increasing tensions, conflicts and violence, to make peace a tangible reality is of critical importance. Ethnonationalism, xenophobia, racism and discrimination against minority groups, religious extremism and violations of human rights are the cause of an increasing number of local and regional conflicts. Violence fuelled by hate and directed

---

*   Director of UNESCO's Division of Human Rights, Democracy and Peace.
** Programme Specialist in the same Division.

against non-nationals, refugees and asylum-seekers, and immigrant workers is a serious threat to domestic security and the very fabric of states themselves. At the same time, exclusion, poverty, urban decay, mass migration, environmental degradation and new pandemic diseases, as well as terrorism and traffic in drugs, create very real threats to internal and international security.

The present culture of violence based on distrust, suspicion, intolerance and hatred, on the inability to interact constructively with all those who are different, must be replaced by a new culture based on non-violence, tolerance, mutual understanding and solidarity, on the ability to solve peacefully disputes and conflicts. The world is in need of such a new culture and of a common system of values and new behavioural patterns for individuals, groups and nations, for, without them, the major problems of international and internal peace and security cannot be solved.

The end of the Cold War and of ideological confrontation between East and West created new possibilities for the United Nations system and for the whole of the international community to move towards a culture of peace. Not only has the threat of a global nuclear war been removed to a great extent but the role of the military factor in international relations is decreasing. This, in consequence, paves the way towards disarmament and demilitarization both internationally and internally and towards the elimination of enemy images, distrust and suspicion. Moreover, the sharp divisions and useless debates concerning the concept of human rights are being replaced by recognition that the promotion and protection of all human rights is an important element of peace and development and, as such, is a great concern of the international community as well as a priority objective of the United Nations.

The process of transition towards democracy is another factor conducive to the construction of a culture of peace. Democracies, as proved by historical experience, not only do not make war against each other but also through their systems of governance – rule of law, participation, transparency and accountability – diminish considerably recourse to violence.

In the new international atmosphere, UNESCO has undertaken a series of activities aimed at the promotion of a culture of peace. It is worth noting that the first call to work in this direction was formulated in July 1989 by the

Constructing a culture of peace: challenges and perspectives – an introductory note

UNESCO International Congress on Peace in the Minds of Men, held in Yamoussoukro, Côte d'Ivoire, which in its declaration proposed to 'help construct a new vision of peace by developing a peace culture . . .'.

At its 140th session in 1992, the UNESCO Executive Board discussed the contribution to be made towards the promotion of a culture of peace, in the light of the United Nations Secretary-General's *An Agenda for Peace*.[1] It decided that an action programme should be established to promote a culture of peace, in particular by strengthening and co-ordinating ongoing activities.

As declared by Federico Mayor, Director-General of UNESCO, at the opening session of the Forum for Education and Culture held in San Salvador, El Salvador, on 28 April 1993, the underlying spirit of a culture of peace is to:

- promote the apprenticeship and practice of a culture of peace, both in the formal and non-formal education process and in all the activities of daily life;
- build and strengthen democracy as a key to a just and peaceful negotiated settlement of conflicts;
- strive towards a form of human development which, with the participation of the entire population, values the social capabilities and the human potential of all members of society;
- give pride of place to cultural contacts, exchanges and creativity, at national and international levels, as a means of encouraging recognition of respect for others and the ways in which they differ; and
- strengthen international co-operation to remove the socio-economic causes of armed conflicts and wars, thereby permitting the building of a better world for humankind as a whole.

In accordance with the resolutions of the twenty-seventh session of the General Conference in 1993, an initial programme was prepared for 1994–95 providing, *inter alia*, the elaboration of two or three country projects aimed at the creation of a climate conducive to reconciliation in countries torn by war or civil strife and where United Nations peace-keeping operations had been or are being

---

1. *An Agenda for Peace*, 2nd ed., New York, United Nations, 1995.

conducted. Such pilot projects were established in El Salvador, Mozambique and Burundi.[2]

Another important step forward was made in 1995 when the twenty-eighth session of the General Conference adopted a transdisciplinary project, 'Towards a Culture of Peace'. This project comprises four parts:

- Education for peace, human rights, democracy, international understanding and tolerance.
- Promotion of human rights and democracy and the struggle against discrimination.
- Cultural pluralism and intercultural dialogue.
- Conflict prevention and post-conflict peace-building.

The implementation of this project will involve all the sectors of the Organization. It will also require increased co-operation with Member States, institutions and organs of the United Nations system, regional and intergovernmental organizations, the relevant non-governmental organizations and the intellectual community.

This present volume of the UNESCO Peace and Conflict Issues Series, *From a Culture of Violence to a Culture of Peace,* should be seen as an example of such co-operation with the intellectual community. Its main purpose is to enable a group of eminent peace researchers, philosophers and jurists to present their views on the 'concept' of a culture of peace, on a common system of values, on ways and means to construct it through the partners and networks which are so vital for its promotion.

THE MAIN CONCEPTUAL ELEMENTS OF A CULTURE OF PEACE

The term 'culture' may be used both in a wide and in a restricted sense. In the wider meaning, 'culture' concerns the sum of human activities, the totality of knowledge and practice, whereas in the restricted sense 'culture' is understood

---

2. A detailed presentation is given in this volume by the UNESCO Culture of Peace Programme, 'UNESCO and a Culture of Peace: Promoting a Global Movement' (p. 251).

Constructing a culture of peace: challenges and perspectives – an introductory note

mainly as the result of creative activities and the highest intellectual achievements, such as music, literature, art or architecture.

A culture of peace should be understood in the broader sense. Such understanding is formulated by several UNESCO documents. The Recommendation on Participation by People at Large in Cultural Life, 1976, explains 'that culture is not merely an accumulation of works and knowledge which an élite produces . . . but is at one and the same time the acquisition of knowledge, the demand for a way of life and the need to 'communicate'. Similarly the World Conference on Cultural Policies (1982) stressed that the term 'culture' was understood by the delegates as 'ways of thinking and organizing people's lives'. Therefore 'culture' is not only a knowledge of certain values but also an adherence to them and a readiness to defend and follow them in everyday life. Thus a culture of peace should be understood as the creation of peaceful, non-violent behavioural patterns and skills.

This aspect is emphasized by Johan Galtung[3] who, in his reflections on ethical, sociocultural and legal dimensions of a culture of peace, underlines the need to enhance paxogenes and pacify bellogenes. As he argues, 'the test of the validity of a culture of peace lies in how it affects behaviour in conflict'.

Elise Boulding[4] analyses behavioural dynamics of 'peaceableness' in selected contemporary societies which set a high value on non-aggression and non-competitiveness. She stresses a need to lay emphasis on the cultural context of peaceful behaviour in everyday life – partnership, family life, celebrations and rituals, trade and exchange, all of which can contribute to peace and non-violence. There is no human occupation which cannot be 're-turned' to peace-building.

Nevertheless, one fundamental question concerning human nature is pertinent. Are human beings capable of peace? The view that man is the source of all evil, including war, has a long tradition. Its advocates include, among others, St Augustine, Hobbes, Luther, Spinoza, Malthus and Freud.

Contemporary research conducted by psychologists, biologists, educators and sociologists does not confirm the thesis about man's unappeased and irresistible drive for war. This position is taken in *The Seville Statement on Violence*,

---

3. See, in this volume, 'Cultural Peace: Some Characteristics' (p. 75).
4. See, in this volume, 'Peace Behaviours in Various Societies' (p. 31).

adopted in 1986 by a meeting of a group of well-known scientists organized by UNESCO, who challenged the biological pessimism based on alleged human aggressiveness which is so frequently used to explain or even to justify war.

Recalling the Statement, Santiago Genovés[5] deals with anthropological and sociological dimensions of a culture of peace. His analysis demonstrates that violence is neither part of our evolutionary legacy nor in our genes; it is in our sociological and cultural roots. Moreover, there is nothing in the neurophysiology of human beings which compels them to react violently and it is possible to create a culture of peace founded on their natural pacific behaviour patterns.

Aggressive behaviour does not stem from human nature but is either a result of a process of education or a response to a painful stimulus. Individuals are normally ready to adapt to their environment and, under normal circumstances, prefer co-operation to aggressiveness. They are also capable of self-control, of love, friendship and tolerance. In the process of their upbringing, these dispositions can be developed.

As the culture which we are discussing here is that of peace, there is a need to elucidate this notion. The word peace has a variety of meanings in different contexts.

In international affairs, it is employed to denote relations between states. Elsewhere, it is associated with internal conditions in a country, in a society, between groups, organizations and social structures or between man and his natural environment. In ethics or morality, the word 'peace' is used to characterize human relationships and attitudes or to determine an individual's frame of mind, often qualified as 'inner peace'. Given its various applications, the term is polysemantic, by its very nature avoiding a univocal definition. In the law of nations, 'peace' denotes the contrary of war, which is most frequently defined as a resort to armed struggle and hostilities. A war is a factual state, an attempt to solve disputes and conflicts and to achieve domination through armed force and violence.

---

5. See, in this volume, 'Social and Cultural Sources of Violence' (p. 93).

Constructing a culture of peace: challenges and perspectives – an introductory note

In general there are two understandings of peace: the 'negative', narrow understanding, reducing peace to a mere absence of war; and the 'positive', defining peace as a lack of war often enriched by further elements and guarantees which make peace constructive, just and democratic. In its second sense, peace is not a static state but a dynamically conceived aim of international and national communities.

What are the main, indispensable values on which a positive peace can be built? As the first preambulary phrase of the Universal Declaration of Human Rights states, 'the recognition of the inherent dignity and of the equal and inalienable rights of all members of the human family is the foundation of freedom, justice and peace in the world'. The Yamoussoukro Declaration proposed to base a peace culture 'on the universal values of respect for life, liberty, justice, solidarity, tolerance, human rights and equality between women and men'. If we add democracy, development, burden-sharing and responsibility as well as non-violence and peaceful resolution and transformation of conflicts, the list can be seen as relatively exhaustive.[6]

All these values may be grouped around such key notions as justice, human rights, democracy, development, non-violence and peaceful resolution of conflicts. Though their underlying message appears clear, their interpretations are nevertheless not free from controversy.

As Linda Groff and Paul Smoker[7] observe, a concept of non-violence, for example, has different meanings in different cultural and political contexts. Different interpretations of non-violence can be advanced: non-violence as any action to prevent war, non-violence as action to maintain a system, structural non-violence and holistic inner and outer peace and non-violence.

A culture of peace cannot be built during the arms race and militarization

---

6. During the twenty-eighth session of the General Conference on 31 October 1995, the Group of 77 adopted the Paris Declaration which, in paragraph 10, states: 'We attach high priority to promoting a culture of peace, which includes freedom from all forms of economic and social deprivation, poverty, social injustices, such as exclusion and discrimination, and redresses flagrant asymmetries of wealth and opportunity, both within and between countries.'
7. See, in this volume, 'Creating Global/Local Cultures of Peace' (p. 103).

of societies which unavoidably generate enemy images, suspicions and threats. Therefore disarmament and demilitarization are conditions *sine qua non*. Positive peace assumes not only absence of war but also absence of the instruments and institutions of war.[8] In this context, Keith Suter[9] suggests that a culture of peace must completely reshape the military-industrial complexes built during the Cold War period, sustained by scientists, media and trade unions. One possibility is linked with military conversion.

The diminishing role of military factors, resulting in disarmament and demilitarization, gives new importance to non-military dimensions of security. This applies in particular to the notion of 'human security' introduced in the *Human Development Report 1994*, presented by the United Nations Development Programme (UNDP). Indeed, the human being must be considered as the central subject and ultimate beneficiary of all efforts aimed at the creation of a common and co-operative system of security. 'Human security' in particular implies the right to live in dignity. This cannot be achieved simply through the implementation of political and civil rights but also through that of economic, social and cultural rights, including the right to development.[10]

A culture of peace is intimately linked with a culture of human rights and democracy. Peace cannot be preserved if the basic rights and fundamental freedoms of individuals or groups are violated and when discrimination and exclusion generate conflict. Therefore the protection of human rights and the promotion of a culture of democracy which imply, *inter alia*, the formation of well-informed, democratically-minded and responsible citizens become important elements for the construction of internal and international peace.

---

8. Asbjorn Eide, 'Methods and Problems in Peace Research', *International Social Science Journal*, Vol. 24, No. 1, 1974, pp. 121–2.
9. See, in this volume, 'The Role of Education for a Culture of Peace' (p. 209).
10. See Janusz Symonides and Vladimir Volodin, 'Concept and New Dimensions of Security: Introductory Remarks', *Non-military Aspects of International Security*, pp. 9–21, Paris, UNESCO, 1995. (Peace and Conflict Issues Series.)

Constructing a culture of peace: challenges and perspectives – an introductory note

A NORMATIVE BASIS FOR A CULTURE OF PEACE

An analysis of the concept of a culture of peace shows that it cannot be achieved without normative bases and universally recognized moral and ethical principles. Such norms and values are necessary for all levels of peace relations between states, groups and individuals.

The question at this moment is: do we already have certain elements of these normative bases and shared values or is this only a postulate? Fortunately the former is indeed true.

As regards inter-state relations, international law has outlawed aggression and use of force. States are duty-bound, according to the provisions of Article 2 of the Charter of the United Nations, to 'settle their international disputes by peaceful means in such a manner that international peace and security are not endangered'.

The United Nations Charter provides for a system of collective security: in cases of threats to peace, or acts of aggression, the Security Council of the United Nations is invested with the authority to take the necessary measures. It can, in the last resort, legitimately use force for restoring or maintaining international peace and security.

However, the fact that present-day conflicts are preponderantly intra-state or internal points to the need for adjusting the structure of the United Nations to permit adequate reaction to new challenges. The effectiveness of the United Nations action is primarily determined by the will of Member States. This inevitably poses the question of the acceptance of the limitation of state sovereignty. Further reflection on the concept of domestic jurisdiction, on the acceptance of the supremacy of international law, as well as on a new interpretation of the principle of non-interference in internal affairs, is needed to increase the possibility of effective United Nations action in cases of internal conflicts and massive violations of human rights.

A number of instruments also exist for promoting peaceful relations between different groups. Thus Article 20 of the International Covenant on Civil and Political Rights (1966) condemns incitement to war, the advocacy of national, racial or religious hatred and any form of discrimination, hostility or violence. Furthermore, states parties to the International Convention on the Elimination of All Forms of Racial Discrimination (1965) undertake to adopt immediate and positive measures to eradicate all incitement to, or acts of, racial discrimination.

The Declaration on the Preparation of Societies for Life in Peace, adopted by the United Nations General Assembly (1978), stipulates certain duties and obligations for states in order to promote peace and calls upon all states to discourage and eliminate incitement to racial hatred, national or other discrimination, injustice or advocacy of violence and war.[11]

As regards inter-human relations, the international law of human rights embodies relevant values, norms and principles. States are duty-bound, as the World Conference on Human Rights declared, to implement universally recognized human rights and fundamental freedoms, to develop and encourage respect for these, without distinction as to race, sex, language or religion.

The Vienna Declaration and Programme of Action stresses that:

> All human rights are universal, indivisible and interdependent and interrelated. The international community must treat human rights globally in a fair and equal manner, on the same footing, and with the same emphasis. While the significance of national and regional particularities and various historical, cultural and religious backgrounds must be borne in mind, it is the duty of States, regardless of their political, economic and cultural systems, to promote and protect all human rights and fundamental freedoms.

Human rights instruments also provide monitoring procedures for which the treaty bodies are responsible. Procedures for safeguarding human rights and for examining alleged cases of their violation exist at both regional and global levels. Besides, there are also national mechanisms in the form of constitutional or administrative tribunals, ombudsmen, commissions, etc. However, these procedures, cannot be seen as being fully satisfactory. There is an obvious need to increase their effectiveness.

As Marek Thee's[12] analysis shows, human rights instruments as a standard-setting guide already provide a framework for a new, just and peaceful world order. A culture of peace must be viewed in its interface with democracy and

---

11. J. Symonides, 'Education for Peace', *Bulletin of Peace Proposals*, No. 2, 1980, pp. 234–41.
12. See, in this volume, 'Towards a Culture of Peace Based on Human Rights' (p. 229).

Constructing a culture of peace: challenges and perspectives – an introductory note

paramountcy of the rule of law. In the context of positive peace theory, one must focus on social development and on the normative bases of the right to development and the right to peace as solidarity rights.[13]

Emmanuel Decaux's[14] contribution underlines the primacy of international law and universal human rights and elucidates existing legal frameworks and positive obligations for a culture of peace. By examining the formulation of substantive provisions in relevant instruments, Decaux brings into focus what he calls 'struggles against a culture of hate'.

Further work on the normative framework for a culture of peace is of vital significance. It must recognize various critical issues: the need to strengthen domestic laws, to favour legal harmonization at the regional level and to encourage co-operation between states in the fight against increasing crime. A legal framework must be comprehensive in providing both negative and positive obligations which must be rooted in the conscience of each person and take into account all levels of human relations. It must involve all possible actors, from grass-roots associations to universal organizations, in a spirit marked by legal pluralism.

A culture of peace includes, by definition, an ethical dimension and principles of solidarity, burden-sharing as well as respect for each other's culture and moral values. This must be recognized as being essential. The normative bases should be complemented and enriched by moral or ethical principles.

The question of global ethics is therefore intimately linked with the normative bases for a culture of peace. Hans Küng[15] pleads for a minimal consensus for the emergence of world global ethics. In this, religions, by virtue of their moral and spiritual values, can give men and women a supreme norm of conscience. Küng suggests that, in the formulation of a planetary code of ethics, four

---

13. United Nations General Assembly Resolution 2037 (XX) of 7 December 1965. For an analysis of United Nations instruments and legal nature of right to peace, see Adrian Nastase, 'The Right to Peace', in Mohammed Bedjaoui (ed.), *International Law: Achievements and Prospects*, Dordrecht/Paris, Martinus Nijhoff Publishers/UNESCO, 1992, pp. 1219–29.
14. See, in this volume, 'Normative Instruments for a Culture of Peace' (p. 55).
15. See, in this volume, 'Towards a Planetary Code of Ethics: Ethical Foundations of a Culture of Peace' (p. 129).

irrevocable directives are useful, necessitating fourfold commitments: to a culture of non-violence and respect for life; to a culture of solidarity and a just economic order; to a culture of tolerance and a life of truthfulness; and to a culture of equal rights and partnership between men and women.

WAYS AND MEANS TO CONSTRUCT A CULTURE OF PEACE

Education

Education is at the heart of any strategy for the construction of a culture of peace. It is through education that the broadest possible introduction can be provided to the values, skills and knowledge which form the basis of respect for peace, human rights and democratic principles. It is an important means to eliminate suspicion, ignorance, stereotypes and enemy images and, at the same time, to promote the ideals of peace, tolerance and non-violence, and mutual appreciation among individuals, groups and nations. Education should not only strengthen the belief that peace is a fundamental value of humankind and create a non-violent mentality, but also mould an attitude of involvement and responsibility for matters relating to peace at the local, national, regional and global levels.

The obligation of states to develop education for peace and human rights is already well established in international law. The Universal Declaration of Human Rights was the first instrument which, in its Article 26, paragraph 2, laid down that:

Education shall be directed to the full development of the human personality and to the strengthening of respect for human rights and fundamental freedoms. It shall promote understanding, tolerance and friendship among all nations, social or religious groups, and shall further the activities of the United Nations for the maintenance of peace.

This formulation was repeated in Article 4 of the Convention against Discrimination in Education (1960) and Article 13 of the International Covenant on Economic, Social and Cultural Rights (1966). The obligation to provide education for peace and human rights is formulated in a more developed form

Constructing a culture of peace: challenges and perspectives – an introductory note

in Article 29 of the Convention on the Rights of the Child (1989) which, *inter alia*, requires the preparation of the child for a responsible life in a free society in the spirit of understanding, peace, tolerance, equality of sexes, and friendship among all peoples, ethnic national and religious groups and persons of indigenous origin.

The special role and the importance of broadly understood education is emphasized by the United Nations Declaration on the Promotion among Youth of the Ideals of Peace, Mutual Respect and Understanding between Peoples (1965). It calls upon governments, non-governmental organizations and youth movements to fulfil by all means of education the postulate to bring up young people in the spirit of peace, justice, freedom, mutual respect and understanding.

Since its inception, UNESCO has devoted itself to promoting education for peace and human rights. In this effort a special role is played by the Recommendation concerning Education for International Understanding, Co-operation and Peace and Education relating to Human Rights and Fundamental Freedoms (1974). It calls upon Member States to take steps to ensure that the principles of the Universal Declaration of Human Rights become an integral part of the developing personality of each child, adolescent, young person or adult, by applying these principles in the daily conduct of education at each level and in all forms. Member States should encourage a wider exchange of textbooks, especially those concerning history and geography, and should take measures for the reciprocal study and revision of textbooks and other educational materials in order to ensure that they are accurate, balanced, up-to-date, without prejudice, and enhance mutual knowledge and understanding between different peoples.

The 44th session of the International Conference on Education (October 1994) adopted a declaration which underlines the great responsibility incumbent not only on states and intergovernmental and non-governmental organizations, but also on all members of society as a whole, to work together with those involved in the education system so as to achieve full implementation of the objectives of education for peace, human rights and democracy and to contribute in this way to sustainable development and to a culture of peace.

The long-term goal which UNESCO has set up in its Medium-term Strategy (1996–2001) is the establishment of a comprehensive system of education and training for peace, human rights and democracy that is intended for all groups of people and embraces all levels of education, both formal and non-formal.[16]

Inspired by this goal, the Organization will collaborate with governments in framing national policies, plans, programmes and strategies aimed at the development of peace education. It will foster the elaboration of manuals, textbooks and teaching aids, as well as introducing innovative approaches and providing support to Member States concerning the revision of school textbooks, so as to remove any prejudices or stereotypes *vis-à-vis* other nations or vulnerable groups. In addition, UNESCO will further strengthen and develop its co-operation and partnership with teaching and research institutions and networks.[17]

It is worth noting that the fiftieth session of the United Nations General Assembly (December 1995) adopted a resolution: the United Nations Decade for Human Rights Education: Culture of Peace, which welcomes the adoption of the UNESCO transdisciplinary programme 'Towards a Culture of Peace', and in particular Unit 1, 'Education for Peace, Human Rights, Democracy, International Understanding and Tolerance'. The resolution encourages countries, regional organizations, non-governmental organizations and the Director-General of UNESCO to take all necessary action to ensure such education.

---

16. In 1993–95 the international community adopted a number of plans and programmes which are the basis of UNESCO's activities aimed at the development of education for peace, human rights and democracy: the World Plan of Action on Education for Human Rights and Democracy (Montreal, 1993), the Declaration and Programme of Action of the World Conference on Human Rights (Vienna, 1993); the Declaration on Education for Peace, Human Rights and Democracy and the Integrated Framework of Action (adopted by the International Conference on Education in Geneva in 1994 and approved by the UNESCO General Conference in 1995) and the Plan of Action for the United Nations Decade for Human Rights Education (1995–2004).
17. These networks embrace: Associated Schools Project (now 3,000 schools in 125 states); Associated Universities Project; UNESCO Chairs for Peace, Human Rights and Democracy (eighteen in 1995), Annual Meetings of Directors of Human Rights Institutes.

Constructing a culture of peace: challenges and perspectives – an introductory note

The media

It is commonplace to say that the media, along with education, now exert a predominant influence on the forging of attitudes, judgements and values, that they create images and often determine the relation to 'others'. A dramatic example of the devastating impact that the media has on human behaviour was given in Rwanda, where the broadcasting of hatred incited genocide. Similarly, in former Yugoslavia the media had their share in the incitement to ethnic cleansing and war crimes. One can also find encouraging cases of the positive influence of the media on the process of reconciliation, as in El Salvador and Mozambique.

The importance of the media for the promotion of peace is broadly recognized by international organizations, which have adopted a number of normative instruments dealing with this subject. The first of them, the International Convention concerning the Use of Broadcasting in the Cause of Peace was already adopted by the League of Nations in 1936.

In 1978 the General Conference adopted the UNESCO Declaration on Fundamental Principles concerning the Contribution of the Mass Media to Strengthening Peace and International Understanding, to the Promotion of Human Rights and to Countering Racialism, Apartheid and Incitement to War.

The Declaration states that the strengthening of peace and international understanding demands a free flow and a wider and better balanced dissemination of information. Article II defines the essence and content of the mass media contribution:

In countering aggressive war, racialism, apartheid and other violations of human rights which are, *inter alia,* spawned by prejudice and ignorance, the mass media, by disseminating information on the aims, aspirations, cultures and needs of all peoples, contribute to eliminate ignorance and misunderstanding between people, to make nationals of a country sensitive to the needs and desires of others, to ensure the respect of the rights and dignity of all nations, all peoples and all individuals without distinction of race, sex, language, religion or nationality. . . .

An analysis of the text of the Declaration allows us to conclude that the concept of freedom of information is fully preserved. It does not call for state control or censorship but refers rather to deontology, to professional organizations of educators and journalists.

UNESCO is fully aware of the role played by warmongering propaganda and incitement to hatred in triggering and aggravating conflicts and encourages the action of the media in defending the values of peace and mutual understanding. The Organization sees the media as an important tool for reconstructing civil societies torn apart by conflict, and as crucial to the re-establishment of social bonds and to the reconciliation process.

Freedom of information, plurality of the media, their independence and free democratic access are recognized as necessary conditions but, at the same time, important guarantees of their positive contribution to the shaping of human minds, and propagation of peace and friendship.

The disturbing invasion of 'violence on the screen' cannot be countered by simple censorship and state control. Only by negative reactions and rejection by viewers can their message of violence be abandoned. Another solution may be found in the production of interesting, attractive programmes promoting positive values of non-violence, tolerance and mutual understanding. This is an important challenge for literature, theatre, cinema, graphics and music. The success of rock concerts against racism and xenophobia is a good example of an artistic potential which may be used for the promotion of a culture of peace.

Cultural pluralism and intercultural dialogue

In a world in which the crisis of cultural identities, discrimination and violation of the cultural rights of national, ethnic, religious or linguistic minorities, migrants and indigenous peoples are among the major sources of conflict, recognition of cultural diversity becomes one of the most important factors in their resolution and management. It is worth noting that the states parties to the Convention on the Rights of the Child agreed that education shall be directed to: 'The development of respect for the child's parents, his or her own cultural identity, language and values, for the national values of the country in which the child is living, the country from which he or she may originate, and for the civilizations different from his or her own' (Article 29(c)). Thus the very idea of the recognition and respect of cultural diversity and pluralism is well formulated.

Since its foundation, UNESCO has striven to develop dialogue between cultures as an essential element of peace-building strategy. By encouraging exchanges between the world's prominent cultures and by helping newly independent countries to affirm their cultural identity, the Organization has helped to promote broad awareness of fruitful diversity. The international cultural co-operation which has developed under the impetus of the Organization has helped to bring out the concept of the 'common heritage' of humankind, to make many cultures better acquainted with one another and to promote cultural diversity and cultural interaction, which should be seen as the best way to eliminate prejudices and stereotypes and to promote mutual understanding and confidence.

PARTNERS IN A CULTURE OF PEACE

Global partnership is vital for bringing about a culture of peace. The importance of broader co-operation was stressed by the Yamoussoukro International Congress on Peace in the Minds of Men, which invited states, intergovernmental and non-governmental organizations, the scientific, educational and cultural communities of the world and all individuals to help construct a new vision of peace.

The United Nations

The United Nations, which was created with the main purpose of maintaining international peace and security, has a central role in this domain. During the last fifty years, it has undertaken numerous activities aimed at restoring and maintaining peace and these are being currently reinforced. The work of the United Nations Organization linked with peace-keeping and peace-building have become multifunctional, with co-ordinated programmes for eradicating the original causes of conflict.

The United Nations Secretary-General's *An Agenda for Peace* presented a broad framework and addressed the questions relating to preventive measures as well as post-conflict peace-building. It attached primary importance to action to be undertaken to eliminate sources of conflict which develop in a context of marked social injustice and in the absence of democratic approaches to the resolution of conflicts, as well as the absence of mutual respect for each other's cultures. Recognizing that the sources of conflict and war are pervasive and deep, *An Agenda for Peace*[18] called for the utmost efforts of the international community to enhance respect for human rights and fundamental freedoms, to promote sustainable economic and social development for wider prosperity.

Viewing a culture of peace in its interface with *An Agenda for Peace*, Nazli Moawad[19] put forward the idea that 'the transition from a culture of war to a culture of peace calls for a new approach to conflicts', so that our natural response to conflict would be non-violence. This new approach to a culture of peace implies a shift in the paradigm of peace studies and presents certain dilemmas of a culture of peace: growing cross-cultural conflicts, poor understanding of diversity and the transformation of perceptions of conflict.

Furthermore, the United Nations Secretary-General's *An Agenda for Development*[20] also addressed peace concerns in a development perspective; it acknowledged that only sustained efforts to resolve underlying socio-economic, cultural and humanitarian problems can place peace on a durable foundation.

Intergovernmental and non-governmental organizations

In addition to the United Nations and its Specialized Agencies, intergovernmental and non-governmental organizations must be seen as being important among global partners for creating a culture of peace. Their role has been discussed in the contribution to this volume by the Culture of Peace Programme.[21] One must in particular mention the role of the Council of Europe in promoting respect for cultural identities and cultural pluralism which will pave the way for peaceful relations among communities and peoples.

It is also worth noting that the objectives of the United Nations Year for Tolerance (1995) are to 'educate, inform and empower individuals to assume the responsibilities of dialogue, mutual respect, toleration and non-violence, and to encourage pluralism and tolerance in the policies of Member States'. This

---

18. See note 1 on page 11.
19. See, in this volume, '*An Agenda for Peace* and a Culture of Peace' (p. 177).
20. United Nations document A/48/935.
21. See 'UNESCO and a Culture of Peace: Promoting a Global Movement' (p. 251).

assumed the participation of many institutions and societies, with UNESCO as the lead agency. The follow-up programme for the Year will create a broad coalition, involving wide-ranging actors: Member States, the United Nations system, National Commissions for UNESCO, intergovernmental and non-governmental organizations, municipalities and other actors in public and private life.

States

States have a significant role to play in constructing a culture of peace pursuant to their obligations under international law. Observance and promotion of human rights, democracy and peace primarily calls for state action. Implementation of socio-economic and cultural policies is indispensable for creating conditions for a culture of peace. This is of particular importance in adopting relevant legislative measures and policy mechanisms and in encouraging non-governmental organizations and various members of civil society in their endeavours for a culture of peace.

The intellectual community

The intellectual community in particular deserves to be mentioned among global partners for a culture of peace. UNESCO is co-operating with institutes, associations and research centres, including the International Peace Research Association (IPRA). Peace researchers, jurists, sociologists and scientists can provide valuable analyses, perceptions and perspectives.

In this respect, it is pertinent to mention the Recommendation on the Status of Scientific Researchers, adopted by the General Conference in 1974, which stipulates that

Member States should recognize that scientific researchers encounter, with increasing frequency, situations in which the scientific research and experimental development on which they are engaged has an international dimension; and should endeavour to assist scientific researchers to exploit such situations in the furtherance of international peace, co-operation and understanding, and the common welfare of mankind.

Religions

Religions have a great potential for contributing to a culture of peace. As observed by Felix Marti,[22] religions, understood in their true spirit, can make a valuable contribution to a culture of peace. It is important to reinforce the sanctity of great religious values, and the wisdom of non-violence, thus developing conduct which can deactivate the spiral of violence.

In this respect, as Mrinal Miri[23] shows, Gandhi's contribution to inter-religious harmony and to a culture of non-violence is of paramount importance. Religion for Gandhi meant 'a belief in ordered, moral governance of the Universe'. As his life demonstrated, the power of *ahimsa* (non-violence) is incomparably superior to that of violence.

Following in the footsteps of his mentor Mahatma Gandhi, Martin Luther King embraced non-violent direct action in his civil rights campaign to fight segregationist practices and the evils of racism, as Solomon Nkiwane[24] observes. This was a reaffirmation of the Gandhian philosophy that non-violence evokes the most noble and courageous of human qualities.

In this context, it is befitting to mention the Declaration on the Role of Religion in the Promotion of a Culture of Peace, adopted at a meeting organized in December 1994 by UNESCO and the Centre UNESCO de Catalunya, Barcelona (Spain), where the participants spoke with one voice to spread the message of peace in a violence-riven world. The Declaration has demonstrated that the dialogue with eminent religious figures has a great potential for contributing to UNESCO's ethical mission. An increasing number of its adherents have committed themselves to resolving or transforming conflicts and to building 'a culture of peace based on non-violence, tolerance, dialogue, mutual understanding and justice'. The Declaration, which is the first of its kind with regard to religion and a culture of peace, has thus helped create a network bringing

---

22. See, in this volume, 'Understanding and Dialogue between Religions to Promote the Spirit of Peace' (p. 145).
23. See, in this volume, 'Gandhi on the Moral Life and Plurality of Religions' (p. 163).
24. See, this volume, 'The Teaching of Martin Luther King for a Culture of Peace' (p. 195).

together eminent religious figures, peace researchers, educators and human rights activists for constructing a culture of peace.

CONCLUSIONS

As stated by Federico Mayor, prevention of conflict and building of peace is a long-term process which should address threats to global security at their very roots. We must incorporate in our everyday behaviour attitudes forged through the entire educational process.[25]

A profound transformation of the international community, leading to the elimination of causes of conflict and violence, is by no means an easy task. The replacement of the existing culture of violence by a culture of peace, human rights and democracy can only be achieved in a longer perspective.

By elaborating a transdisciplinary programme on a Culture of Peace for 1996–2001, UNESCO has given impetus to this process. However, the construction of a culture of peace is a task which, in fact, would continue through the next century, far beyond the Medium-Term Strategy.

Experience shows that, though political and economic changes may be rapid, cultural changes, in particular changes in behavioural patterns of individuals, groups and nations, take time. A culture of peace can be achieved only when all potential partners are fully engaged in its realization.

Though the establishment of national programmes for reconciliation and conflict resolution is possible, nevertheless, because we are living in an interdependent world, such culture cannot be set up only in one country or one region. These programmes must be holistic. The construction of a culture of peace assumes a comprehensive approach, both from the point of view of values as well as of the ways and means. The contributors to this volume share these common concerns. They underline the universal nature of a culture of peace. Some of them have delved into the concept of a culture of peace, others into the

---

25. Introductory speech to the debate, 'Towards a Culture of Peace, Human Rights and Democracy through Education for All', during the 44th session of the International Conference on Education, Geneva, October 1994.

manner to achieve it, and yet others have concentrated on the partners of this collective endeavour.

As an attempt to elucidate the concept of a culture of peace, this volume responds to the need expressed by the 145th session of the UNESCO Executive Board (1994) in discussions on the Programme and Budget for 1994–95 and the Medium-Term Strategy (1996–2001).

The richness of the present volume lies not only in the reflections on the multiple facets of a culture of peace but also in making certain constructive suggestions for future work.[26] It is hoped that it will provoke further reflection by researchers, educators and the intellectual community on the very concept, and on the norms and shared values on which a culture of peace is based, and thus contribute to its further promotion.

---

26. Thus, Keith Suter suggests that UNESCO's National Commissions could create a media peace award, using UNESCO's culture of peace as a criterion. Emmanuel Decaux suggests that UNESCO could set up a watchdog committee for cultural rights and a culture of peace, with a resource list of independent experts and rapporteurs and a public assessment of individual or collective claims in regard to violations of cultural rights. Hans Küng proposes that the UN or UNESCO establish a consultative committee to elaborate a first draft of a planetary code of ethics.

Peace behaviours in various societies

Elise Boulding *

HUMANS AS NURTURERS, OR HUMANS AS AGGRESSORS? DILEMMAS AND CONTRADICTIONS IN CONTEMPORARY SOCIETIES

Given the high levels of reported local and national inter-ethnic and intercultural violence and high levels of military preparedness for inter-state violence on every continent, and the images reflected back to each society by the media and images of violence pervading every polity, not only is the present portrayed as violent but the historical record is written as the story of conquest and war from earliest times. The fact that most human activity revolves around raising and feeding families and organizing the work of production and of meeting human needs, interspersed with times of feasting and celebration of human creativity in poetry, song, dance and art, does not show through in our media depictions. Pervasive images of human aggression sap our confidence in the human capacity to create a peaceful international order as we move toward the twenty-first century.

Yet a closer inspection of the historical record, the bias towards reporting wars notwithstanding, reveals a much richer tapestry of human activities. The remarkable historical undertaking of Werner Stein's *Kulturfahrplan,* translated as *The Timetables of History,*[1] is a brave beginning on a fuller account of the range of

---

* Member of Conflict Resolution Consortium, University of Colorado, Boulder, Colorado, USA. This paper was prepared with the help of Patricia Lawrence, graduate student in the Department of Anthropology at the University of Colorado.
1. See Bernard Grun, *The Timetables of History* (based on Werner Stein's *Kulturfahrplan*), New York, Simon & Schuster, 1975.

human doings over time. *Timetables* tabulates events year by year from A.D. 501 (and by half-centuries before that starting at 4000 B.C.). The column entries for the year-by-year record include (1) history and politics, (2) literature, theatre, (3) religion, philosophy, learning, (4) visual arts, (5) music, (6) science, technology, growth and (7) daily life. Column (1), listing the battles and kingdoms won and lost, is the fullest, but the other columns get fuller over time, recording peaceful human activities in civilian society.

That humans are conflict-prone, however, is undeniable. The social ubiquity of conflict stems from the basic fact of human individuality and difference in the context of limited physical and social resources. Conflict itself should not be confused with violence, which is taken here to mean the intentional harming of others for one's own ends. The differences in wants, needs, perceptions and aspirations among individuals and among groups, stemming from individual uniqueness, require a constant process of conflict management in daily life at every level from the intrapersonal (each of us has many selves), the family and the community, to the international community. What keeps this unceasing process of conflict management largely peaceful is the equally ubiquitous need of humans for one another, for social bonding and nurturing, without which no society could function.

Hans Hass[2] has undertaken a remarkable documentation of the universality of human responsiveness to other humans. Travelling around the world with his camera he has photographed a series of expressive human gestures of smiling, greeting with glad surprise (eyebrows raised), comforting another in grief by having the griever's head resting on the comforter's shoulder, a reaching-out gesture to protect a child in danger, in settings as far apart as France, Kenya and Samoa. In cultures which practise disciplined control over such expressive gestures, one finds their fullest expression in children who have not yet learned the discipline. Hass points out that children learn early how much a smile can do. Why do we humans smile so much? – 'because we are not, basically, unfriendly creatures. Thus our smile is a means of eliciting contact readiness

---

2. Hans Hass, *The Human Animal: The Mystery of Man's Behaviour*, New York, G. P. Putnam's Sons, 1970.

with others and of conveying our accessibility to contact'.[3] A smile serves as a social bridge-builder.

This universal need for bonding can be thought of as the key to the survival of the human species. It is what draws humans toward negotiating with one another in the face of conflicting interests, needs, perceptions, whether in settings of family, neighbourhood, workplace or public institutions. The historical fact of war and social violence tells us, however, that negotiation is not the only response to conflict. In fact we may think of responses to conflict as falling on a conflict-management continuum that ranges from destruction of the adversary through mediating-negotiating behaviours to complete union with the other (Fig. 1).

FIG. 1. The conflict-management continuum.

Some societies tend toward the aggressive end of the continuum in their behaviours, others toward the integrative, with many societies falling somewhere in the middle. The historical reasons why different groups pattern their responses to conflict differently lie beyond the scope of this paper, but it is useful to remember that former warrior societies have been known to change and adopt more peaceful ways. It is also true that warrior societies of the past have all had images of living in peace.

Every religion has a vision of a peaceful kingdom. The Greeks pictured Elysian fields, where heroes hung their swords and shields on trees and walked arm in arm, discoursing on philosophy and poetry. The Hebrew Bible gives us Zion, the holy mountain where the lion shall lie down with the lamb and none shall hurt nor destroy. The Koran gives us the sanctuary in the desert, from

---

3. Hass, op. cit., p. 123.

which no one shall be turned away. Even in Valhalla, the warriors who fought each other by day feasted and sang together at night in the great hall of Asgard, drinking mead from a cup that never ran dry.[4]

The wars of ancient China did not prevent Chang Huen-Chu from writing these words: 'Heaven is the Father and Earth the Mother . . . wherefore all included between Heaven and Earth are one body with us and in regard to our dispositions, Heaven and Earth should be our teachers. The People are our brothers and we are united with all things.'[5] The persistence of imagery of 'peaceableness' in the midst of war tells us something about an underlying human longing for peace, about the enduring capacity of the human imagination to visualize the other and better, and the resilience of the bonding impulse even as violence rages all around.

The longing for peace would not be of much use if it could not be translated into the skills of peace-building, however. Here it is instructive to look at an example in the recent historical past of a warrior society turned peaceful: the transformation of the Vikings, the 'scourge of Europe', into the architects not only of the most peaceful region in Europe, Scandinavia, but also as the designers of a set of diplomatic strategies and social institutions important for the development of a peaceful international order. The skills of negotiation developed in the pre-Viking institution of the Thing, the gatherings of landholders to make decisions by consensus, were centuries later discovered to be more useful than the forcible rule of conquered territories, in what became the Danelaw areas of Britain. Similarly, negotiated trade turned out to be more productive than simple pillaging. This new awareness also led to the eventual abandoning of the conquest of Russia and of involvement in the imperial wars of seventeenth- and eighteenth-century Europe. The choice of a peaceful separation of Norway from Sweden in 1905, even though both sides had been armed for war, was a notable example

---

4. References for mythic images of the good society in warrior cultures may be found in Elise Boulding, 'The Dynamics of Reshaping the Social Order: Old Actors, New Actors', in Selo Soemardjan and Kenneth Thompson (eds.), *Culture, Development and Democracy*, p. 203, Tokyo, UNU Press, 1994.
5. Leonard Tomkinson, *Studies in the Theory and Practice of Peace and War in Chinese History and Literature*, Shanghai, Friends Centre, Christian Literature Society, 1940.

of a new style of diplomatic initiatives which was important in the evolution of the League of Nations and its successor, the United Nations.[6]

CULTURAL CONTEXTS FOR PEACEFUL BEHAVIOUR IN EVERYDAY LIFE

The historical record on war/fighting, even if it greatly exaggerates the actual human experience of violence in everyday life, nevertheless makes clear that there are strong cultural values associated with physical dominance and conquest in both tribal and imperial societies. One of the strongest sources for the cultural legitimization of war lies in the teachings of each of the major religions. The holy war culture is a male warrior culture headed by a patriarchal warrior god. In the Hebrew Bible, the Israelites were enjoined to fight bravely in taking possession of the Promised Land and not to turn back, because Jehovah was at the head of their army. In the Koran, Allah enjoined *jihad*, or holy war for faithful Muslims in defence of *dar al-Islam* against its enemies. From the eleventh to the thirteenth century, many European Christians felt called by God to fight the holy war of the crusades, to liberate the Holy Land from Muslims. In the eighteenth century, Japanese Zen Buddhist warrior monks fought for their warlords as part of their spiritual discipline.

Yet in each of these same religions, there are strong teachings about dealing with differences through patience, forgiveness, reconciliation and love. The other face of God is the loving face, of a God who protects the weak, a God who is

---

6. This vastly oversimplified account of a very complex history does not even touch on the special qualities of local democracy in Scandinavia once slavery was abolished, on renewed acknowledgement of an older tradition of strong roles for women, on the fostering of community education programmes that led to high levels of literacy at the local level. See Gro Steinsland and Preben Meulengracht Sorenson, *Menneske og makter i vikingines verden*, Oslo, Universitsforlaget, 1994; Judith Winther, 'Kriegens unnodvendighed, den nordiske unionstrid 1905', *Vandkunsten*, No. 4, 1990, pp. 6–20. Note also a critical essay suggesting that Sweden, at least, may not continue its role as model peace-making state, by Hans Mouritzen, 'The Nordic Model as a Foreign Policy Instrument: Its Rise and Fall', *Journal of Peace Research*, Vol. 32, No. 1, 1995, pp. 9–21.

served through prayer, self-discipline and the doing of good to all God's creatures. These other teachings emphasize an equal partnership between women and men in family and society, give an important place to the nurturing and mediation skills of women and set a high value on the skills of peace-making.

At the grass-roots level, the social bonds of kinship and intergroup alliances, and the need for mutual aid systems in order to survive, whether in inner cities or on overstressed farmlands, are strengthened by these gentler religious teachings. It may be said that women's culture shares with religious culture a primary-level responsibility for the well-being of a people. Women's cultures everywhere are the source of the work of nurturing a society, a reservoir of experience and knowledge in the bearing and rearing of children, in the healing of the sick, in the growing, processing and actual serving of food, and in the providing of clothing and shelter. Traditionally women have had the more difficult role in marriage partnerships through the widespread practice of women moving to the male partner's community and being expected to serve as communication channels and conflict resolvers when differences between the communities arise. It is very often women, therefore, who have had the most experience in doing the background work for negotiation and mediation.

The role of infants and young children in the gentling of the human species is often understated. Adults everywhere tend to respond to infants with smiles and modulated voices. Watching small children discover with delight the most ordinary and humdrum items of daily existence literally refreshes adults, as does seeing children at play, creating a wondrous world of imagination which has no purpose but itself.

Through most of human history people have lived in rural settings and in small-scale societies. Just as each familial household develops its own problem-solving behaviour, so each social group has developed its own strategies of conflict resolution over time, uniquely rooted in local culture and passed on from generation to generation. Similarly each society has its own fund of adaptability, built on knowledge of local environment and the historical memory of times of crisis and change. Such knowledge and experience are represented in familial households as they are organized into communities. The knowledge is woven into religious teachings, ceremonies and celebrations; it is present in women's culture, in the world of work and the world of play, in environmental lore, in the memory of the past. These are the hidden peace-building strengths of every society.

As societies become more complex, and élites become differentiated from 'common people', centre-periphery problems based on mutual ignorance develop. Élites not only cease to share locally based knowledge but cease literally to share a common language with locals. Traditional conflict-resolution methods then break down, and new ones are slow to develop during prolonged periods of transition. Since, in this last decade of the twentieth century, there are only 185 states in the world, and '10,000 societies'[7] – ethnic, religious and cultural groups with significant historical identity – this breakdown of communication and lack of common conflict management practices between ethnic groups and the larger states of which they are a part is one of the major problems contributing to current levels of intra-state as well as inter-state violence. Rediscovery of the hidden strengths of local cultures is one important aspect of peace-building for this painful transitional period in contemporary history.

Given the diversity of negotiation and conflict-resolving behaviours that go on every day in every household and every community in the 185 states of the present international order, how can everyday peace behaviour be illustrated? This will be handled here in two ways. First, the character and dynamics of everyday peace behaviour will be highlighted by choosing societies that set a high value on 'peaceableness', and examining how they go about their conflict-managing/avoiding interactions as adults, and how they train their children in such behaviour.[8] Next we shall take a more general look at peace behaviours to be found in societies in general, and those common elements underlying wide differences in cultural patterns. The advantage of beginning with societies which

---

7. The '10,000 societies' is a term sometimes used by anthropologists to refer to the large number of separate ethnic groups spread across the globe. Estimates of the actual number of societies range from 5,000 to 7,000, varying according to the criteria used for counting.
8. I have drawn heavily on the very fine survey of anthropological studies of peaceful societies, prepared by Bruce D. Bonta and published as *Peaceful Peoples: An Annotated Bibliography* (Metuchen, N.J., The Scarecrow Press, 1993), in making choices on what people select and what social practices are most significant in generating societal 'peaceableness'. I wish to express my appreciation here for his outstanding work.

are known to be peaceful is that this approach offers behavioural specificity. It highlights the strategies and skill-based nature of peaceful behaviour, and its dependence on an explicit set of values about non-aggression. Only after that shall we go on to see how every family in every society in fact gives some degree of skill training to children to achieve the accepted norms of conflict resolution behaviour, whatever they may be. This is the basic process of socialization at work.

In this pursuit of discovering local strengths in 'peaceableness', we shall examine peace behaviours in two types of societies which are alive and functioning at the present time: (1) small pre-industrial societal groups that maintain a distinctive identity and yet also have some degree of contact with the larger world and its urban centres, and (2) inter-faith Irish and North American Anabaptist 'peace church' communities that function actively within industrial core societies but have distinctive ways of life which mark them as separate subcultures within those societies.

THE BEHAVIOURAL DYNAMICS OF 'PEACEABLENESS' IN SELECTED CONTEMPORARY SOCIETIES

The societies selected here set a high value on non-aggression and non-competitiveness, and therefore handle conflict by a variety of non-violent means. The four tribal societies to be examined are the Inuit of the Canadian part of the Circumpolar North, the Mbuti of the north-eastern rainforests of Central African Zaire, the Zuni of the desert Southwest of the United States and the mountain-dwelling Arapesh of New Guinea. Each has distinctive ways of child-rearing which produce distinctive adult behaviour, but they vary in the degree to which these skills are conflict-suppressing or conflict-resolving and in the degree to which the skills are based on a strongly dichotomous in-group/out-group way of thinking in relation to neighbouring peoples. Where there is a strong dichotomous sense, people are free to be aggressive towards outsiders and are only expected to be peaceful in their own community. Where attitudes are more inclusive of other peoples, peaceful behaviour is extended to outsiders.

The Inuit

The Inuit live in the Circumpolar North, spread out from eastern Siberia through Greenland and Canada to Alaska, surviving a harsh and unforgiving winter cold through co-operation and social warmth, a warmth which extends to the baby animals that children bring home from the icy outdoors to cuddle. Violence and aggression are under strong social prohibition. The social values are centred on (1) *isuma*, which involves rationality, impulse control, thinking problems through calmly and being able to predict consequences of behaviour, and (2) *nallik*, which is love, nurturing, protectiveness, concern for others' welfare, and total suppression of hostility.

The distinctive child-rearing which produces these rational, compassionate, controlled adults revolves around what Briggs[9] calls 'benevolent aggression'. This involves an unusual combination of warm affection for infants and a complex kind of teasing which creates real fear in children and then teaches them to laugh at their fears. The title of one of Briggs' studies, *Why Don't You Kill Your Baby Brother?*, suggests the extremes to which the teasing goes, seen from a Western perspective. That it works, in the sense that it produces people with both *isuma* and *nallik*, and a remarkably peaceful society, I would ascribe to the fact that young children are far more socially perceptive, far more sophisticated in their assessment of social situations, than adults usually give them credit for,[10] and that they figure out what is going on and learn to respond creatively. Although it is a tricky kind of socialization that one can imagine going wrong with some individuals, it does make children self-reliant problem-solvers with a well-developed sense of humour, affectionate, and acutely aware of the disciplined anger-control processes going on inside themselves and others. Girls and boys

---

9. Jean Briggs, *Never in Anger: Portrait of an Eskimo Family*, Cambridge, Harvard University Press, 1971. See also Briggs, 'The origins of non-violence: Inuit management of aggression', in Ashley Montagu (ed.), *Learning Non-aggression: The Experience of Non-literate Societies*, pp. 54–93, New York, Oxford University Press, 1978.
10. Susan Isaacs, *Intellectual Growth in Young Children*, London, Routledge & Kegan Paul, 1930. Note also Elise Boulding, 'The Nurture of Adults by Children in Family Settings', in Helen Lopata (ed.), *Research in the Interweave of Social Roles*, Greenwich, Connecticut, Jai Press, 1980.

get the same type of socialization and Inuit men and women are equally resourceful. There is also a parallel process of much fondling of infants and arctic baby animals, much food-sharing and communal eating, a lot of laughter and playfulness. This unusual combination of affection and teasing seems to lead to a high level of conflict awareness and an equally high level of skill in problem-solving. The skill of handling conflict playfully, as in song duels (or drum matches) between offended parties, and other similar rituals, produces enjoyable public events rather than battles.

There is no basic we/they, in/out dichotomy, so the conflict management skills are in theory extendible to conflict with non-Inuits. Conflicts with less aware parties such as the Canadian Government suggest limits to this. In recent years the Inuit have suffered much from forced government resettlement projects and now have their share of problems with unemployment and accompanying dysfunctional behaviour. However, it is also noteworthy that there is now an Inuit who is Canada's first Circumpolar Ambassador, Mary Simon. With her colleagues in the Council of Arctic Peoples, she is showing the hidden strengths and resourcefulness of traditional Inuit culture by applying them to the protection of the fragile arctic environment and the creation of new spaces for reconstructed ways of life to enable the Inuits to maintain a viable society.[11]

The Mbuti

The Mbuti are hunter-gatherer, rainforest-dwelling pygmies in north-eastern Zaire who have long had periodic contact with Bantu villagers, and who have been movingly described by Turnbull.[12] The basis for their peacefulness is their relationship to the rainforest – their mother, father, teacher and metaphoric womb. The family hut is also symbolically a womb. Children grow up listening to the trees, learning to climb them early so they can sit high above the ground,

---

11. Clyde H. Farnsworth, 'Envoy Defends World of Eskimo', *New York Times*, 22 February 1995.
12. Colin Turnbull, *The Forest People,* New York, Simon & Schuster, 1961. See also Turnbull, 'The Politics of Non-aggression', in Ashley Montagu (ed.), *Learning Non-aggression: The Experience of Non-literate Societies*, pp. 161–221, New York, Oxford University Press, 1978.

listening to wind and waving branches. Mbuti is a listening culture, but also a singing and dancing culture, as adults and children sing to and dance with the trees. *Ekimi*, quietness, is highly valued, as opposed to *akami*, disturbance. This preference for quietness and harmony is reinforced at every stage of life, yet does not preclude children's rough-and-tumble play, and a lot of petty squabbling among adults, which tends to be controlled by ridicule. While children are slapped to control forbidden activities and nuisance behaviour, they are also taught interdependence and co-operation. Adults seem to enjoy horseplay and noisy disputes. Semi-humorous 'sex wars' in which men and women line up for a tug of war between the sexes serve as tension dissipaters, as the tugs of war break up with much laughter. They are also an indication of the companionable equality between women and men. Most groups have a 'clown', one person whose antics also help keep conflicts from getting out of hand. For all the squabbling, disagreements rarely get serious.

The contrast between the forest as womb and the love of the silences of the forest on the one hand, and the frequency of arguing and the use of joking and ridicule to keep it under control on the other, is an interesting one. The Mbuti themselves value 'letting it all hang out' in modern parlance, not letting conflicts fester. There seems to be a nature-based social equilibrium here, based on a combination of listening, singing, dancing and squabbling not easy for Westerners to understand.

The Mbuti, like the Inuit, face a modernizing national government which is destroying their environment and require adaptation to the limit of their capability, but the Mbuti 'we' is an inclusive we. This suggests a potential for some degree of long-term survivability, as they link with other rainforest peoples in the new transnational indigenous peoples networks, but the destruction of their lifestyle before other adjustments can be worked out is a very serious threat.[13]

---

13. In 1991, the first representative of the Central African Forest Peoples made his way to Geneva to create a linkage with the UN Working Group on Indigenous Populations. Since then the newsletter of the International Work Group for Indigenous Affairs (IGWIA) has been reporting increasingly on the activities of the African rainforest peoples. A linkage with other rainforest peoples took place during the 1993 International Year of the World's Indigenous Peoples. See the *IGWIA Newsletters* (Copenhagen), Nos. 2 and 3, 1993.

The Zuni

The Zuni live in the arid mountain canyon country of western New Mexico in the United States, many of them on a Zuni Indian reservation. A matrilineal society noted for its peaceful ways of life, its arts and crafts and its antipathy to overt violence, the Zuni are well-known through the writings of Ruth Benedict.[14] As with the Mbuti, the love of harmony is based on a sense of oneness with nature and a sense of place, yet that love of harmony does not preclude habits of gossip and quarrelling.

The war gods who once ensured tribal survival in a period of warfare are now thought to be channelling their sacred energy into the peaceful well-being of the Zuni. Earlier in-group/out-group attitudes which kept that warfare going are no longer salient. The culture devalues authority, leadership and individual success. No one wants to stand out. There are rituals for sharing, for healing, for conflict resolution, which help children to learn appropriate group behaviour. Problem-solving skills are highly developed but without any counterpoint of individualism. There is a continued skill transmission of the remarkable environmental knowledge which enabled a rich Zuni culture to develop in a very arid environment, including traditional agricultural and irrigation practices that are only now coming to be understood by Westerners as representing a very sophisticated technology.

Children, after a very permissive and nurturant infancy, are disciplined by masked demons who make an appearance to scold them for fighting. Sudden withdrawals of goodies by adults prepare children for social obedience and non-aggressive behaviour. Zuni youth therefore do not respond well to the incitements to achievement and competition in use by teachers in Zuni schools, although group performance levels are high. The economic, social and political influences the Zuni have been exposed to in the past half-century have emphasized the Zuni

---

14. Note the following: Ruth Benedict, *Patterns of Culture*, Boston, Houghton Mifflen, 1959; Irving Goldman, 'The Zuni Indians of New Mexico', in Margaret Mead (ed.), *Co-operation and Competition among Primitive Peoples*, pp. 313–53, New York, McGraw Hill, 1937; John Whiting et al., 'The Learning of Values' in Evon Vogt and Ethel Albert (eds.), *People of Rimrock: A Study of Values in Five Cultures*, pp. 83–125, Cambridge, Mass., Harvard University Press, 1967.

value system and have increased local conflict levels. However, the traditional Zuni skills of co-operation are reasserting themselves in recent, very interesting tribal developments, including the launching of a comprehensive Sustainable Resource Development Plan built on a combination of traditional and new scientific knowledge, which is expected to initiate a renaissance of the Zuni way of life.[15]

The Arapesh

The mountain-dwelling Arapesh are one of many tribes living in the highly diverse archipelago of New Guinea. Much has changed since Margaret Mead's study of them in 1930[16] and it should be clear that it is the 1930s Arapesh being described here. This people had in common with the North American Zuni a distaste for standing out, a preference for conformity, and a rejection of violence within the community. This rejection is, however, accompanied by actual hostility towards outsiders and little emphasis on dealing with conflicts in a problem-solving way.

Arapesh children grow up experiencing co-operation as the key mode of life. All tasks are group tasks. Any one household will plant many yam gardens, each with a different group. We now know that this represents a very sophisticated adaptation to a region with great diversity in soil quality and many micro-climates at different altitudes in a bewildering variety of micro-ecosystems. Spreading the risk of poor crop yields over many garden plots planted in different locations at different times during the year ensures that there will be some food at all times.

The major negative factor in the society is fear of sorcery, which is thought to come from outside enemies who have somehow got hold of an individual's personal 'dirt'. Even nature-caused crop failures are thought of as sorcery-induced. There are no gradations in social relations, only friends (insiders) and enemies (outsiders). This leaves the Arapesh without any patterns for incorporating the

---

15. For an account of new Zuni developments, see Derek Denniston's 'High Priorities: Conserving Mountain Ecosystems and Cultures', *Worldwatch Paper,* No. 123, February 1995, pp. 50–1.
16. Margaret Mead, 'Sex and Temperament', *Three Primitive Societies,* New York, Mentor Books, 1950.

other, the different, the stranger, into their lives. This has made them very vulnerable in the turbulent struggles between tribes, against present and former colonial authorities, and against powerful mining companies destroying the mountain environments through open-pit copper and gold mining.

In the four peace-valuing societies we have looked at so far, we have seen a pattern of basic nurturing and sharing behaviour experienced from childhood. Sex-role differentiation has been minimal. However, there has been considerable variation in the ways conflict is managed, from avoidance and suppression, as among the Zuni and Arapesh, to acknowledgement and socialization for managing conflict, as with the Inuit and Mbuti. But all the societies, at the times their behaviour was recorded, were living in relative isolation from the urban and industrial centres of their respective countries. Now we turn to two cultures located within politically modernized states, the rural Irish of Northern Ireland, and the Anabaptist cultures of the historic peace churches in the United States, both rural and urban.

The rural Northern Irish

Some of the rural communities of Ulster exemplify the possibility of non-violence emerging from violence. Extremes of physical aggression experienced in urban areas are rejected by both contending parties, Catholic and Protestant, in some rural areas. In the communities described in Bonta's collection of studies,[17] the Protestants have abandoned their former 'superior' socio-economic status for a more egalitarian stance *vis-à-vis* the Catholics, and communities of both faiths work very hard at developing many joint activities. They deliberately form non-sectarian groups, to prevent the religious polarization prevalent elsewhere in Ulster. They have very self-consciously chosen bridge-building across cultural and religious differences. Joint activities for children and youth as well as adults are carefully planned. Hostile behaviour is quickly dealt with in the interests of community harmony. Social, economic and cultural functions which involve co-operation of Catholic and Protestant farmers and business people are given high priority, and people strongly value good neighbourly relations. When violence

---

17. Bonta, op. cit., note 8.

does occur, it is blamed on outsiders. While locally inclusive in their peace-building, they are threatened and vulnerable in the face of the larger-scale violence taking place in the region. The success of current negotiations in the 1990s between the two parts of Ireland and the United Kingdom may depend on the extent to which other areas are willing to accept these peaceful inter-faith communities as role models for relations on a larger scale.

The Anabaptist historic peace church communities

Anabaptism has its roots in sixteenth-century movements, originating in the Swiss Alps, to defy all outward authority (including infant baptism, which forcibly incorporated each new-born child into the local religious power structure). These movements lived under Christ's authority alone, abjuring all violence as Christ taught. This unusual combination of medieval Christ-mysticism, Reformation social protest and absolute, early Christian pacifism spread through Europe. It resulted in seventeenth-century (and later) migrations to the Americas in search of religious freedom, and freedom from military service. The three main communities presently active in the United States, known as the historic peace churches, are the Brethren, the Mennonites and the Quakers. Other smaller communities include the Amish, the Doukhobors, the Moravians and the Hutterites. We will focus here on the three major Anabaptist communities. Traditionally abstaining from political action because of their rejection of military service,[18] they have nevertheless become increasingly involved in various types of public activity to remove social and economic injustice and to bring an end to war as an instrument of state policy. In the Second World War, the three faith communities co-operated to administer Civilian Public Service Camps for their own young men and other conscientious objectors, as an alternative to military service.

All three communities define themselves as living 'in the world but not of it', holding to testimonies of simplicity, gender and racial equality and personal

---

18. Although Pennsylvania was a colony founded by Quakers who originally constituted a majority in the colony's legislative assembly, the issue of voting appropriations to fulfil military obligations to the King during the French and Indian Wars led most Quakers to resign from the legislature in the later years of the Colony.

and social non-violence, yet finding themselves an increasingly urban and middle-class professional population compared to their earlier, more rural origins. Their challenge is not only to develop strategies for living their witness, but increasingly in the twentieth century they have sought to find ways to work for their vision of a 'peaceable kingdom' on earth and to rear their children to carry on efforts for the social transformation of an increasingly violent larger society.[19]

The three faiths differ in degrees of hierarchical authority, with the Quakers as the most egalitarian, having no 'hireling shepherds' (as ministers are traditionally referred to among Quakers).[20] All three faiths stress democratic participation of all members, including women, and decision-making at the local level. Quakers, however, in the absence of authoritarian figures, developed a special consensus approach to decision-making based on the 'sense of the Meeting', as members sought divine guidance on what was to be done in the face of sometimes conflicting views of participating individuals. While consensus is specifically Quaker, the educational practices described here are also common among Mennonites and Brethren.

Anabaptist testimonies begin in the home. While individual families certainly fall short of the ideal, spouse relations are to be based on a full and equal partnership and parenting is taken seriously by both parents. An important part of parenting is the cultivation of the divine seed in each child, so times of silent worship in the home, as well as discussion and reading, help prepare children for their responsibilities. Explicit training in non-violent responses to conflict, and alternative ways of dealing with conflict, are emphasized. Conflict suppression is not encouraged. Rather, children are urged to 'work things out'. All this is in the context of an affectionate family life and a nurturing local Meeting. 'The chief enjoyment of Friends is connubial bliss', wrote an eighteenth-century observer

---

19. Among studies on the Anabaptist communities, see James Juhnke, *Vision, Doctrine, War: Mennonite Identity and Organization in America*, Scottdale, Pa., Herald Press, 1989, 3 vols.; Duane Friesen, *Christian Peace-making and International Conflict*, Scottdale, Pa., Herald Press, 1986; Elbert Russell, *The History of Quakerism*, New York, Macmillan, 1992.

20. During the nineteenth-century evangelical revival in the United States, a certain number of Quaker meetings shifted to the more usual pattern of having ministers, to cope with rapidly growing numbers of adherents.

of Quakers, and while divorce takes its toll in every religious community today, Anabaptist families on the whole have a lot of fun together. On the other hand, Anabaptist adults, and children too, also carry a certain load of guilt. Given their acceptance of responsibility for peace and justice in the world, and the reality of the huge gap between what any individual, family, or Meeting can do and what is needed, guilt is inevitable. A healthy family and a healthy Meeting keep a sense of humour about this. Laughter is an important safety valve. So are imagination and skill in organizing useful local service projects which can absorb individual energies creatively.

An important institution in the local communities of all three faith groups is the Sunday School (called First-Day School by Quakers), where adults of the congregation do their best to supplement the work of member families in preparing children and young people, spiritually, intellectually and in terms of social skills, for peace-making. Community history, and the stories of Quaker, Mennonite and Brethren heroes and heroines are an important part of this education.

While the forms of worship of the three faith communities are different, all three have a strong emphasis on family life, on individual spiritual development and on training for social service and peace-building. All three have developed remarkable service bodies which do peace-building around the world, and Brethren and Mennonites are particularly strong in non-violence training for their youth, prior to giving a year or more of service in the United States or abroad. The Children's Creative Response to Conflict Program,[21] now used in elementary to middle schools in a number of countries, was first developed by Quakers to help children deal with conflict. A similar programme, Alternatives to Violence, was developed to prepare prisoners for post-prison life. Each faith supports outstanding schools and colleges which educate young people who seek an active and committed social learning.

Because all three Anabaptist communities are committed to being in the world but not of it, and to the work of social transformation toward peace and justice for all peoples, training for dealing creatively with conflict is an important

---

21. The Children's Creative Response to Conflict Program is now housed with the Fellowship of Reconciliation, Box 271, Nyack, NY 10960.

value. 'Enemy' concepts are not used, neither is the language of fighting. There can be no enemies, only strangers with whom a relationship needs to be developed. Peace-making is seen as building bridges across differences, finding solutions to the problems of all disputants in ways which injure none, and reframing disputes so that common interests can be discovered.

The world sometimes overwhelms the sense of faith-based identity, and individuals can feel hopelessly compromised by the world they are trying to change. The three historic peace churches formed the coalition 'New Call to Peacemaking' several decades ago, in order to strengthen each others' resolve to carry on peace-making activities. Currently they jointly support the training and deployment of unarmed peace teams to go into situations of serious violence in Africa and Central and Latin America.

PEACE BEHAVIOURS THAT CAN BE FOUND IN ANY SOCIETY

Micro-societies such as we have been examining, which take peace and non-violence as primary organizing values for their way of life, are rare in the closing years of the twentieth century. Most of humanity lives in societies marked by increasingly high densities of weaponry, from handguns to bombs to the terrors of chemical and biological weapons. But underneath the layers of violence, each society, without exception, has its peace behaviours, precious resources that could be available to help bring about new and more peaceful forms of governance locally and on a larger scale in the next century.

Where do we find these peace behaviours, these peace culture resources? In the recurring cycles, rhythms and rituals of human celebration, with its feasting, singing, dancing and sharing of gifts; in the reproductive cycles of human partnering, of birth, of lifelong everyday chores and the completion of dying, which bind people together across kin groups; in the succession of wounding and healing of human bodies as they move through life's dangers in those cycles; in the labour to produce sustenance from the earth; in the daily round of trade, barter and exchange of goods and services; and perhaps most wonderful of all, in human play, the playing of games, the play of artistic creation, the play of the mind in pursuit of knowledge.

Celebrations are the play-life of a society, as well as occasions for reaffirmation of identity and social values.[22] But play by its very nature performs a serious creative function for each community, as Huizinga[23] has pointed out. Taking place outside the realm of everyday life, play nevertheless creates boundaries, rules and roles ('let's play house – you be Daddy and I'll be Mummy'), and structures within which children can create their own realities in fantasy. Mary Reilly[24] emphasizes the importance of play in learning non-violence and self-control. Watching young monkeys at play, she comments on 'the conversion of aggression into social complexity', as the monkeys learn control over their movements in the course of rough-and-tumble activity. When children's rough-and-tumble dissolves into tears because a child is hurt, the same learning is taking place. A society which encourages the play of the mind encourages the exploration of other and better ways of ordering lifestyles. Polak, the Dutch historian, discovered through his macro-historical studies that societies tended to be empowered by positive images of the future, that visions themselves could act as magnets drawing forth behaviours which could bring the envisioned future into being.[25] Polak wrote *The Image of the Future* in 1950 for a war-paralysed Europe, as a call to begin imagining how things could be, to create visions which could inspire action. A half-century later we have once more reached a state of social despair, in both countries of the North and of the South. What are the possibilities for the twenty-first century?

---

22. For examples, see McKim Marriott, 'The Feast of Love', in Milton Singer (ed.), *Krishnna: Myths, Rites and Attitudes*, Chicago, Ill., University of Chicago Press, 1968. See also Richard Lannoy, *The Speaking Tree: A Study of Indian Culture and Society*, London, Oxford University Press, 1971.
23. Johan Huizinga, *Homo Ludens: A Study of the Play Element in Culture*, Boston, Mass., Beacon Press, 1955.
24. Mary Reilly (ed.), *Play as Exploratory Learning*, Beverly Hills, Calif., Sage Publications, 1974.
25. Fred Polak, *Images of the Future*, translated from Dutch by Elise Boulding, one-volume abridgement, San Francisco, Calif., Jossey-Bass/Elsevier, 1972.

PEACEFUL SOCIETIES IN THE TWENTY-FIRST CENTURY: A POSSIBLE SCENARIO

Kenneth Boulding always used to say that 'what exists is possible'. We have shown in the preceding pages that peaceful behaviours do indeed exist in every society, and that a few societies, and some subcultures within larger societies, actually give peace a high priority. They value 'peaceableness' so much that they have found ways to handle conflicts without violence. Energies which might be channelled into aggression are instead channelled into a range of non-violent activities.

As societies become more complex, there are more occasions for violence at least in part, because equitable sharing of resources becomes more difficult as the scale of social organization increases. Social systems which systematically direct resources away from the poor, from women, from ethnic and religious minorities, are systems characterized by what peace researchers call structural violence. While it is the behaviour of individuals which maintains the systemic injustice, individuals do not specifically intend harm by the way they live. Yet because much harm is done, the conditions for aggressive and violent responses to injustice may be widespread. This is why Anabaptists and other pacifists in contemporary industrialized societies spend so much of their energy working on social and economic injustice.

We should note that this picture of energetic activist pacifists contradicts the prevailing image of pacifists as passive, non-reactive people with an incomprehensible predilection for turning the other cheek. In the four peace-loving tribal societies described, there is a lot of activity going on – not only to keep interpersonal relations in order, but to provide sustenance while maintaining the integrity of the environment. Each of these societies, including the forest-dwelling Mbuti, has to 'struggle' to survive, but the struggle is a non-violent, problem-solving struggle.

Pacifist communities such as the Anabaptists are also characterized by non-violent struggle, in this case not primarily for the survival of their own community but for the survival of the planet. A more realistic image of the non-violent way of life would be one of adventure, a constant taking on of difficult challenges, a life requiring great ingenuity, imagination and problem-solving skills, a life based on a capacity for self-discipline coupled with a great fund of affection for the human species and a love of nature and all living things. Such an image is at least as exciting as the warrior-hero image, and certainly takes as much if not more energy. It is useful to remember that aggression is only one way to use up that remarkable flow of psychic/physical energy which has led to such an extraordinary array of human achievements thus far in the lifespan of the species.

If we put the heroic warrior and heroic peace-maker side by side, what is the future for each in the twenty-first century? In the best possible scenario, the heroic warriors gradually become heroic peace-makers.[26] They can only do this, of course, to the extent that the international community buckles down to the serious work of local, regional and global governance which will reduce the need for arms. This means gradual conversion of weapons production in every country to meeting urgent civilian needs, together with a careful monitoring of the arms trade and the replacement of nuclear non-proliferation agreements by an outlawing of the production and use of nuclear weapons.

Many things have to happen at local and regional levels to make this possible. However, the increasing involvement of transnational peoples' associations in issues of demilitarization and the creation of alternative problem-solving mechanisms in all inter-state arenas concerned with the environment, social and economic development and the peaceful settlement of disputes make this a genuine possibility. Ethnic separatist movements will mature over time. Already new models are developing for ethnic autonomy within existing states, as happened several centuries ago in Switzerland, and is now happening in several European countries, including Spain, even as the European Community itself evolves. It is also happening among indigenous peoples in the Circumpolar North and the tropics. These developments free creative energy

---

26. This is what William James was writing about in his *Moral Equivalent of War*, written in 1910 and just reprinted in *Peace and Conflict: Journal of Peace Psychology*, Vol. 1, No. 1, 1995, pp. 17–29. An interesting exploration of this subject drawing on classical myths and contemporary psychology is found in R. William Botcher and William S. Pollack, *A Time of Fallen Heroes: the Re-creation of Masculinity*, New York, The Guilford Press, 1993.

for dealing with twenty-first century challenges: the more careful use of the earth's limited resources, more attention to human and social development and a more judicious approach to technological development, reducing it to the role of servant rather than master. In this, they will have something in common with the tribal societies and Anabaptist communities which we have been considering.

People's associations and local civic and religious cultures, in this image of the future, will pay increased attention to the education of the young, and the nurturing of family and community life. This shift of focus will be essential to prepare the next generation and generations to come for imaginative, adventurous problem-solving and the resolution of as yet unforeseen conflicts. We are talking about a slow, century-long process; certainly not a rapid one. What is involved is not so much social transformation as a gradual shifting of the balance between violent and non-violent institutional and behavioural patterns over time. The problem-solving and peace-making resources are already there at the local level, however hidden. The role of the transnational associations can be to interface between governmental and civic structures so that peace-building know-how is drawn on with increasing frequency.[27] The role of the media and the arts in reflecting such a shift will be of critical importance if there is to be a beneficial feedback system[28] which mirrors to the general public the actual impact of new behaviours. UNESCO has a very special role to play in helping to bring about this long-term shift, as the Organization works with non-governmental organizations in all social sectors, and at all levels from grass roots to transnational, as well as with governments.

This essay began by indicating how historians have biased our view of history and the human condition by recording mainly wars and conquests. It is fitting to end with praise for that courageous group of historians who founded

---

27. This NGO/IGO/UN interfacing is described in Elise Boulding, *Building a Global Civic Culture*, Syracuse, NY, Syracuse University Press, 1990.
28. Deviation-amplifying feedback loops are a very important aspect of the dynamics of social change, and are brilliantly discussed by Magorah Maruyama in 'The Second Cybernetics: Deviation – Amplifying Mutual Causal Processes', *American Scientist*, No. 51, 1963, pp. 164–79, 250–6.

the Council on Peace Research in History (now the Peace History Society) in the 1960s to direct scholarly research toward removing that bias.[29] They do not work alone, since the task of shifting the cultural balance toward non-violence is a challenge for all, whatever one's walk of life, one's age, one's gender, wherever one lives on the planet we call home. There is no human occupation which cannot be re-tuned to contribute to peace-building. The only limitation on that re-tuning is the willingness to liberate our own imagination.

---

29. The Peace History Society, in addition to having fostered numerous publications on peace-making in history, publishes the bi-monthly journal *Peace and Change* jointly with the Consortium on Peace Research, Education and Development (COPRED).

Normative instruments for a culture of peace

*Emmanuel Decaux**

For centuries, there has been a form of natural coexistence between war and peace, which can be traced back to the roots of public international law. The title of Grotius's most important work, published in 1625 at the dawn of the modern inter-state system, was, significantly, *De jure belli ac pacis*. Three centuries later, in 1922, a great French scholar, Paul Fauchille, devised his *Traité de droit international public* with a similar approach. It is interesting to note that his first tome was entitled *Peace* and comprised three volumes, whereas the second tome, *War and Neutrality,* had only one.[1] After the Second World War, the primacy given to peace was even more spectacular and, after Charles Rousseau's work had been published in five volumes by a single publisher during the 1970s under the title of *Droit international public*, it was another publisher who finally agreed to publish a further volume under the title *Le droit des conflits armés* in 1983. Thus, a major state of the art of modern international law by a French scholar actually covered the law of war.

At the same time, another mainstream which identifies international law and peace exists, according to the old motto of the Institut de Droit International, created in 1873, *Jus ac pax*. This new trend was far-reaching within the circle of

---

* Professor and Head of the International Law Centre (CEDIN) of the University of Paris X.
1. The emphasis was placed on the First World War, as the second tome was first published in 1921, with the three other volumes of the first tome appearing successively from 1922 to 1926.

international lawyers and political figures involved in the Hague Conferences of 1899 and 1907.[2] In France the main spokesman of this great cause was a statesman, Léon Bourgeois, who forcefully defined 'peace' as law enduring in time. Indeed, without law, 'there cannot be a true peace, the peace which resides both in the reality and in the minds, a peace which is grounded in the free consent of consciences'.[3] From a different background, a great physician, Charles Richet, published in 1907 a prophetic book entitled *Le passé de la guerre et l'avenir de la paix*.[4]

After the tragedy of the First World War, the most eloquent affirmation of this culture of peace is not in Part I of the Treaty of Versailles, concerning the League of Nations, but in Part XIII, about the International Labour Organisation: 'peace can be established only if it is based on social justice'. The wording of the Covenant of the League of Nations was more pedestrian; even if speeches about peace flourished in Geneva in the 1930s, it was a culture of war which triumphed until the doomsday of 1945.

The new order in the aftermath of the war gave, for the first time, a legal value to the ideals of peace. The Charter of the United Nations gives expression to the common will of the peoples 'to save succeeding generations from the scourge of war, which twice in our lifetime has brought untold sorrow to mankind, and to reaffirm faith in fundamental human rights, in the dignity and worth of the human person'.[5] Thus the main aims of the peoples of the United Nations, according to the Preamble, are:

---

2. Cf. the anthology by Marcel Merle, *Pacifisme et internationalisme*, Paris, Armand Colin, 1966, and by Charles Zorgbibe, *La Paix*, Paris, PUF, 1984. (Que sais-je?, No. 1600.)
3. Léon Bourgeois, *Pour la société des nations*, Paris, Crès, 1910. This citation comes from a message published in 1901 for the yearbook of the Association de la Paix par le Droit, formed initially in 1887 by a small group of Protestant students in Nîmes in the South of France, which developed worldwide branches.
4. Paris, Ollendorff, 1907. His scientific approach foresees the work of the French sociologist Gaston Bouthoul about war studies, *polémologie*. Cf., inter alia, *Avoir la Paix*, Paris, Grasset, 1967. For a later survey of his method, see *Le défi de la guerre*, Paris, PUF, 1976, and *Essais de polémologie*, Paris, Denoël, 1976.
5. This personal tone was the work of Marshal Smuts, but it was watered down by several amendments. On the legal nature of the Preamble, see Jean-Pierre Cot and Alain Pellet, *La Charte des Nations Unies*, Paris, Economica, 1991.

to practise tolerance and live together in peace with one another as good neighbours, and to unite our strength to maintain international peace and security, and to ensure, by the acceptance of principles and the institution of methods, that armed force shall not be used, save in the common interest, and to employ international machinery for the promotion of the economic and social advancement of all peoples.

At the same time, the Constitution of UNESCO was even more lyrical:[6]

That since wars begin in the minds of men, it is in the minds of men that the defences of peace must be constructed . . . that the wide diffusion of culture, and the education of humanity for justice and liberty and peace are indispensable to the dignity of man and constitute a sacred duty which all the nations must fulfil in a spirit of mutual assistance and concern; that a peace based exclusively upon the political and economic arrangements of governments would not be a peace which would secure the unanimous, lasting and sincere support of the peoples of the world, and that the peace must therefore be founded, if it is not to fail, upon the intellectual and moral solidarity of mankind.

In the same spirit as that of the Charter of the United Nations, UNESCO's Constitution was adopted with the aim 'to contribute to peace and security by promoting collaboration among the nations through education, science and culture, in order to further universal respect for justice, for the rule of law and for the human rights and fundamental freedoms'. Through education, peace and security are thus rooted in law. This mandate focuses on the facets of a new culture of peace: tolerance, the spirit of good neighbourliness, the moral solidarity of mankind, on the one hand, and the will to work towards common interests, to promote collective security and to protect the rule of law, on the other. Thus there is no antithesis between right and might. As Blaise Pascal aptly put it: 'La justice sans la force est impuissante, la force sans la justice est tyrannique.'

The Preamble of the Universal Declaration of Human Rights, adopted in 1948, recognized human rights as 'the foundation of freedom, justice and peace

---

6. The initial draft by Clement Attlee was modified by Archibald MacLeish to give it a lyrical note. See Richard Hoggart, *An Idea and Its Servants, UNESCO from Within*, London, Chatto & Windus, 1978.

in the world'. The Universal Declaration rests on the concept of resistance to oppression, stemming from the French Revolution: 'it is essential, if man is not to be compelled to have recourse, as a last resort, to rebellion against tyranny and oppression, that human rights should be protected by the rule of law'. Therefore, as in the UNESCO Constitution, this long-forgotten reference of the Universal Declaration shows the democratic dimension of international law, long before the modern reference to the *état de droit* in the Charter of Paris for a New Europe of 1990, which was a landmark for the Conference on Security and Co-operation in Europe (CSCE).

The Universal Declaration is intended, as stated in its Preamble, 'to promote the development of friendly relations between nations', and emphasizes in its Article 26 that 'education . . . shall promote understanding, tolerance and friendship among all nations, racial or religious groups, and shall further the activities of the United Nations for the maintenance of peace'. Even if there is no specific provision in it about the right to education on human rights, the Preamble states that 'every individual and every organ of society . . . shall strive by teaching and education to promote respect for these rights and freedoms'. Furthermore, it emphasizes the central role of all human beings, who 'are endowed with reason and conscience and should act towards one another in a spirit of brotherhood'. So, besides the right to liberty and equality, there is the duty of fraternity and solidarity. On this basis, international co-operation between states aims at achieving 'a common standard of achievement for all peoples and all nations'.

The normative instruments for a culture of peace have their foundation in this legal tradition. The Universal Declaration itself does not have a binding force but has great political significance. It expresses the spirit of the constitutive charter of the international order; it is an authentic interpretation of universal norms.

A complete survey of the specific norms adopted to put these general principles into practice is impossible in a short essay. To explore fully the legal field is already a vast exercise, and we shall only try to comment on the main normative references, which are threefold:
1. The general texts lay stress upon the primacy of international law and of universal human rights.

2. In this basic framework, they imply negative aspects in order to prohibit war and hate, racial propaganda and intolerance.
3. They lay stress upon positive obligations, through peaceful co-operation, friendship between peoples, good neighbourliness and tolerance.

THE PRIMACY OF UNIVERSAL HUMAN RIGHTS

The need to protect law against misuses of law was at the origin of several escape clauses. Within the Universal Declaration, Articles 29 and 30 set the main limits to these rights: 'These rights and freedoms may in no case be exercised contrary to the purposes and principles of the United Nations' (Article 29(3)); and, more precisely: 'Nothing in this Declaration may be interpreted as implying for any State, group or person any right to engage in any activity or to perform any act aimed at the destruction of any of the rights and freedoms set forth herein' (Article 30). Accordingly, two similar articles, Articles 5 and 20, of the two International Covenants on Human Rights of 1966 need closer examination.

We find the same escape clauses in the Covenants. The formulation of Article 5(1) is common to both the International Covenant on Civil and Political Rights and the International Covenant on Economic, Social and Cultural Rights: 'Nothing in the present Covenant may be interpreted as implying for any State, group or person any right to engage in any activity or perform any act aimed at the destruction of any of the rights and freedoms recognized herein or at their limitation to a greater extent than is provided for in the present Covenant.'

The aim of these clauses is to prevent the abuse of freedom to destroy freedom – 'no freedom for the enemies of freedom' – and specifically to check the growth of nascent nazi, fascist or other totalitarian ideologies.[7] There was some concern about the vagueness of the clause, notably from the former Soviet Union which thought 'it was open to abuse', but also from the United States with its tradition of freedom of speech: it was thought that, widely interpreted, the paragraph might permit a State, which so desired, to curtail very considerably

---

7. Marc Bossuyt, *Guide to the 'Travaux Préparatoires' of the International Covenant on Civil and Political Rights*, p. 105, Dordrecht, Nijhoff, 1987.

the exercise of certain rights. In particular, a State might place undesirable restrictions on the freedom of expression guaranteed in the draft Covenant. An American proposal to delete these paragraphs was rejected by six votes to four at the sixth session of the Commission on Human Rights in 1950.

There was also some discussion inside the Commission on Human Rights about the inclusion of the word 'State' as part of the objectives of the clause, as well as 'group or person'. The opinion was expressed that states were hardly likely to undertake the obligations under the Covenant and then attempt to destroy the rights or limit them to a greater extent than provided in it. It was observed that states were already empowered to limit many rights, for such reasons as the protection of 'public order' or 'national security' and that they should not be encouraged to restrict further the provisions of the Covenants. However, the draft of the International Covenant on Civil and Political Rights was unanimously adopted in 1951 and translated into the International Covenant on Economic, Social and Cultural Rights in 1962. The two Covenants were finally adopted in 1966 and entered into force in 1976.

Reference to the clause was made by the UN Human Rights Committee[8] in regard to extraterritorial activities by the security and intelligence forces of Uruguay: Article 2(1) of the International Covenant on Civil and Political Rights places an obligation upon a state party to respect and to ensure rights 'to all individuals within its territory and subject to its jurisdiction', but it does not imply that the State Party concerned cannot be held accountable for violations of rights under the Covenant which its agents commit upon the territory of another state, whether with the acquiescence of the government of that state or in opposition to it. According to Article 5(1) of the Covenant: 'Nothing in the present Covenant may be interpreted as implying for any State, group or person any right to engage in any activity or perform any act aimed at the destruction of any of the rights and freedoms recognized herein or at their limitation to a greater extent than is provided for in the present Covenant.' In line with this, it would be inconceivable to so interpret the responsibility under Article 2 of the Covenant as to permit a State Party to perpetrate on the territory of another state, a violation of the

---

8. This committee is responsible for the monitoring of the International Covenant on Civil and Political Rights.

Covenant which it could not perpetrate on its own territory.⁹ But, in an individual opinion, the German expert, Christian Tomuschat, made a useful clarification:

In principle, the scope of application of the Covenant is not susceptible to being extended by reference to Article 5, a provision designed to cover instances where formally rules under the Covenant seem to legitimize actions which substantially run counter to its purposes and general spirit. Thus, Governments may never use the limitation clauses supplementing the protected rights and freedoms to such an extent that the very substance of those rights and freedoms would be annihilated; individuals are legally barred from availing themselves of the same rights and freedoms with a view to overthrowing the regime of the rule of law which constitutes the basic philosophy of the Covenant. In the present case, however, the Covenant does not even provide the pretext for a 'right' to perpetrate the criminal acts which, according to the Committee's conviction, have been perpetrated by the Uruguayan authorities.

On another occasion, the Committee used the disposition of Article 5 to narrow the scope of the Covenant against an Italian neo-fascist. In a decision of inadmissibility, the Committee demonstrated the incompetence *ratione temporis*. It stressed also an incompetence *ratione materiae*:

Moreover, it would appear to the Committee that the acts for which M.A. was convicted (reorganizing the dissolved fascist party) were of a kind which are removed from the protection of the Covenant by Article 5 thereof and which were, in any event, justifiably prohibited by Italian law having regard to the limitations and restrictions applicable to the rights in question under the provisions of Articles 18(3), 19(3), 22(2) and 25 of the Covenant.[10]

---

9. Human Rights Committee, *Selected Decisions under the Optional Protocol,* Vol. 1, United Nations, 1985. See also Communication No. 52/1979 on behalf of Sergio Ruben Lopez Burgos against Uruguay, decision adopted on 29 July 1981, p. 91, para. 12.3, as well as Communication No. 56/1979 by Llian Celiberti de Casariego against Uruguay, decision adopted the same day, p. 94, para.10.3.
10. Human Rights Committee, *Selected Decisions under the Optional Protocol,* Vol. 2, United Nations, 1989. See also Communication No. 117/1981, M.A. against Italy, decision (inadmissibility) of 10 April 1984, p. 33.

THE STRUGGLE AGAINST A CULTURE OF HATE

The International Covenant on Civil and Political Rights has another more specific clause to limit the scope of freedom of speech. It is Article 20, which follows Article 19 devoted to the freedom of opinion: 'Any propaganda for war shall be prohibited by law. Any advocacy of national, racial or religious hatred that constitutes incitement to discrimination, hostility or violence shall be prohibited by law.'

In 1947, the former Soviet Union was behind a more radical draft which qualified as 'crime' these actions, without any mention of 'incitement to violence'. The proposal of the former Soviet Union was rejected by ten votes to four.

In 1949, the debate shifted to the Commission on Human Rights, with a more balanced perspective: 'On the one hand, the opinion was expressed that legislation was not the most effective means to deal with the matter, and that if propaganda should constitute a menace to public peace, Article 19(3) of the draft International Covenant on Civil and Political Rights would be applicable.' This was the position of several Member States, such as the United States and the United Kingdom, but also Poland. 'On the other hand, it was emphasised that the strong influence of propaganda on the minds of men rendered legislative intervention necessary and that the general provisions of Article 19(3) were not adequate, as they did not impose upon States Parties any obligation to prohibit the advocacy of national, racial or religious hostility': this was the thesis of France and of the World Jewish Congress.

Taking into account fears 'that an article prohibiting such advocacy might lead to abuse and would be detrimental to freedom of expression', the Commission specified 'that only such advocacy of national, racial or religious hostility as "constitutes an incitement to violence" should be prohibited by the law of the State'. Some members of the Communist bloc, the former Soviet Union, Poland, Ukraine and Yugoslavia, tried to blame 'the propaganda of fascist-Nazi views', but other states, including France, considered the formulation too vague and it was dropped.

The debate was continued during the 1960s, with the emphasis on freedom of opinion and expression (Belgium, Japan, the United States) and the risk of imposing prior censorship on all forms of expression and suppressing the opinions of opposition groups and parties (Argentina, Ireland, Netherlands, Norway). But, on the other hand, the former Soviet Union and its allies placed the emphasis on the prohibition of war propaganda and racial hatred: 'The Article should contain a specific provision which would prohibit war propaganda in order to put an end to the Cold War and to promote peaceful coexistence.'[11]

Mentioning war propaganda created new legal difficulties of definition and interpretation. However, it was pointed out

that the question of propaganda had been dealt with in national laws and constitutions, as well as in international instruments and documents, such as . . . the judgement of the Nuremberg Tribunal, General Assembly resolutions 110(II) on 'Measures to be taken against propaganda and the inciters of a new war' and 381(V) on 'Condemnation of propaganda against peace, and the draft Convention on Freedom of Information'.[12]

This was an old debate between Western countries and the former Soviet Union. During the preparation of the prosecution for the Nuremberg Tribunal, there was indeed serious disagreement over the American proposal that the indictment should include a general charge of waging a war of aggression. The Soviets wanted to limit the charge to a 'Hitlerite' war only. Were they possibly thinking that any general definition of aggression might give rise to painful memories of their invasion of the Baltic states in 1939? Nikitchenko, the Soviet judge, insisted that, if the wording went beyond a specific condemnation of Nazi aggression to a condemnation of war in general, 'it would not be agreeable to the Soviets', as Lord Shawcross recalled with candour.[13]

The first draft of Article 20 was adopted by eleven votes in 1952 (France, with Soviet bloc and Third World countries) against three (Australia, the United Kingdom and the United States) with three abstentions (Belgium, China, Sweden) and, after the addition of the first paragraph in 1961, the article as a whole was

---

11. Bossuyt, op.cit., p. 403 et seq.
12. Ibid., p. 408.
13. *Life Sentence: The Memoirs of Lord Shawcross*, London, Constable, 1995. See also George Ginsburg and V. N. Kudriavtsev (eds.), *The Nuremberg Trial and International Law*, Dordrecht, Nijhoff, 1990.

adopted by fifty-two to nineteen, with twelve abstentions in the Third Committee.[14]

The vote reflected the split caused by the Cold War. Western countries looked upon the 'peace movement' manipulated by the former Soviet Union as an act of propaganda against the policy of national defence and membership of the Atlantic Alliance, often described as warmongers by the communists and fellow-travellers of the anti-militarist lobby. At the same time, for the former Soviet Union, war propaganda was identified with the nationalism of Western countries, whereas its own internationalist propaganda in other states or the involvement of the Red Army in the Soviet bloc were considered as peaceful activities. We have to place the legal debates of the United Nations in the context of these shifts of propaganda for peace against blunt propaganda of war.

Several states made subsequent declarations and reservations about Article 20(1). The most plain was that of the Netherlands: 'The Kingdom of the Netherlands does not accept the obligation set out in this provision in the case of Netherlands.' Similarly, Norway and Sweden had reservations to Article 20(1). In other cases, states tried either to recast their vote, without any legal implication, or to 'banalize' its scope in respect of their own legislation.

Denmark was more explicit in its reservation to Article 20(1): 'This reservation is in accordance with the vote cast by Denmark in the sixteenth session of the General Assembly of the United Nations in 1961 when the Danish Delegation, referring to the preceding article concerning freedom of expression, voted against the prohibition against propaganda for war.' Finland adopted the same point of view: 'With respect to Article 20(1) of the Covenant, Finland declares that it will not apply the provision of this paragraph, this being compatible with the standpoint Finland already expressed at the sixteenth session of the United Nations General Assembly by voting against the prohibition of propaganda for war, on the grounds that this might endanger the freedom of expression referred to in Article 19 of the Covenant.' Iceland adopted the same position.

On the other hand, in a constructive interpretation, 'The Government of the United Kingdom interprets Article 20 consistently with the rights conferred

---

14. Between the two votes in 1952 and 1961, France drifted between a 'yes' and a 'no' for the first sentence, with an abstention for the second sentence and the whole article.

by Articles 19 and 21 of the Covenant and having legislated in matters of practical concern in the interests of public order (*ordre public*) reserves the right not to introduce any further legislation.' In the same way, 'Australia interprets the rights provided for by Articles 19, 21 and 22 as consistent with Article 20; accordingly, the Commonwealth and the constituent States, having legislated with respect to the subject-matter of the article in matters of practical concern in the interest of law and order (*ordre public*), the right is reserved not to introduce any further legislative provision on these matters.'[15] New Zealand had a very similar position: 'The Government of New Zealand having legislated in the areas of the advocacy of national and racial hatred and the inciting of hostility or ill will against any group of persons and having regard to the right of freedom of speech, reserves the right not to introduce further legislation with regard to Article 20.'

In regard to the same law-making obligation, Belgium made a more radical declaration: 'The Belgian Government declares that it does not consider itself obligated to enact legislation in the field covered by Article 20, paragraph 1, and that Article 20 as a whole shall be applied taking into account the rights to freedom of thought and religion, freedom of opinion and freedom of assembly and association proclaimed in Articles 18, 19 and 20 of the Universal Declaration of Human Rights and reaffirmed in Articles 18, 19, 21 and 22 of the Covenant.' Luxembourg made the same declaration. In its declaration, France added a new restriction to protect itself from these provisions: 'The Government of the (French) Republic declares that the term "war", appearing in Article 20(1), is to be understood to mean war in contravention of international law and considers, in any case, that French legislation in this matter is adequate.'

The Human Rights Committee applied Article 20 in the case of the 'W. G. Party'.[16] The party used tape-recorded messages linked to the telephone system to spread propaganda against 'international finance and international Jewry leading the world into wars'. In application of the Canadian Human Rights Act

---

15. *Human Rights: Status of International Instruments*, p. 28 et seq., New York, United Nations, 1987.
16. Human Rights Committee, *Selected Decisions under the Optional Protocol*, Vol. 2, United Nations, 1989. See also Communication No. 104/1981, J.R.T. and the W.G. Party against Canada, decision (inadmissibility) on 6 April 1983, p. 26.

of 1978, this telephone service was curtailed. Mr T., the leader of this unincorporated political party, claimed a violation of Article 19 of the Covenant by Canadian authorities. But, for the Canadian defence, its domestic law in fact gives effect to Article 20(2) of the Covenant. Thus, not only is the author's 'right' to communicate racist ideas not protected by the Covenant, it is in fact incompatible with its provisions. The Committee ruled the same interpretation: 'However, the opinions which Mr T. seeks to disseminate through the telephone system clearly constitute the advocacy of racial or religious hatred which Canada has an obligation under Article 20(2) of the Covenant to prohibit.'

Perhaps more scope needs to be given to these crucial topics, keeping in view the phenomena of the spread of racism and xenophobia, religious intolerance and nationalist propaganda in various parts of the world. The main issues are not only war propaganda between states, with mobilization and militarization of public opinion, as during the 1930s, but hate and division inside national communities, involving internal conflicts with resurgent political racism. So the legal framework of human rights laid down during the post-war period is fundamental to allow democracies to shield their citizens and to maintain values and principles. Openness is the main strength of democracies, but it is impossible to 'tolerate the intolerable'. In this fight, each state is no longer alone; as the Charter of Paris for a New Europe states: 'Democracy is the best safeguard of freedom of expression, tolerance of all groups of society. . . . Our States will co-operate and support each other with the aim of making democratic gains irreversible.'[17]

The effectiveness of this solemn commitment of European countries is tested with the tragic spread of ethnic cleansing in former Yugoslavia, from a dialogue of hate to actual genocide. For the first time since the creation of the Nuremberg Tribunal fifty years ago, the Security Council created an ad hoc tribunal to judge persons responsible for serious violations of international humanitarian law. The aims of the International Criminal Tribunal for former Yugoslavia, as of the similar International Tribunal for Rwanda, are both repressive and preventive. To fight the cycle of violence and impunity by full individual accountability is

---

17. Arie Bloed, *The Conference on Security and Co-operation in Europe*, p. 538, Dordrecht, Nijhoff, 1993.

indeed also a means of deterring further violations of human rights. But these reactions by the international community are often too late. The first needs are for watchfulness, early warning and preventive action.

So the conflict between freedom of expression and prohibition of racial hate ought to be clearly set by international bodies, such as the Human Rights Committee and the Committee on the Elimination of Racial Discrimination (CERD). Likewise the European Court of Human Rights ruled with some ambivalence on a case involving the modern media.[18] The principal needs are now to strengthen domestic law, to favour legal harmonization at the regional level and to encourage co-operation between states in the fight against crime, as stressed by the European Meeting of the National Institution for the Promotion and Protection of Human Rights in Strasbourg which dealt recently with that topic.[19] The National Institutions themselves, at the crossroads between non-governmental organizations, public institutions and international bodies, are an important mechanism for educating the public at large.

THE DEVELOPMENT OF A CULTURE OF PEACE

Indeed, the constructive aspect of a culture of peace can be traced to the provisions of the Universal Declaration of Human Rights. The Preamble of the Declaration contains an essential objective: 'to promote the development of friendly relations between nations'. In its own way, the International Covenant on Economic, Social and Cultural Rights specifies that 'the States Parties to the present Covenant recognize the benefits to be derived from the encouragement and development of international contacts and co-operation in the scientific and cultural fields' (Article 15). Perhaps more implicitly, the International Covenant on Civil and Political Rights provides the rule that the right of freedom of expression must be applied regardless of frontiers (Article 19). However, general rules in universal

---

18. Concerning the Jersild Case against Denmark, 23 September 1994, see the commentary of Gérard Cohen-Jonathan in *Revue universelle des droits de l'homme*, No. 1–3, 1995.
19. Emmanuel Decaux, 'La lutte contre le racisme et la xénophobie', *Revue universelle des droits de l'homme*, No. 1–3, 1995.

textbooks are rather scarce. The field of international co-operation can be given more focus through regional or specialized approaches.

Effective co-operation must be a grassroots movement. Sometimes states have tried to keep the monopoly of these contacts, in the name of friendship between peoples. There are many bilateral treaties of friendship and co-operation but the words seem besmirched. Only free circulation of persons and ideas can give full meaning to such treaties. To build a culture of peace, one needs to promote democracy and the rule of law, but also to democratize international society.

Friendship is something that should exist not only between states but also between peoples, giving a new meaning to transnational relations across borders. International law has to develop transborder co-operation. The main example is given by the European Outline Convention on Transfrontier Co-operation between Territorial Communities or Authorities, signed in Madrid in 1980 between the States Parties of the Council of Europe, but this Convention is also open to adhesion by non-Member States. With the other recent European conventions, such as the European Charter of Local Self-Government of 1985, the Convention on the Participation of Foreigners in Public Life at Local Level of 1992, the European Charter for Regional or Minority Languages of 1992 and the Framework Convention for the Protection of National Minorities of 1995, there is an impressive network of multilateral treaties giving to persons and to peoples, but also to national minorities or to foreigners who have domiciles in a particular country, a set of legal standards for peaceful activities.

On these grounds, the Member States of the Council of Europe are a dynamic force for Europe as a whole. The Meetings on the Human Dimension of the CSCE in Copenhagen in 1990 and Moscow in 1991 stressed the importance of good neighbourliness and cross-border co-operation, especially in relation to minority rights issues.[20] For example, the Final Document of the Copenhagen Meeting quotes the right for persons belonging to national minorities 'to establish and maintain unimpeded contacts among themselves within their country as well as contacts across frontiers with citizens of other States with whom

---

20. Emmanuel Decaux, *La conférence sur la sécurité et la coopération en Europe,* Paris, PUF, 1992. (Que sais-je? No. 2661.)

they share a common ethnic or national origin, cultural heritage or religious beliefs' (para. 32.4) or 'to establish and maintain organizations or associations within their country and to participate in international non-governmental organizations' (para. 32.6).[21] The Geneva Report on National Minorities in July 1991 referred, *inter alia*, to 'encouragement of grassroots community relations efforts between minorities communities, between majority and minority communities, and between neighbouring communities sharing borders, aimed at helping to prevent local tensions from arising and address conflicts peacefully should they arise; and encouragement of the establishment of permanent mixed commissions, either inter-State or regional, to facilitate continuing dialogue between the border-regions concerned'. Furthermore, the report emphasizes the important part of educational, cultural and religious associations: 'In this regard, they recognize the major and vital role that individuals, non-governmental organizations, and religious and other groups play in fostering cross-cultural understanding and improving relations at all levels of society, as well as across international frontiers.'[22]

However, to develop a network is not enough – one should see what the nature of the new relations will be. Today, the onus is not on the states alone but on each of its citizens. It would be necessary to describe the domestic legislation of the states, the regional or subregional attempts at harmonization, such as the Plan of Action against Racism, Xenophobia, Anti-Semitism and Intolerance which took its impetus from the creation of a European Commission against Racism and Intolerance (ECRI), after the first Summit Meeting of Heads of State and Government of the Council of Europe in Vienna in October 1993. In parallel, during the Summit of Corfu in June 1994, the Members of the European Union created their own Consultative Commission against Racism and Xenophobia. The fifteen members of the Union confirmed its mission at

---

21. Bloed, op. cit., p. 457. Greece made an interpretative statement about this item to stress that the exercise of these rights 'should be in accordance with the relevant provisions of international human rights law and should respect, *inter alia*, the rights and freedoms of others and the principle of territorial integrity of the States concerned'.
22. Ibid., p. 599.

the Summit of Cannes in June 1995, with the purpose of creating a European watchdog against racism.

This is also the main aim of the Pact on Stability in Europe – to transform these good intentions into legal instruments. The Pact was signed in March 1995, under the patronage of the European Union, to promote bilateral arrangements in order to develop transborder co-operation and mutual understanding between peoples and national minorities, in the framework of the Organization for Security and Co-operation in Europe (OSCE).[23] The Concluding Document of its inaugural conference in 1994 had already clearly set the aims and principles of the Pact: 'The objectives of stability will be achieved through the promotion of good neighbourly relations, including questions related to frontiers and minorities, as well as regional co-operation and the strengthening of democratic institutions through co-operation arrangements to be established in the different fields that can contribute to the objective.' The Regional Round Tables for the Baltic Area and for Central and Eastern Europe were the occasion to negotiate far-reaching bilateral treaties, with the collective guarantee of the OSCE.

More recently, in May 1995, the OSCE and the Council of Europe, with the co-operation of UNESCO, organized an international seminar on tolerance in Bucharest. In each of these cases, the need for co-ordination of these various initiatives to avoid duplication and overlapping was a major theme.

There is an urgent need for intercultural education. Already, the Universal Declaration places the emphasis on the collective aims of education, not only on individual achievement but on the full development of the human personality and also its social component: 'It shall promote understanding, tolerance and friendship among all nations, racial or religious groups, and shall further the activities of the United Nations for the maintenance of peace' (Article 26(2)). We find the same spirit in Article 13 of the International Covenant on Economic, Social and Cultural Rights:

The States Parties to the present Covenant recognize the right of everyone to education. They agree that education shall be directed to the full development of the

---

23. The Conference on Security and Co-operation in Europe (CSCE) became the OSCE in 1995, following a decision of the Summit of Budapest in December 1994.

human personality and the sense of its dignity, and shall strengthen the respect for human rights and fundamental freedoms. They further agree that education shall enable all persons to participate effectively in a free society, promote understanding, tolerance and friendship among all nations and all racial, ethnic or religious groups, and further the activities of the United Nations for the maintenance of peace.

The World Conference on Human Rights, held in Vienna in June 1993, was an unparalleled occasion to give new impetus to the long-term aims of education, information and training at large:

The World Conference on Human Rights reaffirms that States are duty-bound, as stipulated in the Universal Declaration of Human Rights and the International Covenant on Economic, Social and Cultural Rights and in other international human rights instruments, to ensure that education is aimed at strengthening the respect of human rights and fundamental freedoms. . . . Education should promote understanding, tolerance, peace and friendly relations between the nations and all racial and religious groups and encourage the development of United Nations activities in pursuance of these objectives. Therefore, education on human rights and the dissemination of proper information, both theoretical and practical, play an important role in the promotion and respect of human rights with regard to all individuals without distinction of any kind such as race, sex, language or religion, and this should be integrated in the education policies at the national as well as international levels.[24]

The World Conference on Human Rights, in its chapter on human rights education, takes into account the World Plan of Action on Education for Human Rights and Democracy adopted in Montreal in March 1993 and 'stresses the contribution of UNESCO to encourage States to develop specific programmes and strategies for ensuring the widest human rights education' and to 'promote an increased awareness of human rights and mutual tolerance'.[25]

UNESCO's Fourth Medium-Term Strategy (1996–2001) with regard to contributing to peace-building gives priority to three main objectives:

---

24. A/CONF.157/23, I para. 33. See World Conference on Human Rights, *The Vienna Declaration and Programme of Action, June 1993*, United Nations, 1995.
25. Ibid., II, paras. 81–2.

1. To encourage education for non-violence, tolerance, human rights, democracy and international understanding.
2. To promote human rights and the struggle against discrimination.
3. To encourage cultural pluralism and intercultural dialogue.

However, at the same time, the interdependence of the objectives of peace and development is emphasized, in order to contribute to peace-building and to the emergence of a culture of peace.

Perhaps it is easier to set negative rather than positive obligations, to fight against intolerance rather than to build tolerance. We cannot separate the two sets of legal obligations. On the domestic level, there are no human rights without equal opportunities, no true equality without effective solidarity. The same is the case at the regional and the international level. Nobody can be free as a lone individual. Nobody can be free if other people are not free, too!

Concluding this general survey of the new trends in positive international law, we can try to offer some new prospects. First of all, a culture of peace is rooted in the conscience of each person, so normative instruments must take into account every level of human relations, from the spirit of brotherhood to international co-operation, from grass-roots associations to universal organizations. A close interaction of these relations and institutions is a major step towards legal pluralism and true democracy in the international system, as a basic condition for a culture of peace.

Within each state, a National Institution for Promotion and Protection of Human Rights should be created and developed, with broad competencies according to the guidelines set by the General Assembly in 1993.[26] Being a focal point between civil society and public authorities, these institutions are able to promote, inside and outside the country, the values of tolerance and solidarity which are the basis of a culture of peace. They already have an important part to play in the fight against racism and xenophobia, but these actions need regional co-ordination and international follow-up. UNESCO could therefore usefully

---

26. The so-called 'Principles of Paris' are incorporated in resolution 48/134 of the General Assembly, adopted by consensus on 20 December 1993. See Human Rights Centre, *National Institutions for the Promotion and Protection of Human Rights,* United Nations, 1993. (Fact Sheet No. 19.)

place emphasis on its own priorities and help promote actions and measures during international or regional meetings of these national institutions.[27]

The second level concerns bilateral relations. Good neighbourliness between states is a prerequisite for a culture of peace. Bilateral treaties of friendship and co-operation are an essential part of international peace networks but they are not isolated. First of all, they refer to and consolidate the more general obligations of umbrella agreements. In this way, the Pact on Stability in Europe is a good example of an empirical joint operation. It brings together a set of confidence-building measures, international guidelines and collective guarantees. In the fields of its competencies, UNESCO could constitute the framework of similar joint operations combining international principles and possible targets. On the other hand, bilateral treaties like international agreements can favour transborder co-operation between local communities, so that borders are no longer a wall of distrust and hate but become a bridge between peoples. A true culture of peace should take place with an erosion of borders and with a new flow of goods, ideas and peoples. Especially in countries with national minorities issues, the development of transborder co-operation is a confidence-building measure of prime significance. In this field also, UNESCO has a central mission to facilitate the flow of mutual information, regardless of frontiers, and promote a dissemination of intercultural education.

It is at the international level that normative principles must be universally established. Several international instruments already exist but need to enter in force or to be strengthened. The aim of universal recognition, set by the Vienna Conference, for the two International Covenants on Human Rights and for the International Convention on the Elimination of All Forms of Racial Discrimination and other relevant instruments must be a high priority for the international community. These instruments share the values embodied in the Universal Declaration and they should share the same international obligations and benefit from the same international monitoring. Nevertheless, there are some gaps in the set of obligations, especially in the field of cultural rights.

---

27. After the Vienna Conference, there were biennial international meetings, Tunis in December 1993 and Manilla in April 1995. The third international meeting will take place in 1997.

In the same way as the OSCE principles for the Pact on Stability in Europe, UNESCO could draft general guidelines and confidence-building measures for the new cultural framework which should combine the pre-eminence of the rule of law and freedom of speech, respect for human dignity and education for tolerance. The actual measures of implementation are as important as general principles. We have to imagine ways and means of monitoring these international obligations. UNESCO could set up a watchdog committee for cultural rights and a culture of peace, with a resource list of independent experts and rapporteurs, and assess individual or collective claims in regard to alleged violations of cultural rights, and also undertake positive actions or policy remedies.

Such a set of commitments and mechanisms is only a reflection of the complexity of the new international system. After the simplification of the post-war culture of peace establishing the monopoly of winners against former enemies, as in Article 107 of the United Nations Charter, and the lip-service paid during that period to peaceful coexistence which too often ignored human rights, a true opportunity has now appeared, through co-operation and interaction with a multiplicity of participants at various levels.

So a culture of peace is not simply another catchword, like the old pacifism of the 1930s and the 1950s, which weakened democracies against dictatorship and which was characterized by more war and more aggression. It is a new ideal rooted in the same democratic values and in an international set of duties and obligations, through international organizations and agencies, human rights monitoring and treaty bodies, mechanisms of preventive diplomacy and pacific settlement of disputes. The vital link between domestic freedom and collective security is the centre of a culture of peace. For the first time, perhaps, since the Abbé de Saint-Pierre[28] and Emmanuel Kant, it is not a moral Utopia but a legal obligation. This will be also the fulfilment of the wish of Franklin D. Roosevelt in 1945: 'More than an end to war, we want an end to the beginning of all wars.'

---

28. Abbé de Saint Pierre, *Projet pour rendre la paix perpétuelle en Europe,* 1713; new edition, Paris, Fayard, 1986.

Cultural peace: some characteristics[1]

*Johan Galtung**

INTRODUCTION: WHAT IS IN A WORD? OR TWO? OR THREE?

With words as rich and important as 'culture' and 'peace', we had better proceed with some care. Consensus about their use is neither possible nor desirable, nor necessary. But the reader has a right to know how the author thinks he is using the words.

'Culture' is the symbolic aspect of human existence. 'Culture' is representation through symbols, usually visual or acoustic, organized diachronically or synchronically.[2] Recently that representation, as on colour TV

---

* Professor of Peace Studies, University of Hawaii, Witten/Herdecke University, European Peace University, Tromsø University.

1. Of course, another title would have used the commonly found expression, 'a culture of peace'. But 'cultural peace' is the homologue of 'cultural violence' (see Johan Galtung, 'Cultural Violence', *Journal of Peace Research*, Vol. 27, No. 3, 1990, pp. 291-305. The problem to be explored is what cultural peace might look like, in order to recognize it if it should appear. The hunch is that there is less cultural peace around than structural peace, and less structural peace than direct peace; in other words, human beings behave remarkably peacefully in spite of negative structural and cultural contexts. For an exploration of these concepts, see Johan Galtung, *Peace by Peaceful Means*, Part I, Ch. 2 and 3, London/New York, Sage, 1995. Here, the book will be referred to as *PBPM*.

2. Thus a text is visual and diachronic; speech is acoustic and diachronic, like music; a painting is visual and synchronic, like a photo; a harmony is acoustic and synchronic. Opera: all of the above. Dark silence: none of the above. The tactile,

in real time, or on the computer screen interactively, has become so close to reality that the term 'virtual reality' is used, an 'as-if' reality. It may be objected that this is not art, that art enhances some aspects of reality and plays down others. But that is no objection: culture is a broader category than art.

Not unlike finance economy relative to real economy, culture takes on a life of its own, with its own logic, in the end even representing nothing but itself; evolving, breeding by cultures meeting and begetting new cultures, budding like a virus drilling itself into human minds, programming those minds to reproduce that culture and occasionally adding and subtracting something. The result is certainly an enormous amount of culture, to speak a truism, one of the most obvious examples being language, spoken and written, for which 'oralcy' and literacy are needed, both as sender and receiver.

Again, to draw on the parallel to finance/real economy: there has to be some kind of synchrony. Humans do not live by bread alone, but they do not live by the word, by symbols alone either. Too much culture relative to what it represents and there is inflation, a state of 'overculturation'; too little and there is 'underculturation', too little meaning available. We often talk about 'inflation in words', like speaking the word 'peace' – not to mention 'love' – too often, with no reality counter-value. The Cold War history of 'peace' is an example.[3] The result can be a lack of confidence, and then a crash on the

---

tasting and olfactory senses seem to be underutilized as carriers of culture, possibly because our discriminatory ability is less than for the visual and auditive senses.

3. Thus in the 1950s and 1960s the word 'peace' was underused in the West partly because it was overused in the East, and even if the socialist countries were serious about international peace (both Hungary in 1956 and Czechoslovakia in 1968 would be counter-indicative), the political repression inside the countries would be good examples of the lack of real world counter-value. However, in the 1970s and 1980s the word 'peace' was used with increasing frequency in the West, for instance by the German Social Democrats, by the non-communist peace movement and increasingly by the governments, probably because of a feeling that the word had retained its value in the population at large in spite of the socialist bloc misuse (which the population recognized as such); and the non-use rather than misuse by the West might backfire because it might also be interpreted as lack of real world counter-value, in other words that the West basically did not want peace. Eventually Reagan had to give in and adapt to Gorbachev's peace/disarmament rhetoric, possibly because people around the world were enthusiastic and believed it reflected some

cultural stock exchange: some words, like stocks, become worthless. The value depletion may be quick or slow, like the Dow Jones Index versus the Nikkei Index.

On the other hand, are there people whose words can always be trusted. And there are even those who can be trusted precisely because they do not talk at all: 'speech is silver, silence is gold'. In economics, gold has played that curious double role of being both a real and a financial good, the 'gold standard' being so attractive precisely because it was its own counter-value. The 'real reality' counter-value of that proverbial gold standard for the verbal market, silence, would obviously be real world, not only symbolic, action.

Culture provides *Homo sapiens*, poor in instincts, with a virtual reality map that serves as a guide to real reality. Deep culture, the crude, unembroidered aspects embedded in individual or collective subconscious, serves to orient human beings – possibly toward the Greek ideals, the true, the good and the beautiful, like a (computer) programme, a (genetic) code.

Peace is, of course, absence of violence of all kinds, direct (physical, and also verbal), structural, cultural, directed at the body, mind or spirit of some other being, human or not. A more pragmatic and dynamic conceptualization of peace would be: peace is the condition for conflicts to be transformed creatively and non-violently. The focus is then on conflict, rather than on peace. Peace is a context (inner and outer) for a constructive way of handling conflict, that human condition that may serve both as a creator and as a destroyer.

Tell me how you behave in conflict and I will tell you how much peace culture you have. A culture of peace is not a set of peaceful, non-violent representations of a reality. The test of the validity of a culture of peace lies in how it affects behaviour in conflict. The finance/real economy parallel is obvious: the test of money is not the quantity of money, stock and bonds, but how much real economy value they can be converted into. And this is the beauty of a peace culture, any culture: it is translated, not converted into real world reality and hence not depleted. The danger is inflation, not depletion. The cash flow may stop, not the flow of symbols.

Soviet reality. Morale: be careful with the big words, define them; but be lavish when there is real world counter-value.

As mentioned, we are all surrounded by an unimaginable amount of culture. There may be a culture of peace somewhere out there in the symbolic realm, even if only some, very few, nobody, living there has internalized that culture of peace to the point of being able to handle conflicts peacefully. Thus, we may distinguish between a potential peace culture that has not entered and configured our minds and mind-sets, and an actual/actuated peace culture that has been enacted.

At this point educators become happy: who else is going to bridge that gap between those who have not (yet) been effectively programmed for peaceful behaviour, and those who have? Between the potential and the actual? If we assume that a culture has to be received before it can be internalized, then a problem is whether that culture has been mediated – the mediator being the educator – or is 'unmediated', meaning, simply, received directly. Thus, I prefer absorbing a Bach cantata without anybody telling me what happens, and how I am supposed to receive. I want it to happen. I happen. I = it, it is part of me and vice versa.

The problem is, of course, that mediated culture differs from the unmediated version, having passed through the mediator. This is what makes schooling so problematic: literature 'taught' at school differs from the unmediated opening up to a novel. A direct reading of Gandhi (or Buddha, or the soft, gentle aspects of Jesus Christ) will always have an impact different from the countless mediated versions.

Does that mean, educators, please stay away? Stay at home, go back to wherever you came from, write texts, make speeches, stay among yourselves, and have a good time! No. Educators may be useful if they have deeper readings of the texts[4] they mediate than most others. But if educators only transmit culture, then education may itself contribute to 'out of sync' detachment of representation from reality; like a moral rascal teaching ethics. This is a heavy argument against peace education conveying peace culture without some practice, including peace action by the educator him/herself.

---

4. 'Text' here taken in a broad sense, including, for instance, music.

CONFLICT TRIANGLES AND CONFLICT TRANSFORMATION TRIANGLES

Above, 'conflict' has been chosen to play an essential role in understanding peace in general, and a culture of peace in particular. So, some words about 'conflict' are needed.

The discourse used here starts with a simple formula:

CONFLICT = $\underline{A}$TTITUDE/ASSUMPTIONS + $\underline{B}$EHAVIOUR + $\underline{C}$ONTRADICTION

The (A,B,C)-triangle, in other words, with B at the top as the only observable part. A and C have to be inferred, usually from violent inter-acts, physical and/or verbal. However, from those acts no automatic inference can be made about hatred, nor about any specific underlying contradiction among any number, n, of goals (be they values, or interests, or both) held by any number, m, of parties. Negative attitudes and contradictions are hypotheses to be tested in the praxis of conflict participation. The general hypothesis would be that violent behaviour is produced by unresolved contradictions and negative attitudes; the problem is which contradictions and which attitudes. There may be many candidates to be tested. But even reduced violence is no guarantee that the candidates have been found. There are many other possibilities: fatigue, a more important conflict has come up, etc.

According to this formula a conflict may start in any corner and spread to the other two. Conversely, it may also be transformed, even dis/re/solved from any corner – although the general advice would be to start in all three corners at the same time: dampening behaviour, modifying attitudes, dissolving contradictions. The question is how: and particularly under what conditions this can be done non-violently and creatively.

Here is a formula derived from the conflict formula:

CONFLICT TRANSFORMATION: EMPATHY + NON-VIOLENCE + CREATIVITY

for attitudes/assumptions, for behaviour, for contradictions.

The formula would apply to any outside conflict/peace worker, and to any inside party wanting to transform the conflict. First, empathy with all parties; not in the cheap sense of imagining 'how would I experience being in their shoes?' but in the sense of 'how do they experience being in their shoes?' Second, the limitation to non-violent action, among other reasons to break the 'violence breeds violence' cycles.

Third, creativity in order to transcend contradictions.

The problem is, of course, where do these 'commodities', as precious as scarce, come from? Answer: from a culture of peace, as three key components of such a culture.

Let us first defend this thesis negatively: what happens if the culture is not only poor in all three but even hostile? Clearly, without empathy, there is no insight in A,B,C as experienced by the other parties (pluralis, the cultural idea of only two parties is already violent.) Then Saddam Hussein becomes only an invader of Kuwait (he was, indeed), not the head of a people that has suffered deep trauma at the hands of the Occident (1258, 1916, 1917, 1922, 1961 to mention some). His behaviour becomes only violent, even malevolent, autistic, a manifestation of Evil. And what he sees as the nature of the contradiction sounds like 'propaganda'. The example is chosen not out of sympathy for any particular person or people, but to show that countries with 'free press', 'rule of law' and democracy are also easy victims of shallow, misleading conflict understanding when empathy is absent.

If non-violence is not in the culture when appeals to reason and settlement of the conflict through direct dialogue, or normal mediation/arbitration/rule-of-law, and even rule-of-man[5] have proved insufficient, then recourse to violence comes too easily, 'to settle the matter once and for all'.

And in a culture that privileges mental inertia over creativity in reconciling incompatible goals, violence also comes easily. If the solution to the conflict were within mainstream thinking, then that solution would probably already have been found, and enacted. When this is not the case, a reasonable hypothesis would be that sufficient creativity is needed to transcend mainstream thinking.[6]

It is also easily seen that one or two of these precious 'commodities' are

---

5. *PBPM*, Part II, Ch. 4.
6. One classical, pedagogical example runs as follows: You are at the South Pole, ordered to move on, but not permitted to move north. Mainstream thinking, knowing that any step is northward, would lead to a standstill. Creative, non-paradigmatic, countertrend thinking might make you jump.

insufficient. Empathy is fine, but it has to be translated into action. For a Gandhi to understand the British, including to respect them and to wish for them an even better future, is beautiful, but hardly sufficient to liberate both India and England from the scourge of the structural and cultural violence known as colonialism. An empathy with Saddam Hussein to the point of understanding that his major goals were not necessarily to keep Kuwait against a coalition headed by the USA, but to stand up against that coalition, in courage, thereby increasing his honour and dignity, makes us understand why both he and Bush declared themselves winners of that Gulf War. But it does not mobilize forces against his crime, like a march of 100,000 unarmed civilians into Kuwait occupied by Iraq, making an occupation meaningless, and also impeding a war that has killed close to one million so far.[7]

Empathy and non-violence together, even under a Gandhi's leadership, were insufficient to find a creative solution to the separatism of the Muslims (Pakistan). History did not move forward. The ability of Mother India to serve as a gracious host to an incredible variety of religions, as long as they did not basically challenge the highly complex cultural nexus conventionally referred to as Hinduism, was insufficient. Ecumenism broke down, European nation-statism prevailed on one side as purity, with ethnic cleansing on both sides.

In short, these three cultural elements, internalized or not, constitute a *holon*, even with highly synergistic properties. Delete one, like non-violence, and you end up with Sun Tzu, or the Israeli Defence Forces: insight into yourself and the enemy, brilliant, but violence none the less. Not peace. If empathy, non-violence and creativity are internalized, then concrete procedures for what to do might look as follows:

- Establish a dialogue with at least one of the parties, but alone rather than with the others. Try to understand what the basic goal is, underneath violent acts and rhetoric.
- Develop together a non-violent process to reach that goal.
- When the basic goals of the parties are incompatible, the outside peace worker may insert into the dialogue levels of creativity unavailable to parties

---

7. Including deaths due to economic sanctions.

blinded by cultural violence in addition to the hatred produced by direct violence.
- Only well-prepared parties should meet 'at the table'.
- Then, let 100, 1,000 peace dialogues blossom lest the misunderstanding prevail that peace equals a document signed by the leaders.[8]

BEYOND EMPATHY, NON-VIOLENCE AND CREATIVITY

Could empathy, non-violence and creativity, as cultural elements, and internalized as personality traits, be part of something more comprehensive? Is there a cultural genus behind each one of them? One possible answer would be: yes, *karma* for empathy, reversibility for non-violence, flexibility for creativity. Let us explore them, starting with empathy.

Empathy would have as one consequence a perception of the violent act, physical or verbal, the way the actor sees it: as the outcome of provocations pushing him beyond a threshold that may already be low, given factors in that person's inner and outer context (a history of violence in the family, being raised in a violent culture, identifying with a nation that has suffered terrible traumas and relates the provoker to the source of the traumas). *Tout comprendre, c'est tout pardonner.* No. At some point there was a choice. All the forces impinging on a person may combine to determine the outcome, except for one force: the capacity of the human spirit to rise above the other forces. But the spirit also needs sustenance. The name of that sustenance is a peace culture.

So let us turn empathy in another direction; not towards one or two Others, trying to understand the Other in Other, not only Self as Other. Let us turn empathy to human life in general, trying to fathom the networks, the couplings in time, forward, sideward, backward – the after-life, the side-life – as a totality. I, mySelf, Other, only small grains in this endless flux of life but endowed with the capacity to steer, to be in charge, to take on responsibility.

---

8. For personal experiences with this kind of approach, see Johan Galtung, 'On the Politics of Peace Action: Non-violence and Creativity', in Judith McKibben (ed.), *Hawaiian Journeys in Non-violence*, Honolulu, Spark M. Matsunaga Institute for Peace, 1995.

Cultural peace: some characteristics

'We are all one in Jesus Christ,' Paul said. Buddhists say: 'Co-arising origination', meaning everything influences everything. 'We are all in the same boat' is not a bad expression for the same idea, adding that, if the boat is leaky even with holes in it and the water is pouring in, the basic problem is not who drilled those holes but what to do. Indeed, we may always identify some knots in this net of life, hang guilt certificates, even ropes around some necks, hanging those selected for guilt-attribution ('I hereby declare . . . guilty of . . . . Date . . . . Signed . . . . '). As usual the basic message is not spoken: 'I . . . am not guilty.' Such certificates serve to glorify Self, not only to condemn Other. They draw fine, mighty lines of ink, building walls of paper.

One way of summarizing this particular syndrome would be the 'Dichotomy-Manicheism-Armageddon' (DMA) syndrome: there are sharp lines dividing human reality into two parts; one part, Other, is pure Evil, and the other, Self, is pure Good; a final, decisive battle is bound to come, better be prepared. A syndrome like that can best be understood in terms of its negation. There are lines but they are fuzzy and criss-crossing, defining more than two parties; no party is only evil or only good, they are all *yin/yang*; there is no final battle. The first syndrome is a part of cultural violence, the second a part of cultural peace. The first leads to clear fronts, polarization, mobilizing for a battle or a stalemate deterred by balance of power; the second to inner and outer dialogues inside Self and with Other over ways of improving the situation; or to inaction, immobilized by doubt.

One way of summarizing the second syndrome has been done for thousands of years already in the concept of *karma*: a shared destiny which is not predetermined but can be improved at any time. The approach is exactly through the inner dialogue which is then usually called meditation, and through the outer dialogue among all parties to the conflict, the 'conflict formation'. To search for an answer to the perennial question of the first syndrome, 'Who started?', is meaningless since life is interactive, co-dependent origination anyhow. Somebody may have fired the first shot, but then somebody else did something before that and so on backward and sideward, till time immemorial, and out in the remotest geographical and social periphery. There is no denial of Evil but denial of the possibility of locating it neatly at one space point, and of allocating the First Evil Act to one point in time.

How, then, about forward in time? If time is finite, then there is a final state, the state arrived at when time stops (or, more precisely, when change stops). But if there is a final state, then obviously that state is irreversible, otherwise it would not have been final. If it is irreversible, then obviously it is engraved, mildly speaking, in stone, in steel. Any move away from the final state, or efforts in that direction, would be like crimes against History, Time, Nature. The step from that idea to the use of violence to arrive at and uphold the final state is short, and is a major part of the Orwellian idea of irreversible society, exemplified in this century in the violence of Nazism (*Tausendjähriges Reich*), global communism and capitalism (End of History).

Posited against this would be the idea of reversibility: do nothing that cannot be undone. If nothing is final, nothing should be done as if it were. This can be interpreted as leading to fatalism. But a stronger interpretation would be: any state of affairs can be improved, hence do not make it irreversible.[9]

There are some important implications that follow. One implication is non-violence. Violence is so terribly irreversible. Only in Disney-type cartoons do flattened, pierced beings, those crosses between humans and animals, rise from the dead, given new life by their creator as if the Bible were born again; in real, empirical life not.[10]

This also applies, even if less so, to non-lethal violence because, by definition, it leaves traumas behind. The verbs used for violence, to harm, to hurt, already carry this connotation of wounds, somatic and/or mental; and any physician of the body and/or the soul knows that wounds are not easily localized (except superficially) but tend to spread all over; moreover, they are not easily erased. Both body and mind have memory, maybe particularly so of trauma, even if a strong Self may rise to the occasion and process and erase, not only suppress,

---

9. Not, incidentally, to be confused with a Pareto optimum from which any move makes nobody worse off. A Pareto optimum is, obviously, compatible with changes so that some stand still and some move ahead, increasing the distance, which very often means increasing the conflict potential. Thus, a Pareto optimum does not serve as an example of something that should be made irreversible.
10. It is hardly too far-fetched to suggest that this is one of the many reasons behind the enormity of US violence: people may simply believe that life is reversible if cartoon virtual reality stands out as more real than empirical reality.

even heavy traumas. The key probably lies in making them meaningful, learning from them, turning them into sources of enrichment.

This also applies to traumas of the significant Others, of those directly hit and hurt: the bereaved, the friends and relatives of the wounded (crippled in body or mind): their grief may also carry elements of irreversibility.

The second implication is ecological: do unto nature nothing irreversible like killing a species; only take from nature what nature can renew, making your take reversible. A simpler formulation would be: extend non-violence as theory and practice to the non-human part of nature.

It is worth noting that a philosophy of reversibility differs from Kant's philosophy of universalizability.[11] Kant may be interpreted as saying that the principle underlying your action should be generalizable, even universalizable, to the whole world (potentially to the whole universe), meaning: do only that which others (all others) could also do. If every family on earth cannot have a fridge without the ozone layer breaking down, then abstain from it yourself. If your spiritual development does not reduce the possibilities of a similar development for others, then no problem, do it.

Obviously, Kant's dictum serves well to regulate behaviour in a materially finite world, and steers activities towards that which is not or less limited: the non-material. But does it rule out violence? Or is it more like 'engage only in the (quality and quantity) of violence that you would be willing to permit universally'? Like 'peace enforcement',[12] defensive violence, violence according to Augustinian Rules for Just War or Islamic Rules for Holy War (fourth stage of *jihad*)? This is actually in one sense the world in which we live; war being legitimized through the idea that 'I now go to war, but under the same or similar circumstances I would also have granted you the right to do so'. Obviously this does not rule out war, and universalization may even serve legitimization.

Finally, the search for an overarching concept for creativity. Above, the word 'flexibility' has been given as an indicator, a road-sign, so to speak. The idea is as follows. The action-space for a person P, in search of a way out of a

---

11. In *Zum ewigen Frieden*, first published two centuries ago in 1795.
12. According to Chapter 7 of the UN Charter, the expression being a good example of a *contradictio in adjecto*.

conflict, for instance, in a point in space, S, at a point in time, T, can generally be divided into three subspaces: the conventionally possible, the potentially possible, and the impossible – CP, PP and IM for short. P searches CP and finds nothing. Creativity not being his strong side – among other reasons because he lives in a culture where the world is seen as inflexible, as governed by ironclad laws of nature and laws of society enforced by iron fists – he gives up, assuming PP to be empty and IM to start where CP ends. It goes without saying that, if violence is in CP – and it usually is, most peoples around the world have heard about it and learnt some by now, however innocent they may have been at some point in time – if CP is very limited and PP non-existing, then violence would come at an early stage. Question: what is underlying these kinds of attitudes?

One culturally embedded assumption has been indicated above: the faith in iron laws, not of nature and of society. It is not by chance that we use the same word (law, *Gesetz, lov, loi, legge, ley,* etc.) both for those of society and those of nature. The origin for that sameness in the doubleness is easily seen: God prescribed not only laws for man/humans but also for nature; to study nature, hence, was to study God. Today, after the Enlightenment, we see the former as given (by law-givers) and the latter as found (by scientists).

But the result is the same in all three cases, whether laws are given by God or the successors to the theologians, the jurists and the scientists: action-spaces are limited. There are constraints: laws of nature, laws of society. If people believe these constraints to be inflexible, immutable (or irreversible, to refer to the preceding point), then so they are in their consequences (the Znaniecki-Thomas theorem).

The negation of this would be a less God-given nature with laws established once and for all, and less immutable social laws. To start with the latter: an interesting characteristic of Anglo-Saxon common law, as opposed to Roman law, is that the laws are themselves on trial because they also serve predictive functions. If people break them *en masse*, then in what sense are they still a law? They are not a social science law in the sense that they can be used to predict normal, average behaviour, nor are they social laws in the sense of something that is obeyed or at least not broken. What remains is an empty formulation, some kind of epitaph over a dead law. A new law has to be born.

Within a culture of that type civil disobedience makes sense. Mass civil disobedience adds a moral dimension to the decline of predictability, indicative of what a new law might look like. That this is politics is beyond doubt: there is nothing so political as a conflict, any conflict,[13] and few ideas so revolutionary as 'peace'. Civil disobedience can also work with one person who says *ich kann nicht anders*,[14] but that person should rather be strong in all possible ways. Gandhi combined Hindu *ahimsa* with Anglo-Saxon common law.

But how about laws of nature, can they also be transcended? A glance at the history of natural sciences and their applications will immediately inform us that the answer is yes: we do all the time. The typical approach is not to change the laws but to introduce more variables so that what was (held to be) impossible suddenly becomes possible, meaning that it was all the time potentially possible.

A good example is the invention of the airplane: the contra-argument was that it was impossible, otherwise it would already have been there; besides, why do we have the laws of gravity anyhow, if not exactly to see to it that things that are heavy are down and things that are light are up? Airplanes are heavy; the conclusion is obvious. Within that single law discourse, yes, but when the buoyancy created by two wings, flat on the underside and curved on the upper side, dragged through the air by even a relatively weak engine is added to the force of gravity, then the thing takes off.

How about social science laws? Of course, they are more rubber and iron laws but nevertheless, perhaps because people believe in them, something that may serve as a barrier between CP and PP, and make PP look like IM. The approach is exactly the same: a third variable is introduced in a relation between two variables, showing that one cannot have industrial development without destruction of the extended family because the workers have to move to the cities and cannot bring all thirty members of the extended family. Solution: bring the

---

13. For that reason, slogans like 'the politics of everyday life' and 'the politics of inner life' make complete sense and should not be regarded as reductionism. And peace culture is as relevant there as anywhere a conflict can be identified.
14. Luther, who somehow managed, in spite of working inside a Roman rather than an Anglo-Saxon tradition.

industry to the villages, make parts, have a first rate transportation-communication system, like Japan and Switzerland.[15]

WHERE DO WE FIND *KARMA*, REVERSIBILITY AND FLEXIBILITY?

Not much knowledge of culture and macro-culture (civilization) is needed to know that one obvious answer to this question is Buddhism. The *karma* idea is central, not in the frequently misunderstood (in the West) sense of predetermination, but in the sense of 'whatever you say, and whatever you do, sooner or later comes back to you'. You say/do something bad and your *karma* deteriorates; you say/do something good and your *karma* improves. The concept is holistic, it takes anything you say and do (including the 'subvocal speech', the cognitions-thoughts, and the 'subcutanous' acts, the emotions-volitions). Above all, there is a concept of individual *karma* but also of collective *karma* (you did wrong to me/I did wrong to you) the more holistic, and more relational, we did wrong to us, meaning you and I share a bad *karma*. What has to be changed is our relation and through that also you and me. The term 'guilt' locates what is wrong at one *karma* point, in one actor, instead of predicating it of the *karma* as a whole.[16] Therapy follows from what has been said: not by the guilty engaging in a confession-apology-penitence-catharsis sequence but through a process back and forth between inner and outer dialogue to find what went wrong and what can be done.

But Oriental and Occidental approaches can and should be combined. The point can be made that, if the guilty/non-guilty approach is too black-white, then the *karma* approach is too 50/50. There are circumstances, even if the causal nexus is extremely complex and cyclical rather than linear, where some are more responsible (better than guilty) than others.

Interestingly, Buddhism also carries in its epistemology the two pillars of

---

15. For much more about this, see Johan Galtung, 'Science as Invariance-finding and Invariance-breaking', *Methodology and Ideology*, Ch. 3, Copenhagen, Ejlers, 1977.
16. *PBPM,* Part II, Ch. 2.

reversibility and flexibility here seen as essential.[17] In Buddhist thinking, time, being unlimited, has no end, nor any beginning, meaning that there is little or no room for speculation about the state of origin and the final state. From that, however, reversibility does not follow: there could be room for infinite progress or infinite regress, for instance. And there are elements of this in Buddhism as *nirvana* is irreversible. On the other hand, for all of humanity we would be operating with time perspectives of such a duration that 'for all practical purposes' such final states carry few shadows into the present. The quality of the many *karmas* oscillates, even if there is a happy ending in the very long run. There are moral precepts, like the Noble Eight-Fold Path, the *Panch Shila* and the *Panch Dharma*, but the epistemology opens for a never-ending creation process with one possible interpretation being that the task is to identify those external circumstances that favour inner growth.

This opens the cone of possible futures for any P in S, T. No god (or successor) can prescribe forever what the laws of nature and society will be; one reason being there is no god. However, Buddhists have, in practice, been more interested in the laws of the inner human being than in social and natural laws, Hindus and Chinese getting more into the social realm, and the West focusing more on outer nature. Thus, Buddhists and Hindus have been bending the mind like the West has been bending nature. And peace, they say, is located in the minds of men; so reversibility and flexibility of mind matter.

From the point of view of *les sciences de l'homme,* it would be naïve to limit the search for cultural paxogenes to religions alone. Of course paxogenes, peace culture elements, can be found in all religions, in their softer rather than their harder articulations. But culture should not be confused with the cultural products/objects (among them religious texts and symbols) but should rather be seen as the (symbolic) standards generating these products, such as the standards for the true, the good, the right, the beautiful, the sacred. Any human group develops such standards, perhaps not all five types but at least the first three. So does any human category, defined by the lines classifying us humans, sometimes

---

17. For an exploration of Buddhist versus Christian epistemology, see Johan Galtung, *Methodology and Development*, Ch. 1.1, Copenhagen, Ejlers, 1988, or *Buddhism: A Quest for Unity and Peace*, Ch. 5, Colombo, Sarvodaya International, 1993.

also dividing us to the point that we can talk about fault-lines. A short list: gender, generation, race, class, nation, territory (country).

My own experience from nearly fifty years as a peace activist would be that the carriers of peace are found among women more than among men; among women of all ages, among men more among the young and the old (the middle-aged being more dubious); race as such does not matter; among the middle class more than in the upper and lower classes; certainly not among nations ridden by Chosenness-Myths-Trauma (CMT) complexes, or among those believing they have found the only valid truth for the whole world; and where territory is concerned among the smaller countries rather than the larger, down to the small and underutilized territorial units known as municipalities. And, among non-territorial units, meaning non-governmental organizations, civil society.

Let us regard these as hypotheses and try to identify underlying peace cultures that may explain such findings, even if it has to be done negatively in the sense of postulating the absence of bellogenes rather than the presence of paxogenes in category deep culture.

Gender

In patriarchies, males competing for positions might develop zero-sum views of conflicts more than women in an incessant search for ways of harmonizing the goals of family members. It becomes 'me or you', not 'us'. In that struggle there is little or no room for admitting weakness, even to oneself. If there is imperfection around the tendency, it will be to project it on the Other and attribute guilt rather than to assume shared responsibility. Reversibility of any decision is tantamount to the admission that the decision may have been wrong, a difficult position to assume for the gender closer to the Omniscient/Omnipotent. Knowing their own latent aggressiveness, men may, more than women, construct and embed themselves in rigid hierarchies of ideas/theses (cultural violence, such as deductive law) and of positions (structural violence, such as found in military-bureaucratic hierarchies). Conclusion: no guarantee that women are carriers of peace cultures, but the hypothesis that men in patriarchies are not.

Generation

Since much of what has been said about males above derives from positions in society outside the family and as *pater familias,* it should apply less to the young male on the way up but still a subordinate family member, and the old male on the way down in society and family. Example: peace messages from retired senior officers or defence ministers.

Race

No reason to assume any difference in the distribution of paxogenes and bellogenes as long as gender, generation, class and nation are kept constant.

Class

The basic point to be made here is that class, as we know, it is basically defined within a 'society', which up till now in practice means some combination of nation and country. A person derives élite status from nation/country, for instance through birth or education, and it is not automatically transmitted around the world (not even for royalty). High at home, a nobody abroad; the opposite applies more to the individual than to the socially construed person ('nobody is a prophet in his own country'). As a consequence, élites would be particularly inclined to play leading roles in inter-state and inter-nation conflict for mutual enhancement. And they will most easily be able to command the allegiance of the segments of society most vulnerable to the lures of the carrot (for instance because they may be starving, or at least unemployed) and the threats of the stick (having little power). The result is an élite-working class national alliance, and an inter-élite tacit alliance in sacrificing workers.[18]

Not so, or less so, for the middle class. As opposed to the other two they, the bourgeoisie, have a very similar lifestyle around the world: four members in the family, four-room apartment, four-wheels on the car (the 4-4-4 syndrome).

---

18. A point often made about the First World War: the generals who sent the working class across the trenches to kill each other were operating across considerable class divides. In the end (1918) the soldiers revolted; in France that revolt was crushed by Maréchal Pétain.

They are the mass members of the people's organizations, and at least potentially cosmopolitan rather than nationalist.[19] They can still be mobilized for war, but they will try to avoid conscription, and seek peace-building roles instead.

Nation

By definition nations are carriers of cultures, since that is how nations are defined. However, I would prefer to build the definition of a nation and its culture around something more primordial than language and religion, namely space and time, and more particularly around the *kairos* points where glory and trauma, secular and/or sacred, are defined. To protect the points in space, contiguous territory around us seems to be the rational approach and, to protect the recurring points in time, the memory, continuity of that territory in time. In short, the country, with an organization of the state in its midst, even as a nation-state. At the micro-level the family farm/estate/castle play the same role.

Territory

The essence has already been said: territory as the abode of the nation. A basic problem, then, is whether territories and nations exclude each other. Drawing borders, using rulers to rule, certainly makes territories look mutually exclusive, although condominium, where administration is concerned and double citizenship would still be possible. And the same would apply to nation: people are known to speak more languages than one, some even to hold more religions than one, and in multinational societies (like Hawaii) people can develop polynational styles (like polyglot people), being conversant with more nations than one, distributing their joy and grief more equally among the *kairos* points. One condition for this, it might seem, is that there is no single nation dominating, statistically or otherwise, the territory.

And here we choose to end. The theme is endless. So is the search to enhance the paxogenes and pacify the bellogenes.

---

19. One reason why so much scorn was heaped upon them until the 1970s when the potential usefulness for peace of these people's organizations was discovered in the Soviet Union.

Social and cultural sources of violence

Santiago Genovés *

BACKGROUND

Since the moment I participated in the UNESCO meeting organized to adopt the Statement on Race and Racism in Moscow in 1964, I realized we had to work towards a Statement on Violence. That is the reason why I published a series of books and works, as a result of direct or indirect experimentation with regard to the contributions of other scholars on this subject. Furthermore, the film *Pax* and the animated cartoon *Muscle and Culture* (Genovés, 1976) were prepared in the same spirit. While participating in another assembly on race and racism in Athens in 1981, which was also organized under the auspices of UNESCO, I became deeply convinced of the need for carrying this work further.

Hence, based on my own research and that of others, I continued in the same direction and tried to fight against taboos, prejudices, mistakes and misunderstandings concerning the origins and sources of violence (Genovés, 1982, 1984a, 1984b, 1985, etc.). In general terms, a group of well-known researchers (such as Lorenz, 1966, 1970; Lorenz and Leyhausen, 1973; Eibl-Eibesfeldt, 1970; Ardrey, 1970; Storr, 1968; and, up to a certain point, others like Fromm, 1973; Morris, 1969; Moyer, 1976; Ortega, 1982) maintained a different ethnological, psychoanalytic and physiological point of view: that is, fundamentally, that

---

* Dean of the Institute for Anthropological Research, University of Mexico.

violence is something innate to man.[1] However, investigations by other authors indicated that this was not so. Subsequently, a meeting between scholars in different fields was held at the Monastery of la Rábida, near Seville in Spain, in order to elaborate a statement on violence, *The Seville Statement on Violence*, which has now been adopted by more than 100 international and national scientific organizations, including UNESCO.

It is based on five points:
1. It is scientifically incorrect to say that violence is genetically determined.
2. It is scientifically incorrect to say that it comes from our animal past.
3. It is scientifically incorrect to say that, in the process of human evolution, there has been a greater selection for aggressive behaviour than for other kinds of behaviour.
4. It is scientifically incorrect to say that humans have a 'violent brain'.
5. It is scientifically incorrect to say that violent behaviour is genetically inherited.

Thus, just as 'wars begin in the minds of men', peace also begins in our minds. The same species which invented war is capable of inventing peace. The responsibility lies with each of us.

The Seville Statement was prepared by nineteen scientists from different parts of the world and from many disciplines (genetics, neurophysiology, anthropology, sociology, history, psychology, ethnology, palaeoanthropology, psychiatry).

The film *Pax*, as well as a television series entitled *Expedition to Violence*,[2] comprising five one-hour parts, constitutes the most evident antecedents to *The Seville Statement on Violence*.[3]

It is evident (Genovés, 1994; de Saint Blanquat, 1989) that we have not had a palaeoanthropologically true proof of generalized, institutionalized violence

---

1. For contrary views, beyond my own, see among others: Mead, 1940; Roe and Simpson, 1958; Scott, 1990; Alland, 1967; Montagu, 1976; Dastague, 1982; Messmacher et al., 1986; Hinde and Groebel, 1988; de Saint Blanquat, 1989.
2. Spain, UNESCO-Mexico, produced by Televisa.
3. This is intended to give the scholar essential data which lead, historically and scientifically, to a 180° change about what we know today of the origins and sources of violence and, starting from the integrative and interdisciplinary *Seville Statement on Violence*, to dedicate ourselves fundamentally to its social and cultural aspects.

during the process of hominization over the last 5 million years. Generalized, institutionalized violence started with a great revolution of man, the Agricultural Revolution approximately 7,000 years ago, and was exacerbated by the Industrial Revolution approximately 200 hundred years ago.

SOCIAL AND CULTURAL ASPECTS OF VIOLENCE

It is clear that to exert violence, we use biology or its technological extensions. However, the origin of generalized and institutionalized violence is not biological; it is a phenomenon with which we are preoccupied, for we should certainly deal with its sociological and cultural aspects.[4]

Even before civilization, evolution propelled by chance and need followed a pattern going beyond what was logical or reasonable. Let us not return any further to the past but start with the first vertebrate, the amphioxus, found on sandy beaches in Italy and subsequently elsewhere. We can say the world was theirs. But, no, in time amphioxus became fish and owned three-quarters of the earth. As time went by, fish became amphibious and owned both sea and land. Again, in time, reptiles, in turn, became birds and other mammals. Birds remained in the air, but mammals became primates, primates became hominoids and hominoids became hominids and hominids became *Homo faber*,[5] and ... here we are.

Thus the impulse to go further appears before culture, which constitutes, nevertheless, a greater leap than any taken in all of the stages mentioned above. It is an extra-biological leap which in some way continues the biological impulse to go beyond what is known.

Culture, as we know it, starts when we begin to play with pebbles. This game implicitly leads to the constant adventure of proceeding further and further,

---

4. Findings at the beginning of the 1950s are of questionable value, particularly in the medico-genetic field, and have led to a supposed biological determinism of all behaviour, including violent behaviour; see Genovés, 1994.
5. Whether we have or have not reached the stage of *Homo sapiens*, as we pompously call ourselves, remains still to be seen. The intraspecific violence can finish us all, before we reach the stage *sapiens*.

always searching for Utopia, the unknown which frequently we reach. In the pursuit of this exclusively cultural and perennial search through ignorance, like a child who sticks his finger into the eye of another child, we are hurt and it is intraspecific violence which we perpetrate. Owing to cultural (historical, linguistic, religious, economic, political, etc.) reasons or absurdities, we kill one another, for all those reasons which elephants, sharks, tigers, etc., cannot discern. I insist: cultural differences are the main motives of intraspecific violence today – and have been since the Agricultural Revolution. In the very first place, the conscious or unconscious search for leadership and power. Conscious or not, we are here to know ourselves and to be appreciated by others. The more people who see us, in the scope of our inalienable human egocentrism, the more reflections we obtain in the mirror made by others. But we also hope for respect, thus we seek for leadership.[6]

Secondly, the constant change of roles, hour by hour, day by day, week by week. Others frequently cannot adapt or understand these fast changes to new roles, new masks: violence.

Thirdly, every day we are aware of greater differences in levels of information, which create envy, uneasiness and violence among individuals or groups possessing wide cultural information as opposed to those with almost none, who are close to us, both at individual levels and in the extended social environments.[7]

Fourthly, the deficit in processes of socialization during the first years of life. This deficit is reflected, by cultural inheritance, in the way children with an initial deficit act when they become adult (abused child syndrome, violence towards women and the weak, etc.).

Subsequently, depending both on geographical zones and on differing circumstances, lack of culture (which includes many of the so-called 'cultivated', that is, those who have studied, attended university, etc.), obvious external differences caused by genetic realities, such as the colour of the skin and hair,

---

6. The other way to know ourselves, by slow, arduous and persistent introspection, is a long process to which few can dedicate themselves.
7. The struggles, until a point of near death, both in science and the humanities and arts, are daily examples. The two world wars are painful examples of this.

sex, height, language, produce violence and racism follows. There is a reason for this: taxonomically, we have linear categories: gender, species, race. It is a law of nature that everybody feeds off other species, including vegetarians. Racism is therefore a natural consequence which prevails, owing to lack of culture.

An idea akin to this is found in what constitutes the essence of Sartre's existentialism: to refer to the 'others' as 'objects'. And the more they are biologically different from us, the more we think of them as 'objects': the soldier 'object'; the woman 'object'; the negro 'object' – or, for the negro, the white 'object', etc. When we consider other human beings as 'objects', violence is caused, for reasons which are obvious.

CULTURE AND TECHNOLOGY

On the other hand, when we have become slaves of the massive means of communication (direct: trains, ships, aeroplanes, automobiles; or indirect: radio and television), we lose the possibility which formed us palaeoanthropologically and made us ready for physical adventure. Suddenly, great ships, great trains, great automobiles, great planes. To go today from Mexico to China does not represent more than having the money for the ticket. Yet, suddenly the true physical adventure which we lived over hundreds of thousands of years is over. We live today in a world in direct need of adventure. We live by projection of what we see on television happening to Robert Redford or to Peter O'Toole, usually in distant lands; unusual adventures, while we only live 'subway-work-sleep', 'subway-work-sleep'.

From the taste for television, the taste for exciting and massive 'rock' concerts, drugs, indiscriminate sex, all of which spring from a yearning for real communication, such as when we go to great stadiums to live, by empathy and projection, the adventure of the match. Thus, to outlandish dress with knee-length boots, greatcoats and cowboy hats in the middle of the city, in Chelsea, in Montmartre, as if we were to hunt lions in Africa. And all we can do is have a Coca-Cola in a nearby bar, etc.

Yes, physical adventure is over and we search everywhere for the way to recover it. We look for it as we looked unsuccessfully for violence in biology.

Nothing else exists but a fictitious, controlled, domestically prepared physical adventure. There are many authors who have demonstrated each of these points. We have corroborated this in three experiments with rafts, with a total of 212 days' isolation at sea for twenty-six human beings.

Yes, the first great leap was the interaction of biology and pebbles, and the second the Agricultural Revolution; the third is the other adventure, already dawning: the 'Adventure of Thought', through knowledge, science, humanism and technology, integrated and in constant feedback. We are, even though it does not seem so, at the beginning of this huge adventure: that of culture, which possesses flights beyond those already imagined by the limited physical adventure, circumscribed within our planet up to now, or to some of the closer planets for a selected few in the future.

The adventure of creation through thought, of investigation and experimentation, does not have limits, though it seems limited by violence, wars, inhuman and anti-ethical mortality, attributed wrongly to destiny and biological fatality. This is not so! As Léon Felipe[8] would say:

> Tell me no more tales
> for I come from afar
> and I know all the tales
> tell me no more tales
>
> that I do not want to be lulled with tales
> that I do not want to,
> that I do not want to,
> that I do not want to
> that I do not want my mouth and eyes to be sealed with tales,
> that I do not want to
> that I do not want to,
> that I do not want to,
> that I do not want to be buried with tales . . .

To obtain the true adventure of thought, it is necessary to tell the tale we have

---

8. Spanish poet. Born in 1884 in Tabara (Province of Zamora). Died in Mexico in 1968.

told, from knowledge, from science. Let us tell it to friends and people around us so that instead of throwing deadly stones at one another, we use them to build energy, a new world. By opening space to man, the process of evolution has, for the first time, become self-conscious. This finally gave us the possibility of having evolution directed by man, when the absurd prevails. The absurd was to think that we had to kill each other because of biological fatalism. We have told ourselves that this is not so. But the tales are over.

Since the beginning of the century, it has been demonstrated that intraspecific survival is fundamentally due to processes of co-operation and not of intraspecific struggle. Otherwise, from the Australopithecids till now, we would not be here. Owing to lack of culture, this has still not been acknowledged, except by certain limited human groups.

CONCLUSION

The present UNESCO study constitutes a step forward since the 1986 *Seville Statement on Violence*. Just as UNESCO arrived at successive statements on the broadened and improved concepts of race as new scientific knowledge appeared, let us hope, in the same way, that this will be the first step to obtain a Second Statement on Violence. Such a statement should determine the cultural and social processes which are at the root of the present constant state of violence and which threaten to end the solitary raft on which we live, planet Earth, beyond most valuable biological aspects and processes which, in a natural and general form, determine our behaviour: birds fly; fish swim, which our species cannot do biologically. Or the discoveries of genetics and molecular biology which increasingly help us every day to know, or even prevent, situations which harm health. But:

> What is broken is not
> the water the glass holds.
> What is broken is the glass
> and the water spills on to the floor

We therefore now definitely need an extensive and profound Second Statement on Violence concerning sociocultural environments; this is a difficult task for a bioethical culture, but it is possible.

BIBLIOGRAPHY

ALLAND, A. 1967. *Evolution of Human Behavior*. Garden City, N.Y., American Museum Science Books.
ARDREY, R. 1970. *The Social Contract*. New York, Atheneum.
DASTAGUE, J. 1982. Les maladies de nos ancêtres. *La Recherche*, No. 13, pp. 980–8.
EIBL-EIBESFELDT, I. 1970. *Ethology: The Science of Behaviour*. New York, Holt, Rinehart & Winston.
FROMM, E. 1973. *The Anatomy of Human Destructiveness*. New York, Holt, Rinehart & Winston. 478 pp.
GENOVÉS, S. 1976. El experimento acali. *Ciencia y dessarrollo* (CONACYT), Vol. II, No. 8, pp. 4–7.
——. 1982. A propósito de Darwin: una crítica sin sentido. *Información científica y tecnológica*, Vol. 4, No. 63, pp. 20–21.
——. 1984a. Igualdad y desigualdad en el tiempo: antropología. *Ciencia y desarrollo*, No. 55, pp. 9–17.
——. 1984b. De profundia: genética y ambiente. *Información científica y tecnológica* (CONACYT), Vol. 6, No. 9, pp. 12–13.
——. 1985. Human Evolution and Human Behavior. Rethinking Some Particular Paleanthropological Point about Evolution, with Special Reference to Human Behavior. Proceedings of 3rd European and 1st Panhellenic Anthropological Congress, Athens. *Anthropos*, Vol. 10, pp. 195–204.
——. 1994. *Violence Revisited*. UNESCO, Paris. 232 pp.
HINDE, R. A.; GROEBEL, J. (eds.). 1988. The Problem of Aggression. In: *Aggression and War – Their Biological and Social Bases*, pp. 3–9. Cambridge, Cambridge University Press.
LORENZ, K. 1966. *On Aggression*. New York, Harcourt, Brace & World.
——. 1970. *Studies in Animal and Human Behavior*, Vol. 1. Cambridge, Mass., Harvard University Press. 366 pp.
LORENZ, K.; LEYHAUSEN, P. 1973. *Motivation of Human and Animal Behavior: An Ecological View*. New York, D. Van Nostrand.
MEAD, M. 1940. Warfare: Only an Invention – Not a Biological Necessity. *Asia*, No. 40, pp. 402–5.
MESSMACHER, M.; GENOVÉS, S.; NOLASCO, M. 1986. *Dinámica Maya*. Mexico City, FCE.

Montagu, M. F. A. 1976. *The Nature of Human Aggression*. New York, Oxford Ross.
Morris, D. 1969. *The Human Zoo*. Toronto, Clark, Irwin & Co. 256 pp.
Moyer, K. E. 1976. *The Psychobiology of Aggression*. New York, Harper & Row.
Ortega, A. 1982. *La agresividad, el instinto de la muerte*. Mexico City, Universidad Autónoma del Estado de México.
Roe, A. G.; Simpson, G. (eds.). 1958. *Behavior and Evolution*. New Haven, Conn., Yale University Press.
Saint Blanquat, H. de. 1989. L'invention de la guerre. *Sciences et avenir*, No. 506, pp. 81–86.
Scott, J. P. 1990. Ethology and Aggression. *Para conocer al hombre*, pp. 93–114. Mexico City, Universidad Autónoma de México.
Storr, A. 1992. *Human Aggression*. London, Penguin.
Wilson, E. O. 1975. *Sociobiology: The New Synthesis*. Cambridge, Mass., Harvard University Press.

Creating global/local cultures of peace

Linda Groff* and Paul Smoker**

INTRODUCTION

During recent years, the term 'a culture of peace' has become increasingly popular, thanks to UNESCO's initiative, but there is at present no clear consensus as to how the term should be interpreted. Should it be the culture of peace, or should it be a culture of peace, or should we think in a more pluralistic fashion about cultures of peace, thus incorporating part of UNESCO's operational definition that a culture of peace cannot be imported or imposed from outside, but must develop from the culture of the people concerned? There are many different ways to define the concept 'cultures of peace', and we shall consider some of them in this article, but whichever definition is used, it is important to recognize that culture has both micro or local aspects, as well as macro or global aspects, for example Western or Eastern, and that there are many different cultural traditions which need to be included in any 'cultures of peace' concept. This also raises the issue of peace within cultures and peace between cultures. There are too many historical examples of a nation or group co-operating and organizing internally in order to undertake violence or wage war on an external group; indeed, inner cohesion and collaboration is often a necessary condition for such actions. From a systems point of view, every 'cultures of peace' concept

---

* Professor of Political Science and Future Studies, California State University, Carson, California, USA.
** Professor, Antioch College, Yellow Springs, Ohio, USA.

needs to apply within and between cultures, to be a property of both the local parts and the global whole. UNESCO recognizes this fact in its operational definition of a culture of peace, when it stresses that local programmes are embedded in a national and perhaps subregional context, as well as the global context of the United Nations and its Specialized Agencies.

The problem of deciding what we mean by the term 'culture(s) of peace' is further complicated by the various interpretations of the two key elements 'culture' and 'peace', as noted below. After looking at different definitions of culture, and the evolution of six different perspectives on peace, largely within Western peace research, this paper will then discuss six perspectives on a culture of peace and six perspectives on non-violence as they relate to peace in each of these six areas.

CULTURE: DIFFERENT DEFINITIONS

There are a number of different definitions of culture, a few of which will be explored here. First, it must be noted that there are both narrow and broad definitions of culture. Narrow definitions focus on the arts, including literature, poetry, music, theatre, painting, dance, etc. Broader definitions, which are used in anthropology and intercultural communication fields, include all our socially learned behaviour. Thus one anthropological definition of culture is that it is 'learned, shared, patterned behaviour, as reflected in technology/tools, social organizations (including economic, political, social, religious, educational, family, and other organizations) and ideas/beliefs'. The key point is that culture is not something one is born with but something that is learned after one is born; it is also passed down from one generation to the next. Culture is also shared by a group of people together, and all the different aspects of one's culture must somehow fit together into an overall pattern.

Another definition of culture is 'what gives meaning to life'. A third definition of culture looks at deeper, hidden levels of meaning, in addition to surface-level, more apparent meanings. Here culture is defined as 'common symbols, rituals and hero figures (visible), shared by a group of people, based on a set of values and underlying assumptions about reality (hidden)'. This definition is illustrated in Figure 1.

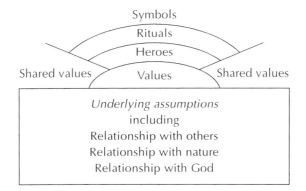

FIG. 1. Culture: visible and hidden dimensions.

EVOLUTION OF THE PEACE CONCEPT, ESPECIALLY IN WESTERN PEACE RESEARCH: SIX STAGES

The term 'peace', like 'culture', has a wide range of interpretations. This section outlines six broad categories of peace-thinking which have emerged historically within Western peace research, especially over the past fifty years (since the end of the Second World War). These six categories roughly correspond to the evolution of peace-thinking in Western peace research. This does not mean that all scholars once thought one way and now think another, nor that the majority of peace researchers now adopt the sixth type of peace-thinking, the holistic inner/outer peace paradigm. Rather it argues that overall there has been a trend in peace research away from the traditional idea that peace is simply the absence of war towards a more holistic view, as seen in Figure 2.

These stages in the evolution of the peace concept include the following.

1. Peace as absence of war

Figure 2 summarizes six perspectives on peace in terms of the levels of analysis and theoretical focus which each includes. The first perspective, peace as the absence of war, is applied to violent conflict between and within states: war and civil war. This view of peace is still widely held among the population in general and politicians. In certain situations, it can be argued that this is still a legitimate

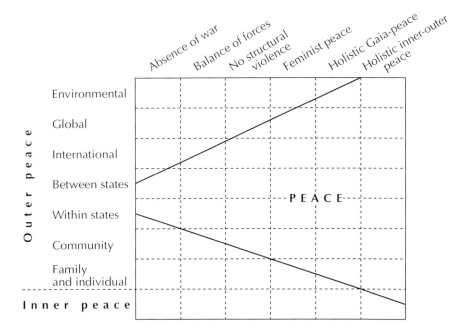

FIG. 2. Six concepts in the evolution of peace.

objective, at least until the killing stops and it is possible to ask for more out of life than avoiding death in war. Furthermore, all six definitions of peace discussed here require absence of war as a necessary precondition for peace.

2. Peace as the balance of forces in the international system

Quincy Wright (1941) modified this idea of absence of war to suggest that peace was a dynamic balance involving political, social, cultural and technological factors, and that war occurred when this balance broke down. Wright argued that this balance of forces occurred in the international system, defined in terms of the overall pattern of relationships between states and international governmental organizations (IGOs), as well as between and within states. Wright also discussed the role of domestic public opinion within a state, which involves the community level of analysis. His model assumed that any significant change in one of the factors involved in the peace balance would require corresponding changes in other factors to restore the balance. For example, Robert Oppenheimer, the much misunderstood 'father of the atomic bomb', adopted Wright's view when he insisted on continuing to develop the bomb so that a global political institution, the United Nations, would have to be created to help control the new global military technology.

3. Peace as negative peace (no war) and positive peace (no structural violence)

Galtung (1969) further modified Wright's view, using the categories 'negative peace' and 'positive peace' which Wright had first put forward some twenty-eight years earlier. Galtung developed a third position and argued that negative peace was the absence of war and that positive peace was the absence of 'structural violence', a concept defined in terms of the numbers of avoidable deaths caused simply by the way social, economic and other structures were organized. Thus if people starve to death when there is food to feed them somewhere in the world, or die from sickness when there is medicine to cure them, then structural violence exists, since alternative structures could, in theory, prevent such deaths. Peace under this rubric involves both positive and negative peace being present. Galtung's model (in addition to the community, within states, between states, and international levels of analysis) includes the global level of analysis, such as the global economy which is influenced by non-state actors, for example non-governmental organizations (NGOs) and multinational corporations (MNCs).

4. Feminist peace: macro and micro levels of peace

During the 1970s and 1980s, a fourth perspective was ushered in by feminist peace researchers, who extended both negative peace and positive peace to include violence and structural violence down to the individual level (Brock-Utne, 1989). The new definition of peace then included not only the abolition of macro-level organized violence, such as war, but also doing away with micro-level unorganized violence, such as rape in war or in the home. In addition, the concept of structural violence was similarly expanded to include personal, micro- and macro-level structures which harm or discriminate against particular individuals or groups. This feminist peace model came to include all types of violence, broadly defined, against people, from the individual to the global level, arguing that this is a necessary condition for a peaceful planet.

5. Holistic Gaia-peace:[1] peace with the environment

The 1990s have seen the emergence of two types of holistic peace-thinking (Dreher, 1991; Macy, 1991; Smoker, 1991). Here, as with the feminist model, peace between people applies across all levels of analysis, from the family and individual level to the global level. In addition, the Gaia-peace theory places a very high value on the relationship of humans to bio-environmental systems, the environmental level of analysis. Peace with the environment is seen as central for this type of holistic peace theory, where human beings are seen as one of many species inhabiting the earth, and the fate of the planet is seen as the most important goal. This type of holistic peace-thinking does not have a spiritual dimension, peace being defined in terms of all forms of physical violence against people and the environment.

6. Holistic inner and outer peace

This sixth view of peace sees inner, esoteric (spiritual) aspects of peace as essential. Spiritually based peace theory stresses the centrality of inner peace, believing that all aspects of outer peace, from the individual to the environmental levels, must be based on inner peace. In addition to the relationships of human beings with each other and the world, including the environment, a spiritual dimension is added to Gaia-peace theory. This dimension is expressed in different ways by peace researchers, depending on their cultural context. As in Fritjof Capra's *The Tao of Physics*, where new paradigms in physics resonate with world-views found in Eastern mysticism, this new paradigm in peace research resonates with much

---

1. In Greek mythology, Gaia symbolized the 'Earth conceived as the primordial element from which sprang the divine races. . . . Earth, the power and inexhaustible reserve of fecundity, gradually became known as the Universal Mother and the mother of the gods' (Pierre Grimal, *The Dictionary of Classical Mythology,* trans. A. R. Maxwell-Hyslop, Oxford, Blackwell, 1986).

thinking in world spiritual and religious traditions. Peace has truly become indivisible.

Summary on evolution of the peace concept:
from single to multifactored definitions;
from single to multiple (macro and micro) levels;
from negative to positive conceptions; and
from outer peace only to both inner and outer peace

The above discussion illustrates a number of important changes in the peace concept in Western peace research during the last fifty years. The idea that peace can be defined in terms of a single factor, 'absence of war', has been replaced in subsequent peace theories by multifactored theories which include a number of other requirements, such as no structural violence and peace with the environment. While the absence of war remains a necessary condition for all peace definitions, it is no longer sufficient in most formulations of peace. At the same time, there has been a shift from including just the state level of analysis in absence of war definitions, to peace theories which include (for outer peace) multiple levels of analysis from the individual to the environmental. Multi-factor, multi-level concepts of peace are, as a consequence, considerably more complex than simple, absence of war theories.

Two other important issues in the evolution of the Western peace concept concern the various interpretations of 'positive peace' (which, after Galtung, was expressed in terms of absence of structural violence) and 'non-violence' (the verbal construction of which suggests an 'absence of violence' framework, that is non-violence, somewhat parallel to the peace as absence of war perspective). In this section of the paper, we would like to consider the evolution from negative to positive views of peace, including the evolution of the 'positive peace' concept itself.

Schmidt, in his critical Marxist analysis, 'Politics and Peace Research' (1968), argued that value-positive concepts of peace were doomed to failure within peace research, because it would not be possible for peace researchers to achieve a consensus on what constituted a positive view of peace. He put forward the view that peace researchers could only agree on what they were against, for example war, starvation and poverty. Schmidt's article was arguably the main stimulus to

Galtung's 1969 rejoinder, in which he redefined Quincy Wright's concept 'positive peace' to mean the absence of 'structural violence', that is the harmful social, political and economic structures which are responsible for avoidable human deaths through preventable starvation or treatable illness. Galtung's positive peace concept, the absence of structural violence, like his negative peace concept, the absence of war, did not include an inner or spiritual dimension. Peace of both sorts took place in the outer world and positive peace was a function of human social structures.

Feminist theory, the fourth perspective defined above, broadened the positive peace concept to include micro-structures, such as the family, as well as Galtung's macro-structures, but, for the most part, it still emphasized the elimination of the undesirable, such as war and wife-beating. At the same time, however, there was an increasing emphasis on value-positive thinking (stressing desirable alternatives, such as visualizing alternative futures as a part of the process of moving towards those futures – the work on imaging positive futures by Elise Boulding in the peace research community being an excellent example).

An earlier paper (Smoker, 1981) discussed the extent to which peace research, as reflected in the pages of a defining journal, such as the *Journal of Peace Research*, had focused almost entirely on negative concerns, such as how to avoid or control war, aggression, physical violence and structural violence. Since that article, which was part of a special issue of the *Journal of Peace Research* on peace, the situation has not changed significantly.

This has not been true in futures studies, where a focus not only on trends (negative and positive) but also on creating desirable, alternative futures has contributed towards the development of both negative and positive conceptualizations. There is a sizeable group of people within the Western futures community, but by no means all futurists, whose visioning of positive alternative futures is also based, at least in part, on a spiritual, holistic, perspective. The works of Barbara Marx Hubbard, Marilyn Ferguson and Jean Houston, an outstanding group of women futurists, are particularly notable examples.

The emergence of holistic peace paradigms in peace research, whether spiritual and/or environmental, has included an increasing emphasis on positive conceptions of peace. In part, this is because of our realization that, whatever our nationality, culture or religious tradition, we are all interconnected and interdependent. Viewed from space, planet Earth is a blue-green sphere; we cannot see national boundaries, but we can see the land and the water, ice-caps, deserts and forests. The Earth is clearly a whole complex system, a living being perhaps. We, as individuals and groups, are but a part of the planet, as the planet itself is a part of the solar system, galaxy and universe. The new thinking, it can be argued, represents a return to wholeness, not in the sense of uniformity, but in the sense of complexity dynamically balanced in interaction, the whole as integrated synergy. This mind-set enables an appreciation of the interdependence of species in the global ecosystem, of particular cultural meanings in the context of the total global cultural system, and of particular faiths in the rich diversity of global religions. The whole is more than the sum of the parts, and the greater the variety of the parts, the richer the expression of the global whole.

Whereas 'peace as absence of war' typifies the conceptual framework for most popular 'peace-thinking', there are other aspects to peace. The answer to the question 'If you think about peace, how would you define it?' might, in the majority of cases, very well be 'absence of war' or 'absence of violence'. But the answer to the question 'When you are at peace, what does it feel like?' will almost certainly describe some form of inner peace experience involving 'being at one with', or being 'peaceful' or 'calm'. This is because the actual experiences of peace which most, if not all, of us have as human beings in Western or Eastern culture are related to inner peace. Inner peace also involves an inner knowing or intuitive dimension, beyond the feeling dimension where one suddenly understands patterns and relationships between things which were not understood before. This type of classical experience is the basis for creativity, and tapping this source would also do much to enrich peace researchers' visions of a positive future world at peace.

Holistic peace paradigms which include spiritual and/or environmental concerns resonate with our positive peace experiences and, as a result, are better able to add value-positive images to their intellectual frameworks. Positive peace can therefore be seen as an evolving concept, a concept which does not yet exist in the initial 'peace as absence of war' definition but a concept that subsequently takes on different meanings as the peace concept expands.

CULTURES OF PEACE : SIX PERSPECTIVES (BASED ON THE EVOLUTION OF THE PEACE CONCEPT)

The term 'a culture of peace' has recently become an important focus for UNESCO, both in academic terms, as witnessed by the 1993 and 1994 Barcelona conferences on 'Contribution by Religions to the Culture of Peace' and, in practical terms, as evidenced by the launching of UNESCO field projects in the developing countries around this concept. An important theoretical question concerns the possible meanings of the term 'cultures of peace', particularly since the previous sections of this paper illustrated the broad range of interpretations given to the words 'culture' and 'peace'. Therefore this section is best seen as a contribution to a preliminary discussion of cultures of peace concepts, a discussion which is likely to continue for some time.

Earlier in this paper, we noted that culture can be defined as learned, shared, patterned behaviour, as reflected in technology and tools, social organizations, including economics, politics, religion, media, education and the family, as well as ideas. From this point of view, socialization is the process through which culture is learned, including our religious beliefs and practices. The agents of socialization include language, politics, economics, religion, education, family and the media. Culture here provides the medium through which we interpret the world, the context of meanings – small and large – which makes coherence possible. A culture of peace, therefore, would be a culture which makes peace possible and, as we have seen in the previous section, what is meant by a culture of peace will almost certainly vary according to the concept of peace used.

1. Culture of peace as absence of war

If peace is just the absence of war between and within states, then a culture of peace would be a culture that made war between or within states increasingly unlikely, until eventually inter-state and intra-state war would cease. Such a culture of peace has long been established in certain parts of the world and between certain states, for example, between Canada and the United States, the United Kingdom and France, and Australia and New Zealand. It has been argued elsewhere that there has been a worldwide trend towards such a culture of peace for some centuries (Smoker, 1984). The steadily decreasing frequency of inter-state warfare in Europe, for example, has taken place over a period of some hundreds of years, so that there is now this sort of culture of peace between all members of the European Community. Similarly, worldwide, there has been a clear trend away from inter-state warfare being the dominant mode, as was the case before 1938; through intra-state armed conflict with foreign military intervention being the dominant mode, for example the Viet Nam or Afghanistan wars, as was the case up to the middle 1980s; to the present situation, in which intra-state armed conflict, usually between nations (as distinct from states) or culturally distinct ethnic groups, without armed foreign military intervention, is the dominant form of violent conflict, for example, in former Yugoslavia, Myanmar and Rwanda.

So while at one level, that is, between states, much progress towards a culture of peace (as absence of war) has been made, the same is not true within states, particularly where culturally distinct nations or ethnic groups are concerned. A consideration of a culture of peace as the balance of forces in the international system is necessary to explore this problem.

2. A culture of peace as the balance of forces in the international system

The establishment of a balance of forces for peace has been explained by various theorists in terms of increased economic, social and political interdependencies between states in the international system, making violent conflict between them less likely. Thus the idea of a war between France and Germany is now unthinkable to either side, despite the fact that just fifty years ago these two states provided a battlefield for the bloodiest war in human history. The same is probably not true for India and Pakistan, Argentina and Chile, or the Democratic People's Republic of Korea and the Republic of Korea, although integration theorists would and do argue that the danger of war between any of these states has in most cases lessened and will certainly diminish in the future with increased economic, social and political interdependencies. This functional integration argument, which is closely related to the balance of forces point of view, suggests that if peace is seen as a balance of forces in the international system which enables change to be dealt with non-violently at the state level, then the globalization process, in line with the integrationist arguments detailed above, should strengthen a culture of peace. This is particularly true for the period since the Second World War, following the establishment of the United Nations and the dramatic expansion in international governmental organizations (IGOs), international non-governmental organizations (INGOs) and multinational (MNCs) and transnational corporations (TNCs). During this period, a 'balance of forces' culture of peace has grown substantially, as indicated by the dramatic fall in cross-border wars between states. A culture of peace in this sense refers to the structures, norms and customs which have grown up in the international system, and within states, and which are increasingly accepted as appropriate, if not yet required, conditions to be an accepted member of the 'community of states'.

Theorists such as Kenneth Boulding have argued that the development of zones of peace, in the sense of peace as absence of war, has in part resulted from the 'movement for peace'. For Boulding, the movement for peace is an indirect consequence of increased economic and social interdependencies between two states in the international system, while the 'peace movement' is represented by individuals and groups who actively campaign against war, nuclear weapons and other undesirable features of the international system. Zones of peace are areas in which war between, or within, states has become increasingly unlikely, because of the multiple interdependencies between both states and nations within the zone.

3. A culture of peace for negative peace (no war) and positive peace (no structural violence)

If we turn to a culture of peace in the Galtungian framework, and we focus on the issue of structural violence, then the world picture is less positive, but by no means entirely negative. At the non-governmental level, large numbers of international citizens' groups have emerged which struggle to create the economic, social and political context to overcome the harshest manifestations of structural violence, namely poverty, starvation and preventable disease. In addition, many governments contribute to humanitarian missions worldwide as a matter of duty, accepting some measure of shared responsibility for the human tragedies which appear daily on our television screens. While it can, with some legitimacy, be argued that the global economic and political structures of the world continue to contribute substantially to global structural violence through the activities of multinational and transnational corporations and the inevitable consequences of the current international economic system, it has to be recognized that a number of multi-million-dollar private enterprises, and thousands of similar smaller groups, work to overcome 'structural violence' using economic, social and political approaches. While this interpretation of a culture of peace has not yet succeeded in changing values or economic, political and social structures sufficiently to create a world in which structural violence becomes progressively less likely, there is strong evidence to suggest the emergence of a culture of peace of this sort. The actions of citizens and governments in humanitarian aid, while often inadequate, are nevertheless an established part of international relations: they are the norm, rather than the exception.

4. A culture of peace for feminist peace on macro and micro levels

If the concept of a culture of peace is interpreted in the feminist framework, then the cultural conditions necessary for peace do not exist in any country. Physical and structural violence at the micro level, in the community and family, on the streets and in the schools, is widespread, and the cultural, social, political and economic changes required to create a feminist culture of peace represent a major challenge to every national society, as well as in most, if not all, institutions, including many religious ones. While the three previously discussed models of peace have stressed peace at macro levels of analysis, the feminist models are firmly rooted in personal experience, and are based upon how peace feels to individuals. The evolution of the peace concept towards holistic peace, which includes both inner and outer aspects, required this shift which, it can be argued, represented the biggest single contribution of feminist peace theory. Whereas the three previous models tended to conceptualize peace using abstract, general concepts applied towards the more global level, the feminist models turned these conceptions upside down and clearly defined peace from the personal, experiential level. Feminist notions of 'structure' stress circular complex patterns as opposed to the complex, hierarchical notions associated with Galtungian definitions of structural violence. In this regard, the feminist theories also represent a shift towards value-positive perceptions of peace which stress holistic, non-hierarchical interaction between human beings.

A feminist culture of peace, based on personal analyses, requires fundamental changes in societal values, in the North as well as the South, if the conditions conducive to the creation of peace, in the feminist sense, are to be achieved. The AIDS issue highlights the centrality of culture in overcoming micro level structural violence. Likewise, issues such as domestic violence and child abuse, which have been highlighted by feminist scholars, will require similar fundamental changes in cultural values. While much feminist scholarship has stressed micro-violence, such as wife-beating, there has also been a focus on macro-structural questions, such as the pervasive effects of patriarchal structures. As a consequence, feminist conceptions of a culture of peace will also require wide societal changes in personal cultural values.

5. A culture of peace for holistic Gaia-peace: peace with the environment

A holistic Gaia-peace interpretation of a culture of peace presents an even broader set of concerns which must be brought into play. Whereas the environment, until fairly recently in Western civilization, was seen as a resource to exploit, separate from human beings, it is now seen as connected to us. The extension of outer peace to include peace with the environment represents an important and necessary evolution of the peace concept, whether the environment is seen as just a tightly integrated biochemical system or as the Goddess Gaia, a living being, a whole system integrated both in functional and meaningful terms. The shift in values towards a concern for peace with the environment has not yet led to widespread, radical changes in cultural values, but perhaps that process has begun. In a period of less than twenty years, there has been a shift towards environmentalism in most societies on the planet, 'green peace' has become more than the name of an important environmental pressure group, and there is now widespread verbal recognition of the need to live in harmony with the environment, a need that for some may be purely functional but which for many, if not most, is based on a vision of planet Earth as sacred.

6. A culture of peace for holistic inner and outer peace

For Western peace research, this represents a shift from secular towards spiritual peace paradigms, a realization that inner peace and outer peace, spiritual and material, are interconnected and interdependent. It is here that the contributions of the world's religious and spiritual traditions can help us better understand holistic peace. For example, the idea that the collective external world of outer peace is in some way a representation or image of the collective inner world of spiritual peace may be of particular importance in the creation of a holistic, inner and outer global culture of peace. The variety and diversity of humanity's religious life, as celebrated in the ecumenical tradition, would then provide a dynamic link between the inner and outer worlds, so that inner/outer peace would be manifest in all aspects of a culture of peace, including macro- and micro-social and economic institutions, local and global values, art, literature, music, technology, meditation and prayer. The resulting culture of peace would display a Gaia-like global pattern, where the interacting local cultures are manifestations of an inner unity and outer diversity principle spread throughout the whole system. Definitions of reality would be fundamentally different under such a paradigm. Whereas 'reality' in Western peace theory has previously been defined in terms of aspects of the material world, leading to a concentration on economic, military and political questions, 'reality' under a holistic peace paradigm includes both material and spiritual components. A holistic culture of peace (balancing inner and outer, feminine and masculine, material and spiritual in a both/and framework) will lead to a completely different outcome to peace theories which concentrate on changing the outer world but do not balance such concerns with a parallel and interdependent exploration of the inner world.

Conclusions on the cultures of peace

The previous sections describe various interpretations of the culture of peace concept, ranging from a narrow view which stresses the creation of cultural conditions to make war between states impossible, to a broad view which requires the transformation of every culture to a state that makes holistic inner/outer peace achievable. If we use this framework, then there are, in practical terms, at least three strategies which can be followed to create global cultures of peace.

The first strategy would emphasize the importance of the international system in creating global cultures of peace. In the short term, the existing trends towards an international society in which war between states is no longer seen as acceptable can be strengthened, which, in the longer term, would make it possible to work for local cultural conditions to support broader definitions of peace, such as feminist ideas that include eliminating micro-level physical and structural violence against individuals as well as against nations and states. The second strategy would stress the bottom-up approach to creating global cultures of peace, arguing that we should, as individuals, work in the short term in our own cultural communities and contexts to transform our own local cultures into cultures of peace and, in this way, in the long term, build a global culture of peace. The third strategy would combine both global and local initiatives, working with international, national and local organizations and groups to create appropriate cultural conditions for peace. At the global level, peace might be more appropriately defined, at least to begin with, in terms of eliminating large-scale physical and structural violence. At the local level, peace might initially be defined more in terms of eliminating individual or small-scale physical and structural violence, as well as in terms of creating inner and outer aspects of peace.

NON-VIOLENCE : SIX PERSPECTIVES (BASED ON THE EVOLUTION OF THE PEACE CONCEPT)

The concept 'non-violence', like the concept 'peace', has various meanings in different cultural and political contexts. In this section, we would like to describe briefly six different interpretations of non-violence, using the peace theories framework developed above.

1. Non-violence as any action to prevent war

During the period of the Cold War, the theory of nuclear deterrence adopted by the United States and the former Soviet Union required each side to develop and maintain substantial military forces, including nuclear weapons arsenals capable of destroying the world several times over. Strategists on both sides argued that the nuclear deterrent kept the peace in Europe and prevented a nuclear or conventional war between the then two military superpowers. Peace can be defined as a state of non-war, as we have discussed above, and actions which maintain such a peace can similarly be defined as non-violent, even when they involve threatening to use military force. So nuclear deterrence is an example of non-violent action under this view of peace. The United States Strategic Air Command, which helped implement nuclear deterrence through its state of constant readiness to launch a massive nuclear attack against the Soviet Union, adopted this view of non-violent action, as illustrated in its motto: 'Peace is our profession'. The film *Dr Strangelove* was a spoof of this interpretation of peace. None the less, many actors, both military and political in both countries and among their allies, given the dynamics of the Cold War, sincerely believed that nuclear weapons were a necessary deterrent to war.

2. Non-violence as actions to maintain the balance in the international system

For Quincy Wright's 'balance of forces' perspective, in which public opinion at the 'within states' level is also seen as important, the idea of non-violence as 'war without weapons' (Boserup and Mack, 1975), based on Gene Sharp's functional interpretation of non-violence (Sharp, 1973), becomes appropriate for maintaining and adjusting the balance of forces. Sharp's model of fragile power, as opposed to the monolith model of power assumed in nuclear deterrence, argues that power is fragile because the balance of social forces which maintains it can be changed by concerted, group non-violent action. Wright similarly assumed that peace involved a dynamic balance between various social, economic, political and technological forces, although he placed more emphasis on the international-system level of analysis, and Sharp focused more on the community level of analysis.

3. Structural non-violence

Galtung's structural view added the idea that certain structures, both in the international system and in the community, can be either violent or non-violent, and that changing such structures was a fundamental task for peace research. Non-violence under this rubric expands beyond Sharp's original conception, as he himself did in his study of social power and political freedom (1980), to include not only group actions but also the social, economic and political structures within which they occur. For example, the international system, which prior to Galtung's theory had been viewed by most peace researchers as a positive contribution to peace, was the focus of intense criticism from peace researchers after the theory was published in 1969. Previously it had been seen as evidence of increased co-operation between states but, after 1969, it was redefined as an oppressive, violent, macro-structure which caused the deaths of millions of people each year through the starvation and inequalities it caused. For example, even though there is enough food in the world to feed everyone, millions die from starvation every year because of the structure of the international economic system. A non-violent international (or domestic) economic system would ensure that no one would starve as long as there was enough food in the world (or country) to feed them.

4. Feminist non-violence on macro and micro levels

The feminist perspective further extended the concept of non-violence, in keeping with its extension of the concept of peace, to include non-violent relationships and structures on all levels of human society, both macro and micro. Feminist non-violence is not limited to the behaviour of states or the structure of the international system; it includes non-violent behaviour in the community and the home, and non-violent political, economic and social structures at all levels of society. The feminist critique of patriarchy provides a good illustration of the extension of the idea of non-violence to include all levels and institutions of society. Patriarchy is seen as a pervasive violent structure which acts against women in all of society's major institutions, including marriage, business institutions, churches, community organizations and even peace movements. Feminist non-violence also involves peaceful behaviour between individuals, as well as between states.

5. Holistic Gaia-peace and non-violence

The Gaia-peace view of non-violence is a natural extension of the original feminist position. Indeed, many feminists (following Rachel Carson's lead) have expanded their original ideas into eco-feminism, where a peaceful relationship with the environment is seen as paramount, embodying, as it does, the central feminist principle of 'power with' rather than 'power over'. This view of non-violence includes non-violent actions at every level, non-violent structures at every level, and non-violent processes and relationships between all living beings. Non-violence of this sort is clearly visible in the West, where environmentalism, vegetarianism and animal welfare issues are becoming increasingly popular.

6. Holistic inner and outer peace and non-violence

Holistic definitions of non-violence have of course been present in Western literature for a considerable time, within Eastern traditions in general, and with Gandhi in particular having made the greatest contribution to our understanding of this spiritually based type of non-violence. The distinction between non-violent action as a technique of struggle versus non-violence as a philosophy and way of life has provided the basis for discussing non-violence in the West, thanks to the work of Gene Sharp in the West and Mahatma Gandhi in the East, and their respective perspectives. Whereas Sharp has stressed the functionality of non-violent action and its value as a technique for waging conflicts, a technique he believes to be superior in pragmatic terms to violence, the Gandhian non-violence-as-a-way-of-life school has always adopted a deeper view of non-violence, based on a centuries-old Eastern tradition which stresses an inner, spiritual peace component.

GANDHI'S SPIRITUALLY BASED NON-VIOLENCE: NON-VIOLENCE AS A PHILOSOPHY OF LIFE – A LINK BETWEEN INNER AND OUTER FORMS OF PEACE

One of Mahatma Gandhi's most important statements was that 'the means are as important as the ends'. This is a central part of using non-violence as part of a whole philosophy of life, rather than as just a temporary tactic. There have been various practitioners of non-violence as a philosophy of life before Gandhi, including Leo Tolstoy in Russia and Henry David Thoreau in the United States as well as, after him, Martin Luther King and Cesar Chavez in the United States. What distinguishes all of these people, besides the fact that they each influenced those who came after them in the use of non-violence, is that their use of non-violence as a philosophy of life was grounded in deep spiritual principles and practices. In short, they all tried to live a life based on these spiritual principles, including the idea that how we live our lives every day is as important as the ends or goals that we seek via these means. In a non-violent struggle, one therefore has the goal of not dehumanizing one's opponent and also trying not to let one's opponent dehumanize oneself, since this dehumanization is part of the process which people go through before justifying the use of violence against other human beings in the world.

Gandhi never took action in the world until he had first meditated and asked for inner guidance on what to do. When Gandhi's movement also became violent, he called off further action until people could be adequately trained in non-violence. Gandhi did not see non-violence as passive, but rather as an active struggle against unjust laws or policies. Gandhi also believed that one should not oppose all laws, only the unjust ones. Gandhi had five stages in his non-violent struggle, as noted below, and believed that one must exhaust all possibilities of each stage before going on to the next stage.

Gandhi's five stages in a non-violent struggle

Stage 1: Utilization of all regular constitutional machinery. In this first stage, the existing legal constitutional machinery is used to try and deal with the conflict within the system and achieve a satisfactory resolution.

Stage 2: Agitation. If stage 1 was fruitless, a stage of agitation is undertaken to heighten the awareness and educate the people as to what the conflict is all about. In a totalitarian society, the network of communication which is established to implement this phase is built outside the normal channels and is thus more difficult, since it must be undertaken in secret.

Stage 3: Ultimatum. This stage involves the presentation to the Establishment of a document listing the people's needs and stating that continued opposition would produce some sort of direct action. If, however, this document fails to produce a favourable response, then members of the movement begin their preparation for direct action.

Stage 4: Self-purification. This stage is used by those preparing for non-violent action to develop *ahimsa* (the spirit of harmlessness), which is seen as a prerequisite to action which is untainted with self-interest. During this time members question their inner strength, noting if they have enough self-respect to command the respect of the opposition. The ability of each member to avoid the pitfall of reducing the opponent to an 'enemy', thereby dehumanizing him/her and allowing violence to occur as a result, is of the greatest importance.

Stage 5: Direct action. In this fifth stage, after exhausting all regular constitutional machinery, heightening the awareness of the population at large about the issue, and undertaking intensive soul-searching and inner preparedness, non-violent action is undertaken. This action can take many forms, including economic boycotts, sit-down strikes, non-payment of taxes, mass resignations from public office, and deliberate and organized disobedience to certain laws which are considered unjust. Gandhi, relying heavily on his opponents' lack of preparation, felt that some combination of these methods, coupled with sympathy from within the ranks of the authority being challenged, could open channels for discussion. On the other hand, if resistance continued, the end result could be the complete collapse of the government's power, shifting power to the Satyagrahis, who could then constitute a new government.

Relevance of Gandhi today

Having explored Gandhi's philosophy and practice of non-violence above, as he used it against the British first in South Africa and then in India, an interesting question is: what relevance do Gandhi's ideas have for today? The first obvious answer is that, with the destructive potential of nuclear weapons today, we can no longer afford to solve conflicts via violence and weapons of mass destruction, if we want a future for ourselves, our children and the Earth. Gandhi was the first person to take ideas of non-violence and apply them in a mass movement for social and political change, which showed that a party to a conflict can win via non-violent means against a much stronger party, 'if' the former can appeal to the moral conscience of their opponent and of the world, and convince them that they have a just cause which deserves to be listened to and addressed in a constructive manner. Certainly the world can use such an approach today. Being willing to listen to inner spiritual guidance, and then undergoing purification (to be sure one's motives are pure) before embarking on political action in the world, are other characteristics of spiritually based non-violence, which distinguish it from both temporary uses of non-violence for functional purposes and from violent efforts at social-political change. Such spiritually based non-violence carries greater moral authority and influence because it is not undertaken for personal power or egotistical reasons, and because it does not dehumanize one's opponent, which is a necessary step before people can justify killing other human beings. All of these values, if adopted by the world's different peoples, cultures and religions today, would do much to create a more peaceful world in the twenty-first century. It is also significant that religious leaders of many of the world's religions would agree today that, when violent actions are undertaken in the name of religion, the party concerned is not being true to the spirit or the letter of that religion. Certainly religious cults today or fundamentalist religious factions which advocate and engage in violence against others with different perspectives than their own are not true to the spirit of the original founders of their professed religions.

SUMMARY: DEVELOPING INDICATORS OF POSITIVE, MULTICULTURAL VISIONS OF PEACE

Concerning each of the areas of peace, it is interesting that, from the examples cited above, Eastern cultures have made especially strong contributions in the last two, more holistic areas of peace (environmental and inner spiritual), while Western cultures have made especially strong contributions in the previous four areas, focusing more on changes in the external world, including social justice, human rights and women's issues. There are also a number of Western activists in the environmental area. In the anti-war/peace area, there is especially strong citizens' support for peace in both Japan and Germany in the form of opposing the sending of national troops abroad, owing to the consequences of such actions in the past. It would appear that there are important things that we can all learn from each other as we come from different cultures and countries about the many dimensions of creating a peaceful world. Let us hope we can move towards some kind of a global consensus on these issues over time.

Once some kind of global consensus is developed which transcends different cultures but yet is based on input from the best ideas and traditions from various cultures around the world, the next step could be to try and develop indicators to measure movement in a positive direction in each of the six different areas of peace discussed here. Then some kind of international United Nations or private body could monitor events and activities around the world for progress in each area. These positive developments could then be highlighted by the world's media and by the UN to give publicity to what is working in a positive sense in the world; this could serve as possible models for others to emulate or learn from. International recognition and awards or prizes could also be offered to groups and people making the most progress in developing new ways to create the foundations and conditions for peace in a positive sense in each of the six areas. In this regard, even behavioural, social learning theory notes that people are more likely to change their behaviour, especially over the long run, if they are rewarded for positive behaviour than if they are just punished for negative behaviour. A more permanent modification of behaviour in a positive direction requires that people be recognized and positively rewarded when they do things which contribute positively to world peace. Beyond this external recognition for positive behaviour which contributes to peace, it is of course also desirable and ultimately necessary that people develop internalized peaceful values to which they are willing to commit their lives.

There is no time in this paper to articulate adequate indicators for creating positive conditions for peace in each of the six areas outlined above. Real multicultural dialogue must continue until some kind of global consensus emerges which includes the best ideas from different cultures around the world on how we can best create peace in each of the six areas. This paper suggests only a few multicultural visions of peace in each area of peace; many more good ideas await inclusion in this global, multicultural dialogue. The authors of this paper would welcome further suggestions in each of the above areas.

BIBLIOGRAPHY

APPLEBY, R. S. 1994. *Religious Fundamentalisms and Global Conflict*. New York, Foreign Policy Association.

BADINER, A. H. 1990. *Dharma Gaia: A Harvest of Essays in Buddhism and Ecology*. Berkeley, Calif., Parallax Press.

BOSERUP, A.; MACK, A. 1975. *War Without Weapons: Non Violence in National Defense*. New York, Schocken.

BOULDING, E. 1992. *The Underside of History: A View of Women through Time*, Vols. 1 and 2. Rev. ed. Newbury Park, Calif., Sage Publications.

BOULDING, K. 1990. Foreword to: Norman Myers (ed.), *The Gaia Atlas of Future Worlds*. New York, Anchor Books/Doubleday.

BROCK-UTNE, B. 1989. *Feminist Perspectives on Peace and Peace Education*. Oxford, Pergamon Press.

CAPRA, F. 1982. *The Turning Point: Science, Society, and the Rising Culture*. New York, Bantam.

——. 1991. *The Tao of Physics: An Exploration of the Parallels between Modern Physics and Eastern Mysticism*. 3rd updated ed. Boston, Mass., Shambhala.

CLARK, P. B. (ed.). 1993. *The World's Religions: Understanding the Living Faiths*. Pleasantville, N.Y., Reader's Digest.

DREHER, D. 1991. *The Tao of Inner Peace*. HarperCollins Pubs., Inc.

EASWARAN, E. 1978. *Gandhi the Man*. 2nd ed. Petaluma, Calif., Nilgiri Press.

ELIADE, M. (ed.). 1986. *Encyclopedia of Religion*. New York, Macmillan.

FISHER, L. 1954. *Gandhi: His Life and Message for the World*. New York, New American Library.

GALTUNG, J. 1969. Violence, Peace and Peace Research. *Journal of Peace Research*, No. 3.

GAWAIN, S. 1993. *The Path of Transformation: How Healing Ourselves Can Change the World*. Mill Valley, Calif., Nataraj Publishing.

GROFF, L. 1991. Global Unity and Diversity: Creating Tolerance for Cultural, Religious, and National Diversity in an Interdependent World. (Paper for Third International Conference on Building Understanding and Respect between People of Diverse Religions or Beliefs, New Delhi, India, January.)

——. 1992. Intercultural Communication, Negotiation, and Conflict Management: Insights on the United States/Japanese Relationship. (Paper for the International Studies Association Conference, Atlanta, Georgia, 31 March–4 April.)

——. 1993. On the Values of Cultural and Ecological Diversity and their Importance to an Effectively Functioning World, Including the UN and UNESCO. (Paper and testimony, US Commission on Improving the Effectiveness of the United Nations, Los Angeles, Calif., February.)

HUNTER, D.; MALLICK, K. 1990. *Non-Violence: A Reader in the Ethics of Action*. 2nd ed. Lanham, Md., University Press of America.

HUNTINGTON, S. 1993. The Clash of Civilizations? *Foreign Affairs*, Summer, pp. 21–49.

KUNG, H.; KUSCHEL, K.-J. (eds.). *A Global Ethic: The Declaration of the Parliament of the World's Religions.* New York, Continuum Publishing Co.

LARSON, J.; MICHELS-CYRUS, M. 1987. *Seeds of Peace: A Catalogue of Quotations.* Philadelphia, Pa., New Society Publishers.

LOVELOCK, J. E. 1991. *Gaia: A New Look at Life on Earth.* 5th ed. Oxford, Oxford University Press.

MACY, J. 1991. *World as Lover, World as Self.* Berkeley, Calif., Parallax Press.

MENDLOVITZ, S. H. 1975. *On the Creation of a Just World Order.* New York, The Free Press (Macmillan).

MOYNIHAN, D. P. 1994. *Pandaemonium: Ethnicity in International Politics.* New York, Oxford University Press.

NICHOLSON, S. (ed.). 1989. *The Goddess Re-Awakening: The Feminine Principle Today.* Wheaten, Ill., Theosophical Publishing House.

Non-violence. 1992. *Gandhi Marg,* Vol. 14, No. 1. (Special Issue.)

O'GORMAN, A. (ed.). 1990. *The Universe Bends toward Justice: A Reader on Christian Non-Violence in the US.* Philadelphia/Santa Cruz, New Society Publishers.

PAIGE, G. D.; SATHA-ANAND C.; GILLIATT S. (eds.). 1993. *Islam and Non-Violence.* Honolulu, Center for Global Non-Violence Planning Project, Matsunaga Institute for Peace, University of Hawaii.

PANIKKAR, R. 1989. Epistula de pace. Response to: *Philosophia pacis. Homenaje a Raimon Panikkar.* Madrid, Simbolo Editorial.

POLAK, F. 1973. *The Image of the Future.* New York, Elsevier. (Translated and abridged edition by Elise Boulding.)

RICHARDSON, L. F. 1960. *Statistics of Deadly Quarrels.* Chicago, Ill., Quadrangle Books.

RUETHER, R. R. 1992. *Gaia and God: An Ecofeminist Theology of Earth Healing.* San Francisco, Calif., Harper.

SCHMIDT, H. 1968. Politics and Peace Research. *Journal of Peace Research.* Vol. 5, No. 3.

SCHUON, F. 1984. *The Transcendent Unity of Religions.* Wheaton, Ill., Theosophical Publishing House.

SHARP, G. 1973. *The Politics of Non-Violent Action.* Boston, Mass., Porter Sargent.

––. 1980. *Social Power and Political Freedom.* Boston, Mass., Porter Sargent.

SIBLEY, M. Q. (ed.). 1963. *The Quiet Battle: Writings on the Theory and Practice of Non-Violent Resistance.* Garden City, N.Y., Doubleday & Co.

SMITH, H. 1976. *Forgotten Truth: The Common Vision of the World's Religions.* San Francisco, Calif., Harper.

SMITH, H. 1991. *The World's Religions: Our Great Wisdom Traditions.* San Francisco, Calif., Harper. (Completely revised and updated edition of *The Religions of Man.*)

SMOKER, P. 1965. A Preliminary Empirical Study of an International Integrative Subsystem. *International Associations*, No. 11, pp. 638–46.

——. 1969. Social Research for Social Anticipation. *American Behavorial Scientist*, Vol. XII, No. 6, pp. 7–13.

——. 1981. Small Peace. *Journal of Peace Research*, Vol. 18, No. 2, pp. 149–57.

——. 1984. Exploding Nuclear Myths: Evidence from Conflict Research. *Coexistence*, Vol. 21, pp. 93–106.

——. 1991. Towards a New Definition of Global Security. *Ritsumeikan Review*.

SMOKER, P.; GROFF, L. 1995. *Spirituality, Religion, and Peace: Exploring the Foundations for Inner-Outer Peace in the 21st Century.* (Conference Proceedings, Second UNESCO Conference on Contributions of Religions to a Culture of Peace, Barcelona, December 1994.)

World Scripture: A Comparative Anthology of Sacred Texts. 1991. New York, Paragon House. (A Project of the International Religious Foundation. Quotations from sacred scriptures of different religions around the world organized by different topics.)

What Does Science Tell Us About God? 1992. *Time Magazine*, Vol. 140, No. 26, 28 December, pp. 38–44.

WRIGHT, Q. 1941. *A Study of War.* Chicago, Ill., University of Chicago Press.

Towards a planetary code of ethics: ethical foundations of a culture of peace

*Hans Küng**

Most commentators of our time agree that, in the wake of the unexpected events of 1989, the world political situation as a whole has become more unstable, more uncertain. No one thought it possible that the world historical scene would change so rapidly: the collapse of the Soviet system, the reunification of Germany, the democratization of the former Eastern Bloc states, the Gulf War, the civil war in former Yugoslavia. No one can as yet say definitively where all these developments are leading. But one thing seems certain: the collapse of Marxist socialism in 1989 and the break-up of the antagonistic military blocks afford a third opportunity for a new world order, following those which were missed after the First World War in 1918 and the Second World War in 1945.

MISSED OPPORTUNITIES FOR A NEW WORLD ORDER: 1918–1945–1989

Opportunity 1: 1918

After the First World War, the League of Nations was founded on the instigation of the then American President Wilson (1920). This was based on the vision of the nations finally arriving at a shared, peaceful and just conduct of world affairs. But Europe and the world missed this first opportunity: above all with Fascism and National Socialism, but also with communism and Japanese militarism, and

---

* Professor and Director of the Institute of Ecumenical Research, University of Tübingen, Germany.

following them with the Second World War, the Holocaust, the Gulag Archipelago and Hiroshima. Instead of a world order, there was world chaos.

Opportunity 2: 1945

At that time, there was another opportunity for such a new world order, and the United Nations which was now founded was to help towards this. But this new attempt, too, proved divided and it was above all the Stalinist Soviet Union which prevented a better order in Eastern Europe and elsewhere and dug its own grave by internal totalitarianism and external hegemonism. Instead of a world order, there was a division of the world. Now, to an unbridled capitalism with negative results, above all in Latin America and Africa, there was added a socialism which, from the Elbe to Vladivostok, led to an unprecedented enslaving of human beings and exploitation of nature until it could go on no longer.

Opportunity 3: 1989

Now we have the third opportunity of what I would call a 'post-modern' world order. Politically, it presupposes the democratic state and, economically, a market economy with both a social and ecological orientation (not to be confused with 'capitalism', which is neither social nor ecological), at least as it is affirmed in principle from Washington via Brussels to Moscow, even if it is far from being developed. However, such a world order will not come into being without a new relationship between the nations. And who could have guessed that once again within Europe a war of unimaginable cruelty would be waged? Other regions, too, are far from being pacified. Is there a new world disorder instead of a new world order?

If we look at today's world, there is no getting round the terrifying fact that at present approximately thirty armed conflicts are going on. The UN is already overtaxed with thirteen peace-keeping missions under way. At present the UN numbers 184 Member States (as compared with fifty-one in 1945). The unofficial estimate is that, if Africa were also to be divided up by ethnic boundaries, the number of sovereign states could approach 450. If smaller and smaller ethnic and religious units want to win the status of a sovereign state, not only Africa but also Europe from Spain to Russia will be thrown into disorder by the splintering. The future will then be more insecure than ever. There will no longer be any question of stability if the units get smaller and smaller, the perspectives narrower and narrower, the pressures towards national demarcation more and more fanatical. Yugoslavia is a warning. What has also been happening in Germany between Rostock, Solingen and Constance is a cruel warning of the need to rethink and to arrive at better rules for society in this one world and one humankind. But how?

NO NEW WORLD ORDER WITHOUT A WORLD ETHIC

First of all, a negative statement: a new, better world order will not be introduced on the basis of:
- solely diplomatic offensives, which all too often are addressed only to governments and not to peoples, and which also are unable to guarantee the peace and stability of a region;
- simply humanitarian help, which cannot replace political action;
- primarily military interventions, the consequences of which tend to be more negative than positive;
- solely international law, as long as this rests on the unlimited sovereignty of states and is focused more on the rights of states than on the rights of peoples and individuals, that is human rights.

Then a positive statement: a new world order will ultimately be brought in only on the basis of:
- more common visions, ideals, values, aims and criteria;
- a strong sense of global responsibility on the part of peoples and their leaders;
- a new binding and uniting ethic for all humankind, including states and those in power in them, which embraces cultures and religions. No new world order can be envisaged and created without a new world ethic.

Someone may object: given the war in Yugoslavia, where Orthodox Serbs, Catholic Croats and Muslim Bosnians have been engaging in a cruel and bloody slaughter; given the situation in the Middle East; given the tensions between Christian Armenians and Muslim Azerbaijanis; between Hindus, Muslims and Sikhs in India; between Buddhist Singhalese and Hindu Tamils in Sri Lanka; and not least given the unresolved conflict in Northern Ireland between Catholics and Protestants, is it not crazy, in order to safeguard the future of this earth, to call for a world ethic to which the religions are to make a decisive contribution? My counter-question would be: when could such a demand be more urgent than today? In any event, 'world ethic' is not a fairweather slogan, a luxury which might arouse academic interest or give one a good profile as a ceremonial speaker. It arises out of the bitter experiences of the past, the bloody crises of yesterday, in which religions have often played a fatal role. Crisis means not only danger but also opportunity.

NOT A SINGLE WORLD CULTURE OR WORLD RELIGION

World politics, the world economy and the world financial system play an essential part in determining our national and regional destiny. Even in Switzerland, people are slowly beginning to see that there are no longer any national or regional islands of stability. Despite the marked splintering of national and regional interests, there is already such a strong political, economic and financial world network that economists are speaking of a world society and sociologists of a world civilization (in the technical, economic and social sense): a world society and world civilization as a coherent world of interaction in which all are involved, either directly or indirectly.

But this world society and technological world civilization, which are coming into being, in no way mean merely a single world culture (in the spiritual–artistic–formative sense) or even a world religion. Rather, world society and world civilization include a multiplicity of cultures and religions, some of which even have new emphases. To hope for a single world religion is an illusion; to be afraid of it is nonsense. The multiplicity of religions, confessions and denominations, of religious sects, groups and movements in today's world is still perplexing. They form a complex phenomenon, geographically, historically and culturally, which cannot and must not be put in a single category.

However, if we do not want to reduce this overcomplexity which has grown up through the centuries and want to adopt an approach which is not only regional or national but world-historical and worldwide, and in this sense planetary; if, given the present complexity which is particularly to be found in matters of religion, we are seeking a new orientation also and particularly in matters of religion; then in view of what Wilfrid Cantwell Smith has called the

Towards a planetary code of ethics: ethical foundations of a culture of peace

'one religious history of humankind', we shall do best to keep to the great religious river systems of the high religions which still exist today and which have also inundated the nature religions of Africa, America and Oceania. If we look at the world today, seeing our globe as it were from a satellite, in the cultural landscape of this earth we can at present distinguish three great religious river systems with their areas of entry, transcending individuals, nations and cultures, all of which have their own genesis and morphology:

- The religions of Semitic origin: these have a prophetic character, always begin from a contrast between God and human beings, and are predominantly marked by religious confrontation: Judaism, Christianity and Islam.
- The religions of Indian origin: they basically tend towards union, and are characterized more by spiritual values: the early Indian religion of the Upanishads, Buddhism and Hinduism.
- The religions of the Chinese tradition: these are stamped by wisdom and are fundamentally characterized by harmony: Confucianism and Taoism.

Older, stronger and more constant than many dynasties and empires, these great religious systems have modelled the cultural landscape of this globe over the millennia. In an incessant rhythm of change, sporadically new mountain chains and high plateaux have thrust themselves up on the different continents, but the great rivers, older, stronger and more constant, have kept making ever-new cuts in the rising landscape. Similarly, in our cultural landscape, ever-new social systems, states and ruling houses have arisen, but the great old rivers of the religions have been able – despite all the rises and falls – to maintain themselves with a few adaptations and deviations and have shaped the features of the cultural landscape in a new way. Simply because of that, because of the far-reaching ways in which cultures have been shaped by religions, it would make no sense to speak of a single world culture or world religion or even to attempt to.

And yet, there are features which the religions have in common. Just as the natural river systems of this earth and the landscapes shaped by them are extremely different and the rivers and streams of the different continents all have similar profiles and patterns of flow, obey similar laws, cut clefts in the hills, wind in the plains and inexorably seek a way to the sea, so too it is with the religious river systems of this earth. Although they are extremely different, in many respects they display similar profiles, regularities and effects. Confusingly different though religions all are, they are all messages of salvation which respond to similar basic human questions, to the eternal questions of love and sorrow, guilt and atonement, life and death. Where does the world and its order come from? Why are we born and why must we die? What determines the destiny of the individual and of humankind? What is the basis of moral awareness and of the presence of ethical norms? And over and above their interpretation of the world, all also offer similar ways of salvation: ways out of the distress, suffering and guilt of being, pointers towards meaningful and responsible action in this life, towards a permanent, lasting eternal salvation, redemption from all suffering, from guilt and death.

Now all this means that even those who reject the religions (and, in my book *Does God Exist?*, I have subjected all the arguments of the modern criticism of religion to a thorough examination) will have to take them seriously as a fundamental social and existential reality; they all have to do with meaning and meaninglessness in life, with human freedom and slavery, with justice and the oppression of peoples, with war and peace in history and the present.

TAKING THE RELIGIOUS DIMENSION SERIOUSLY

There is no doubt about it: any religion is ambivalent as a human phenomenon – as ambivalent as art or music, which also have been and are massively misused. Sociologically, religions too are systems of power concerned for stabilization and the extension of power. They have a high potential for conflict but they also have an often overlooked potential for peace. Religion can stir things up certainly, but it can also calm them down. Religion can motivate, foment and prolong wars, but it can also prevent wars and curtail them.

The foundations for the peace between France, Germany and Italy were laid by convinced Christians (and Catholics): Charles de Gaulle, Konrad Adenauer, Robert Schumann, Alcide de Gasperi. Peace between Germany and Poland was prepared for by a memorandum drafted by the Protestant Church (the Evangelical Church of Germany). Peaceful revolutions in Poland, the German Democratic Republic and Czechoslovakia, and also in South Africa and the Philippines, have shown that religion can also serve to bring about peace.

Clearly, the purely strategic, economic and political aspects of such crises must not be allowed to overshadow their social, moral and religious aspects. Here is just one example, from what used to be Yugoslavia. Anyone who is not blind to history will have noticed that the modern state frontiers in Eastern Europe seem pale in comparison with the age-old frontiers which were once drawn by religions and faiths: between Armenia and Azerbaijan, between Georgia and Russia, the Ukraine and Russia, and similarly also between the different peoples in Yugoslavia. It is possible to understand the complexity of the problems in Yugoslavia only if one knows that, for a thousand years, basically since the division between Western and Eastern Rome, two different religions have been meeting in the middle of Yugoslavia; the Eastern Byzantine paradigm with Serbia and the Roman Catholic paradigm with Croatia. Catholic Croats could get on better with Muslims than with Orthodox fellow Christians. In addition, there are the problems of the 500-year occupation of Serbian territory by the Turks (since the defeat at Kosovo Polje in 1389) which, among the Serbs, produced the ideology of a lasting suffering and endurance which very often does not (or does not any longer) correspond to reality.

Now the Serbs, Croats and Bosnians (the only indigenous Muslims in Europe) are all southern Slavs. For centuries Serbs have lived among Croats, originally recruited against the Turks, as ethnic cousins. So today the three groups are highly mixed in the state territory of what once was Yugoslavia, most of all in Bosnia. Thus it was wrong after 1989 first of all to defend a single uniform Yugoslav state (Phase 1 of the EC and US policy), but also wrong then to go to the opposite extreme and split the whole of Yugoslavia into national states (Phase 2, especially German and then also EC and US policy). A confederation (with cantons or whatever) would have been the right course to take from the beginning and not just now, when it is too late.

Will there ever be peace in such a region if the religious dimension of the conflict is not taken seriously? In the present conflict my sympathies were first of all with Croatia (not because it was Catholic but because it had been attacked) and then, above all, with the Muslims. Nevertheless may I, as a Catholic theologian, keep silent about the fact that the Catholic Croatian Ustasha state under the Nazi protectorate killed tens of thousands (some say hundreds of thousands) of Serbs without a single protest at the time from Archbishop Stepinac of Zagreb or Pope Pius XII, both of whom were very well informed?

Over forty years both churches could have found time to sort out the situation, concede guilt, ask for forgiveness and prepare for a political peace. The World Council of Churches, often more concerned with the world than with churches, certainly meant well when, in the middle of the civil war, it brought together bishops from both sides, though their ecumenical discourses ended in unecumenical accusations. Indeed, whether one speaks today with a Serb or a Croat, each talks about the crimes of the other side and says nothing about the crimes of his own side – just like the Germans and French of old. Will Serbs and Croats need yet another war of revenge before they become aware that such thought and policy, dominated by revenge, will never lead to peace but always only to new destruction? If a cease-fire should finally be achieved, will there still be no bishops or theologians who can begin to talk to one another with understanding? Self-critical recollection is unavoidable.

A basic question is: must these religions inevitably be engaged in conflict and strife? Peace *(shalom, salam, eirene, pax) is* a main feature of their programmes. Their first task at this time must be to make peace among themselves, in order, with all the means which the media offer,

- to remove misunderstandings;
- to work through traumatic memories;
- to dissolve stereotyped images of enemies;
- to come to terms with the conflicts of guilt, socially and as individuals;
- to break down hatred and destructiveness;
- to reflect on what they have in common. Are the members of the different religions aware of the ethos they have in common – despite their great 'dogmatic' differences? Not at all.

THE NEED FOR A MINIMAL CONSENSUS ON ETHICS

First of all, understanding among the religions does not require believers to line up against unbelievers. The Roman campaign for re-Catholicization, especially in Eastern Europe, euphemistically called re-evangelization, only leads to a re-opening of the old war graves: we do not need another division of society and political parties into clerical and anticlerical (as for, example, in Poland). The project of a world ethic, a global ethic, calls rather for an alliance of believers and non-believers over a new common basic ethic.

Secondly, religions without doubt have a special function and responsibility when it comes to binding criteria and personal basic convictions. What unites all the great religions needs to be worked out carefully and in detail on the basis of the sources – a significant and enjoyable task for the scholars of the different religions which is still at its beginnings but has aroused much interest amazingly quickly and produced some initial results.

At a more fundamental level one can ask: what can religions contribute to the furthering of an ethic, despite their very different systems of dogmas and symbols, which distinguishes them from philosophy, political pragmatism, international organizations, philanthropic concerns of all kinds? Granted, in the past religions have always made absolute their traditions, fixed mysterious dogmas and ritual prescriptions and set themselves apart from any others. Yet where they want to, they can present fundamental maxims of elementary humanity with a quite different authority and power of conviction from that of politicians, lawyers and philosophers.

A SUPREME NORM OF CONSCIENCE AND A LEADING FIGURE

Granted, religions were and always are tempted to lose themselves in an infinite jungle of commandments and prescriptions, canons and paragraphs. Yet where they want to, they can demonstrate, with quite different authority from any philosophy, that the application of their norms does not apply to individual cases but is categorical. Religions can give men and women a supreme norm of conscience, that categorical imperative that is still important for today's society, which imposes an obligation at a quite different depth and on quite different foundations. For all the great religions call for the observance of something like a 'Golden Rule', which is not just a hypothetical and conditional norm but one that is a categorical, apodeictic and unconditional norm, one that is quite practicable in highly complex situations where individuals or groups must often act.

This Golden Rule is already attested in Confucius (*c.* 551–489 B.C.): 'What you yourself do not want, do not do to another person'; and also in Judaism (in a negative formulation): 'Do not do to others what you would not want them to do to you' (Rabbi Hillel, 60 B.C.–A.D. 10); and finally also in the Sermon on the Mount (in a positive formulation): 'Whatever you want people to do to you, do also to them.'

This Golden Rule could be a safeguard against a crude ethics of success which is not an ethic at all; it does not need to be understood as a pure dispositional ethic which does not perceive realities, but could become the centre of an ethics of responsibility (the term used by Max Weber and Hans Jonas) which always reflects on the consequences of what we do and allow.

The reference to Confucius and Jesus of Nazareth also already indicates something else: unlike philosophies, religions do not just offer abstract models of life. They can refer to specific individuals who have already gone that way: what Karl Jaspers calls 'normative people'. So the normative leading figures in the world religions are of the utmost significance: Buddha, Jesus of Nazareth, Confucius, Lao-tse or Muhammad. It makes a crucial difference whether one pontificates to people about a new form of life in the abstract or whether one can introduce them to such a form of life by means of a compelling concrete model: as followers of Buddha, Jesus Christ, Confucius, Lao-tse or the Prophet Muhammad. For a Christian, Jesus Christ is and remains the way, the truth and the life. Similarly 'the way, the truth and the life' for believing Jews is the Torah, for Muslims the Koran and for other religions someone or something else.

THE PROCESS OF FORMING AN AWARENESS OF A WORLD ETHIC

But is the working out of such an ethic realistic? Is it perhaps just the undertaking of a few Western intellectuals who once again want to 'export' their project? No, the call for a world ethic is not a matter of the 'exporting' of a model, an artificial 'globalization' or the 'idea of universality' as opposed to the 'idea of regionality'. Here we have neither a radical universalism, which takes no note of the actual plurality in our world, nor a radical relativism, which does not contribute towards the common life of different groups, but rather to what Wolfgang Huber calls a 'relative universality', which, despite all cultural and religious differences, recognizes some principles which transcend culture and religion. Indeed, to be

Towards a planetary code of ethics: ethical foundations of a culture of peace

more precise, it is a matter of becoming aware of what culture and religions already have in common: the formation of an awareness and hence a change of awareness in the sphere of ethics of the kind that has come about in, say, ecology or disarmament.

But is there even the slightest sign that anything is actually happening? At the centenary celebration of the Parliament of the World's Religions in Chicago at the beginning of September 1993, a Declaration towards a Global Ethic[1] was presented which I had the honour and the toil of drafting. It was accepted by the vast majority of the delegates and, in the end, ceremonially promulgated. For the first time in the history of world religions, this Parliament undertook to formulate a basic consensus over binding values, irrevocable criteria and basic personal attitudes. Granted, such a declaration will not change the world overnight, but it will encourage all those who are already committed to it and put to shame those who tend rather ironically to ridicule, to dismiss or, from confessional egoism, declare impossible anything that religions may have in common.

The significance of the Declaration towards a Global Ethic can be illustrated at one point in particular in the context of Islam. For the 'four irrevocable directives' which are elucidated in this declaration include a 'commitment to a culture of non-violence and respect for life'. There was serious discussion of this point during the Parliament. For specifically, in view of the desperate situation of the Muslims in Bosnia, too little emphasis seemed to be placed here on the right to self-defence (which is also affirmed by the United Nations Charter).

However, on closer reading, these fears proved to be ungrounded. For the Declaration deliberately took a middle way which was capable of achieving a consensus between a *Realpolitik* of the use of violence to resolve conflicts and an unrealistic unconditional pacifism which, when confronted with devastation, expulsion, violence, death, or mass murder, unconditionally renounces the use of violence. The right to self-defence to which the Muslims attach importance is

---

1. There is a commentary on the Declaration in Hans Küng and Karl-Josef Kuschel (eds.), *A Global Ethic. The Declaration of the Parliament of the World's Religions,* London/New York, SCM Press/Continuum, 1993. Editions in other languages are available or are under preparation.

thus clearly affirmed both for the individual and the collective. But, within the framework of a culture of non-violence, it applies only *in extremis,* when non-violent resistance is meaningless. In the face of brutality, barbarism and genocide, self-defence has to be allowed. No further holocaust of any people whatsoever can simply be accepted pacifically. On the other hand, no simple formula of legitimization can be offered for military intervention of any kind; no 'just wars' in the service of all too evident economic, political and military interests are to be justified in this way.

TOWARDS A CULTURE OF NON-VIOLENCE

This is what the Global Ethic Declaration says about non-violence:

Numberless women and men of all regions and religions strive to lead lives not determined by egoism but by commitment to their fellow humans and to the world around them. Nevertheless, all over the world we find endless hatred, envy, jealousy and violence, not only between individuals but also between social and ethnic groups, between classes, races, nations, and religions. The use of violence, drug trafficking and organized crime, often equipped with new technical possibilities, has reached global proportions. Many places are still ruled by terror 'from above', dictators oppress their own people, and institutional violence is widespread. Even in some countries where laws exist to protect individual freedoms, prisoners are tortured, men and women are mutilated, hostages are killed.

1. In the great ancient religious and ethical traditions of humankind we find the directive: You shall not kill! Or, in positive terms: Have respect for life! Let us reflect anew on the consequences of this ancient directive: all people have a right to life, safety and the free development of personality in so far as they do not injure the rights of others. No one has the right physically or psychologically to torture, injure, much less kill, any other human being. And no people, no state, no race, no religion has the right to hate, to discriminate against, to 'cleanse', to exile, much less to liquidate a 'foreign' minority which is different in behaviour or holds different beliefs.
2. Of course, wherever there are humans there will be conflicts. Such conflicts, however, should be resolved without violence within a framework of justice.

This is true for states as well as for individuals. Persons who hold political power must work within this framework of a just order and commit themselves to the most non-violent, peaceful solutions possible. And they should work for this within an international order of peace which itself has need of protection and defence against perpetrators of violence. Armament is a mistaken path; disarmament is the commandment of the times. Let no one be deceived; there is no survival for humanity without global peace!

3. Young people must learn at home and in school that violence must not be a means of settling differences with others. Only thus can a culture of non-violence be created.

4. A human person is infinitely precious and must be unconditionally protected. But likewise the lives of animals and plants which inhabit this planet with us deserve protection, preservation and care. Limitless exploitation of the natural foundations of life, ruthless destruction of the biosphere and militarization of the cosmos are all outrages. As human beings we have a special responsibility – especially with a view to future generations – for Earth and the cosmos, for the air, water and soil. We are all intertwined together in this cosmos and we are all dependent on each other. Each one of us depends on the welfare of all. Therefore the dominance of humanity over nature and the cosmos must not be encouraged. Instead, we must cultivate living in harmony with nature and the cosmos.

5. To be authentically human in the spirit of our great religious and ethical traditions means that in public as well as in private life we must be concerned for others and ready to help. We must never be ruthless and brutal. Every people, every race, every religion must show tolerance and respect – indeed high appreciation – for every other. Minorities need protection and support, whether they be racial, ethnic or religious.

Undoubtedly the new world order will only be a better order if, as a result thereof, we have a pluralistic world society characterized by partnership, which encourages peace and is nature-friendly and ecumenical. That is why even now many people are committing themselves on the basis of their religious or human convictions to a common world ethic and are calling on all people of goodwill to contribute to a change of awareness in matters of ethics.

TOWARD A PLANETARY CODE OF ETHICS

With the Chicago Declaration, religions demonstrated that it is in principle possible to formulate a planetary code of ethics. Nevertheless, it certainly makes a difference whether a Parliament of Religions or an international community, through UNESCO or the United Nations, formulates such a consensus.

It is therefore worth discussing how different a planetary code of ethics of UNESCO or the United Nations has to be in terms of style and content. Already in the Chicago Declaration it is emphasized: 'The principles expressed in this Global Ethic can be affirmed by all persons with ethical convictions, whether religiously grounded or not.' In other words: all that is said about the 'vision of peoples living peacefully together' and the 'responsibility for the care of Earth' is said for all ethically committed human beings, whether they are religious or not.

It is also important to note that the Chicago Declaration recalls the 1948 Universal Declaration of Human Rights of the United Nations. The Chicago Declaration stipulates: 'What it (the Universal Declaration) formally proclaimed on the level of rights we wish to confirm and deepen here from the perspective of an ethic: the full realization of the intrinsic dignity of the human person, the inalienable freedom and equality in principle of all humans, and the necessary solidarity and interdependence of all humans with each other.'

On the basis of their own document, the leaders of religions will certainly welcome the possibility of the world organizations trying to formulate a planetary code of ethics. The fundamental demand of this declaration, 'every human being must be treated humanely', should be taken over in this code of ethics and also, if possible, the Golden Rule, which is found and has persisted in many religious and ethical traditions of humankind for thousands of years: 'What you do not wish done to yourself, do not do to others!' Above all, the 'four irrevocable directives' could serve as a structure for this new document:

1. Commitment to a culture of non-violence and respect for life.
2. Commitment to a culture of solidarity and a just economic order.
3. Commitment to a culture of tolerance and a life of truthfulness.
4. Commitment to a culture of equal rights and partnership between men and women.

I would therefore like to propose that a body of the United Nations or UNESCO establish a consultative committee to elaborate a first draft of such a planetary code of ethics. The matter is urgent. There is no time to lose.

BIBLIOGRAPHY

KÜNG, H. 1991. *Global Responsibility. In Search of a New World Ethic.* London/New York, SCM Press/Continuum.
——. 1992. *Judaism.* London/New York, SCM Press/Crossroad.
——. 1995. *Christianity. Essence and History.* London/New York, SCM Press/Continuum.
——. *Islam.* In preparation.

Understanding and dialogue between religions to promote the spirit of peace

*Félix Marti**

THE OBSTACLES

I am using the term 'religions' to refer to a very varied set of experiences which cannot be reduced to a single model. From outside, they can be seen to share certain characteristics which make them similar, but there are also highly original elements in each religious tradition which make it difficult to express such an abundance of human experiences with a single concept. Religions can probably only be properly understood from within. For this reason, the various sociologies of religion are valuable but insufficient approximations. Any attempt at understanding religions must respect and take an interest in the irreducible aspects of the religious experience. It is not possible to understand religions if we approach them with the intention only of discovering their ideological, political, psychological, philosophical, economical nature or any other aspect which would reduce religion to one of these dimensions of human and social reality. Contemporary culture now looks on the religious phenomenon with greater humility than a few decades ago and calmly questions itself as to the type of knowledge religions have to offer, the degree to which they can play a part in people's freedom and responsibilities and the way in which each tradition explores the secrets of the cosmos, the frontiers of life and death, the wonders of human creativity.

---

*   Director, Centre UNESCO de Catalunya, Barcelona, Spain.

Religions in other ages lived in separate territories. There were divisions as a result of their implantation in different geographical spaces. Above all, there was a separation caused by the fact that the cultures within which religions express themselves were until very recently highly impermeable spaces. This lack of communication has changed radically in recent decades. Now religious offers are not made from a monopolistic standpoint; it is becoming easier and easier to decide for ourselves what religion we want to believe in or practise. It is also now usual for believers of any religion to see the usefulness of contributions from other religions rather than limiting themselves to receiving the spiritual traditions of their own religion. At the same time, in societies which are increasingly proclaiming religious freedom as a positive criterion for survival, people also exercise the freedom not to believe – that is, the search for vital orientations and ethical criteria which do not originate in religion. All these facts outline the importance of dialogue between religions. Dialogue allows a clearer picture of what each religious tradition has to offer in relation to the others and also helps discover points in common or shared responsibilities.

Historically, religions have not always contributed to tolerance and peace. One could list many examples of intolerance and warmongering in most religions. One of the reasons why religions turn to violence is connected with the claim of owning an exclusive truth or one that is superior to the others. From this point of view, human groups who do not belong to the community of believers supposedly in possession of the truth may be treated as inferior. Believers who see themselves as superior think they can legitimately force others to submit to the truth even if it means using violence. Religions often offer their followers a doctrinal, moral and pragmatic package that is so complete it becomes a closed universe totally indisposed to dialogue. When a believer has a closed mind, he experiences a comforting psychological security, but the problem is that his faith can take the form of submission to a doctrine which has become an ideology. In ideologies, the coherence of the system is more important than openness to the truth. Ideologies can lead to fanaticism. Religions, unlike ideologies, are like a pilgrimage towards the truth.

The temptation of violence often has another origin. Religions let themselves be used by power structures and then find themselves obliged to legitimize the violence exercised by power. This is something that goes back a long way and seems difficult to change. Political authorities want to use religion to achieve their objectives. They know that religion conditions the conscience of citizens and they attempt an alliance which will eliminate criticism and stimulate conformity. For their own part, religious leaders have often felt that their orientations would be more effective if they had the help of the established powers, and have jeopardized the freedom of religious communities in exchange for power. There is then a confusion between political authority and religious leadership. In this way religious communities can easily come to share the violent methods so characteristic of political life and can be called on to sanctify war. The right solution to the problem of the confusion between power and religion poses serious difficulties. In those religions which profess an all-powerful God, it is easy to imagine social structures in which religious leaders wield effective political power. Reducing religious life to the sphere of the individual's feelings does not solve the problem either. Religion can take on a public dimension, but a public presence for religions has to be found that is coherent with their theologies but avoids confusions harmful both to social life and to the true nature of religions.

Religion is a decisive element in the formation of the images, symbols and values at the heart of individuals and social groups. Religion has an enormous ability to mobilize individual and collective energy. No other cultural reference has the roots or the strength that characterize the religious experience. For this reason, perverting religion can be very dangerous. Religious fervour has often taken the form of fanaticism and extremism. Furthermore, the more religions ask their faithful to attune to realities that are beyond their own control, the easier it is for individuals and religious groups to adopt extravagant and violent conduct. Religions aspire to overcoming the limits to reason and to established social conventions. Religions suggest ways of overcoming the illusions of anthropocentrism. However, sometimes these invitations degenerate into alienated and psychologically unhealthy ways of life. Violence, supposedly sanctified by religion, is one example of the misuse of religion.

Some religions have elaborated doctrines on justified violence. They criticize violence in general but accept it in a particular set of circumstances. These are doctrines inspired in socially accepted evaluations rather than in the original contributions of religious theologies. Human justice has regulated violence in societies and has fixed criteria and limits to it. It is only able to denounce immoderate or uncontrolled violence. Some religions stay close to the regulated acceptance of violence which is characteristic of human societies. They even present an image of God or of the principle of reality which includes a selective form of violence. They believe that precisely God alone exercises violence with justice, but the acceptance of violence becomes an insoluble problem when we try to set limits to justified violence. How can we know what violence God wants or accepts? Who interprets the justification of violence in each specific case? Everything is clearer when religion shuns all expression of violence and rejects violent means even for the noblest ends.

JUSTICE AND PEACE

Peace is a consequence of justice. In situations where people or groups are oppressed, it is normal that there be violence and wars. Human history shows a series of violent situations because injustices have constantly taken place. The change following the advent of modernity is that injustice is no longer considered to be a consequence of fate, so much as the result of decisions by humans and of structures that can be modified. Freedom and oppression, prosperity and poverty, are social constructs, and violence therefore arises not only as an expression of protest but as a way of breaking down unjust structures. In our age, the desire for justice is now universal. Before, there were above all local claims which aimed at a higher degree of freedom or fraternity within geographically well-defined societies. Today what is really shocking is the injustice that condemns many peoples to live in conditions inferior to those of others and with a very limited level of freedom. Justice must become global. There will have to be changes in the political and economic structures that ensure prosperity for a minority of nations and maintain the underdevelopment of the majority.

Justice has a close relationship with the exercise of power. For centuries the predominant concepts of power attributed to it a role which had little to do with an effective search for justice. Democracy is a recent invention and its implantation has taken place initially in countries of Western culture. However, the aspiration to democratic life can be seen in all cultures, and a link will have to be found between each specific culture and those democratic practices compatible with its essential values. Everyone today believes that power should serve justice and that democratic participation is what can direct any power towards the implantation of justice. Democratic practices are beginning to make headway in the field of conventional political life, but there are still many power structures which have not introduced democratic control systems to ensure their orientation in favour of justice. I am thinking in particular of the international financial forces which no one controls and in the power of the media, governed only by the rules of the market both within states and on an international scale. Any attempt to imagine an economy that is not blind to justice is rejected by the representatives of liberal dogma. Any attempt to imagine the media at the service of justice is accused of jeopardizing freedom of information.

Nevertheless, it is possible to imagine, in any society, a future in which the aspiration for justice is no longer a Utopia but a normal criterion of governability. This development is possible if two complementary criteria are agreed on. For one, mechanisms must be created for recognizing the degree of sovereignty all human groups need to govern themselves according to their own values and priorities. Until now the state has been the only entity to govern itself. But state borders are too artificial and do not show enough respect for the diversity of human communities which should be political subjects in the international concert. In this sense, states represent outdated structures that are too inflexible to allow democratic participation beyond the mere recognition of an exclusively individual version of human rights. Secondly, justice will not be made to advance unless truly international organs of government are established. Until now the United Nations has merely acted as a forum for agreements between states. Its freedom to exert its international authority has been conditioned. The time has come to create a world authority that is democratic and effective.

If political and economic injustices centred the attention of analysts during the nineteenth and twentieth centuries, we are now beginning a period in which we shall have to analyse injustices of a cultural nature. The scientific and technological culture developed by the Western countries has looked upon itself as superior and has believed itself authorized to marginalize or destroy all other cultures. Today there is a growing awareness of the limits to science and technology as forms of culture. Scientists and technicians themselves say the same. Intellectuals, sages and artists of dominated or endangered cultures suffer. It is in the interest of all of us today to establish a cultural coexistence which respects all traditions equally. Obviously all cultures are limited and all have to evolve, taking into account new information, new situations and the dialogue between various traditions. What cannot be accepted is that the self-criticism expected of some cultures cannot be exercised in the dominant cultures. It is also inadmissible that cultures or languages should be rated according to the quantitative criteria that belong to the world of economics or politics. Establishing criteria and rules to defend the equal dignity of all cultures is something we must do urgently if we want to work for peace in the world. Disrespect for cultures and cultural oppression are causes of violence and wars.

In other ages, prestige went to imperialist ideologies. At any rate, the beneficiaries of imperialist practices had managed to convince everyone of the value of their political formulas. Empires aimed to consolidate their power by imposing criteria of uniformity within their territories. The attempt to eliminate diversity is one of the practices that has caused the most pain and violence in human history. Even today, political repression is exercised in many places to eliminate individuals and groups who represent human diversity. People want to resolve complexity through measures that destroy complexity. In some places, it is ethnic diversity people are afraid of; in others, religious diversity, national diversity, or diversity of ideological or political orientations. We are more and more aware that human diversity is something to treasure and that the beauty of social life is the constructive organization of diversity. Obviously, it is more difficult to respect diversity than to govern uniform societies, but it is far more interesting to live in pluralist societies than in uniform ones. The shift from the prestige of imperialist systems to the recognition of the value of complex societies offers a rare opportunity for peace.

One of the consequences of the one-sidedness of technological culture is the aggressiveness we have developed towards the environment. The old forms of communion with nature and of respect for Mother Earth have been replaced by a purely utilitarian treatment. Human societies have not only believed themselves independent of the world of nature, they have abused nature's resources to limits that have upset fundamental aspects of the balance on Planet Earth. We are now beginning to think that the meaning of justice cannot be reduced to a distribution of resources and opportunities to human individuals and groups, but that it must extend throughout the system of relations which connect human life with life in general and with the whole of the planet. This is a very considerable change in outlook. We need new wisdom to help us make a judicious use of nature's resources, to create an alternative industrial system that is sustainable and to substantially modify consumer habits which cannot be shared by all the inhabitants of the planet. At the moment, we are still prisoners of unfair ways of life, because 20 per cent of the world's population consumes 80 per cent of its resources, and the way we exploit the available resources is beyond all measure.

The aims of religion cannot be reduced to achieving justice. Religion tries to make accessible the mysteries at the heart of reality. It offers paths for liberation that do not coincide with visible justice, but this does not mean that it is indifferent to justice. All religions contain clear invitations to practise justice. They express it in various languages: love, compassion, willingness, generosity. Not only do they propose the practice of justice, but they are able to activate powerful energies to make their faithful brave to the point of heroism in the struggle in favour of justice. For these reasons, followers of various religious traditions have become outstanding examples in the fight for human dignity, human rights and liberation processes. In today's world, it does not seem easy to bring about the great changes necessary to establish universal justice, with the characteristics laid out above, unless religions help with their own determined and disinterested contributions. In technologically advanced societies, only religion can make an appeal for the change in life which will lead us towards a model of sustainable development. In poor societies, religion alone feeds the hope of the most desperate.

RELIGIONS AND PEACE

Some writers have intimately tied religion and peace to the extent of saying that they are practically identical experiences. When there is a pacification of hearts and of societies, then there is progress towards a religious experience. When there is genuine religious maturity, the result will be non-violence and peace. In this sense, the best contribution which religions can make to peace is to be true to themselves and reject adulterated versions of their own tradition. It is in the heart of human beings that the basic options on violence and peace are decided. The religious experience is an option against violence and in favour of peace. In today's world, religions must clearly state that violence cannot be legitimated by appeals to them and that, on the contrary, religions are factors of personal and social pacification. This clarification can only come about when religions overcome sectarian temptations, that is, when they are at the service of the spiritual message which characterizes them and not at the service of institutional interests. All religions, at some time or another, fall prey to sectarian orientations. Sectarianism contains the explanation for the violence often exercised by religions. Sects use any means available to them to achieve their ends. They act like coldly calculating businesses that are no longer at the service either of their members or of the general public. Religions must not be confused with sects. Religions are an invitation to spiritual life and are incompatible with the instrumentalization of people and with violence.

It is not enough for religions to be themselves if they want to contribute effectively to peace in the world. They must also make an effort at dialogue to provide a solid foundation for social and political peace: religious peace. Peace between religions does not just mean passive tolerance between communities of believers or between communities of believers and the agnostic or atheist trends which also exist in our societies; it means a common search for proposals of spirituality. I have already pointed out that each religious tradition has an originality that makes it impossible to equate it with the others. They do not make the same proposals and their differences cannot be put down simply to the use of different languages. What we can hope for is that they recognize the similarities between their doctrines and, above all, the spiritual itineraries they propose. There are startling similarities to be observed between the mystics of all religions. It seems by all means that we are beginning a period in which religions must take an interest in dialogue and collaboration. Individual believers and communities of believers from different religions have for some time been working together for progress in justice. But this is not enough. It must also be possible to maintain dialogue on doctrines, spiritual experiences and the ways in which believers want to be present in today's world. Dialogue between religions is still very undeveloped. There should be more spaces and occasions for it to take place as something normal. The more institutionally structured religions will have to overcome the inertia specific to their way of functioning. The religions that have lived in greater isolation or in more closed societies must respond to contemporary cultural realities which, for better or for worse, affect everyone.

Understanding and dialogue between religions to promote the spirit of peace

Religions in dialogue will contribute to peace. Religions which have no wish for dialogue will obstruct peace.

Increasingly, religions live in societies in which the citizens have intellectual, moral and aesthetic points of reference that are not monopolized by religion. Believers themselves share, willingly or unwillingly, symbols, values and ideas which come to all cultures from different sources of inspiration. Religion is only one of these sources, even if the principal one. Religions have always maintained a dialogue with the cultures with which they have coexisted. In fact, religious and spiritual messages are expressed in languages provided by the different cultures. The synthesis is sometimes so strong that it is difficult to distinguish between religion and culture and it is difficult to imagine what religion would be like if it were expressed in a different culture or what would become of specific cultures if they did away with the religion which drives them. It would be true to say that, in general, culture and religion do not coincide. Religions are particularly concerned with the sacred, with the mysterious unity of reality or with the relations between human beings and what is invisible and inexpressible. Religions reach areas that are inaccessible to culture when culture does not include religion. Culture, on the other hand, refers to many other experiences of human life and gives rise to philosophies, ethics and aesthetics with little relation to the messages of religion. Religions make contributions to cultures but they are not the only sources. Some religious traditions are more unitary and some are more dualistic. In all of them, we can discover more distinctly cultural elements alongside genuinely spiritual ones. For these reasons, it is healthy that religions should maintain a dialogue with their cultural context and also with more distant cultures. The great spiritual messages can be recreated in any cultural context and need have no fear of any serious cultural novelty that is open to dialogue. If religions do not remain adamant in the face of new cultural situations, peace will be easier.

One of the most valuable contributions by religions to peace in the world would be for communities of believers to practise experiences of peace within their communities. It is important, for example, that legitimate diversity of believers in the doctrinal field not be repressed, that religious leaders should exercise authority on the basis of agreement on their spiritual maturity and that conflicts within religious groups should be resolved with real feeling for individuals. Very often, the structures of the more institutionalized religions are too much like political structures. There is not enough respect for diversity, religious leaders take on their responsibilities without the participation of their community, and an artificial order is imposed by repressive measures similar to those used by totalitarian powers. Communities of believers should keep their distance from the models and practices societies have used in their political life. Religion must be clearly seen as groups of people practising a spiritual experience and, therefore, as something remote from the passions of power, of social prestige and of visible success. In this respect, individuals and communities with prophetic characteristics, even if they seem unconventional, can inspire justice and peace. Order is a legitimate concern of political leaders, but it must not be a priority for religions. Peace needs people and groups who practise love, forgiveness and reconciliation.

Some specifically religious values appear as decisive contributions on the horizon of problems of violence and peace. The wisdom of non-violence from which conduct develops to deactivate the spiral of violence, the welcome for the foreigner, the invitation to forgive offence, and the relativization of desire are all enormously important contributions in the search for peace. Religions have breathed life into these ideals and many people practise them discreetly but effectively. They are not exclusive to religious people but it is obvious that the religious foundation of these ideals means they can be lived with special strength. In addition, religions propose them to all, because the great religious traditions are open to all citizens and not just to selected circles. In this respect, I must mention the foundation that religions have to offer to human dignity and the dignity of all creatures. Human rights could not be formulated without a basis in the recognition of human dignity. It seems a paradox that religions, which differ from mere humanism in that they are gifts that come from outside the human individual, offer a foundation for human dignity. In fact, the difficulty would be to accept that our dignity is decided only by self-evaluation or by social agreement. Self-evaluation entails the risk of overvaluation or undervaluation. Agreements are too fragile. Religions can give wider meanings to human rights values and the rights of peoples. At the same time, they can help to reformulate in new ways assertions which are still too closely tied to Western culture.

One of the great challenges of our age is the threat of scepticism and nihilism. When all principles are relative to the point of not believing in anything or anyone, when there is no value to give a meaning to life, the chances of accepting violence are very high. There are people who do not believe in the possibility of keeping away from violence. They feel trapped by violence and contribute resignedly to its established forms. This conformity is mainly expressed in two ways. Sometimes there is a selfish acceptance of violence which is accompanied by justifications of a cynical type. Sometimes, violence is lived as an experience rather like a game, without any pretence at theory. At any rate, nihilism is different from the vacuum experienced by mystics of all religious traditions. For mystics, the night is like an expectation, or the first taste of plenitude. Nihilists lose themselves in disorientation. They live in it and sometimes take advantage of it without excluding violence. Religions do a great service to the extent that they are universes of faith and spaces for values. It is true that sometimes religious faith and values have been associated with violence, but the total absence of faith and values is even easier to associate with violence. In our own age, nihilism is often present under a gentle guise. An inordinate passion for distraction, sport or consumption is one manifestation of nihilism. Religion teaches us to lead a life reconciled to reality, without running away from it, without the need to look for artificial paradises to give life a meaning. Religions show us the way to overcome radical mistrust in ourselves and others. Faith and values, that is, trust, generate peace.

SPACES FOR PEACE

Religions know that any reform intended to organize society along fairer lines can fail if it does not take into account human fragility, or individual or group selfishness, the possibility of corruption threatening any political structure. Throughout human history, many reforms have been attempted which aspired to establishing peace based on justice. Their success so far has been very limited. Fairer structures are not enough. It is also necessary for each human being to develop a sense of fraternity and the experience of peace. The inner peace of each individual and the peace of society are interrelated and complementary. Human beings can reach peace under a wide range of conditions. Their most intimate freedom is never held to ransom by the political, economic and social conditions of the world around them. Religions teach ways to maintain dignity, calm and peace in situations of oppression, poverty, ideological control, suffering or collective alienation. Religions are bearers of a special wisdom which saves us from destruction by the forces of evil outside or inside each individual. Inner peace is an innocence which survives the experience of evil. Through working for peace within each individual, religions have done a service of great value to peace in the world. Religions do not have a monopoly, but they are extremely rich in this field.

Peace should be one of the characteristics of family life. Today, there are many different family models. The basic element of the family is the special love between two or more people. Love can be present in many family models. The greatness of human love is considered by religions as a gift from God or an experience related to the fullness of life. For this reason, religions have praised the family and have often granted it a specifically religious status. The family is a space filled with wonders. One feels the joy of giving; one creates a universe of shared values; the corporal relationship becomes spiritual and the spiritual communion is expressed in corporal gestures; sexuality, affection and liberty become one; the passage of time is experienced as maturation. The family is a special place in which to live in peace. Relations between members of the family should be characterized by non-violence, by the festive acceptance of diversity, by harmony between generations, sexes, qualities and defects, joys and sadness, successes and failures. The old model of the patriarchal and authoritarian family is evolving towards fraternal and open ways of life. Religions should come out in favour of a family peace centred on meaningful love. They should also be sympathetic towards processes which allow sexuality to be seen positively, which eliminate the subordination of women and which place reproductive conduct in the sphere of freedom. A family at peace is a valuable contribution to peace in the world.

The spirit of peace must not be restricted to personal life and family life. We all belong to larger communities taking into account our dimensions: we are citizens of an urban or rural community; we are members of a company or of a professional structure; we are members of cultural, sports, charitable or other associations. In each of the communities, we can act in favour of peace or contribute to violence. It is not just a question of maintaining good relations with

Understanding and dialogue between religions to promote the spirit of peace

the people we live with in our neighbourhood, at work or in the organizations of which we are members, but of helping to direct all the structures we take part in towards peace. The options of a city, a company or an association are not neutral. They either favour or complicate coexistence. Today, most of the decisions taken by public and private institutions have financial motivations. The search for financial profit does not guarantee a service to peace. We must denounce the abusive presence of financial interests in public life. Religions can oppose the idolatry of money and can maintain hope for the creation of structures of all sorts at the service of people. The service of religions must not be the construction of parallel structures controlled by religious authorities, but the stimulation of all social structures to place them at the service of human communities. The spirit of peace must give life to cities, businesses and associations. The spirit of peace must guide our conduct as citizens, as consumers, as professionals. The spirit of peace must not be excluded from any sphere of human activity.

States wield enormous responsibility in the field of justice and peace. The number of democratic states is relatively small and it is also a fact that all forms of democracy are limited. Non-democratic states exercise uncontrolled violence within their territories and in relation to other states. The roads to democracy are roads to peace. Democratic states exercise very restricted and relatively controllable violence. It is good that mechanisms for participation should be improved and that residual violence should be deactivated. One of the problems which generates most violence today is the lack of correspondence between state structures and national realities. States accuse nationalist movements of being the cause of violence and war. The truth is that the most obvious cause is the reluctance of many states to recognize the sovereignty of nations. One need only look at the practical difficulties which go with the right to self-determination. The spirit of peace should mean that the interests of states take second place to the right of peoples to self-government. At the same time, states must make a move to cede a part of their functions to international organizations and rethink the traditional structures of defence and security characterizing them. Religions will help spread the spirit of peace if they help to stimulate the awareness of national communities and relativize state structures; if they help to criticize the residual violence still practised by democratic states and are sympathetic towards pacifist movements, conscientious objectors and towards other alternative proposals to militaristic philosophies and conventional concepts of security; if they help make the peaceful transition from authoritarian regimes to democratic life.

One of the basic conditions for peace is the universal spread of solidarity. There are many people and groups prepared to practise solidarity within certain geographical limits. They only defend solidarity within the boundary of their own territory, country or culture. Sometimes they identify the space of their own religion as a space delimiting the exercise of solidarity. However, the most courageous of any of religion's messages is the extension of its invitations to all human beings. The great religious traditions, although they were born in specific cultural spaces, are universal. They are pillars, reminders and promoters of universal fraternity. Their universality must be seen not only as the freedom to offer their wisdom to any human being in any territory, but as the proclamation of the unity of the whole of the human family, of the need for universal justice without exclusions, and of the responsibility of each individual and each group towards all others. The cracks which divide the world today could probably be mended if religions insisted on the universal dimensions of human life. In some societies, only religion can propose a change of lifestyle to reduce inordinate consumption and make universal solidarity viable.

MEANS AND METHODS

The spirit of peace is a very ancient philosophy and, at the same time, a very new one. The aspiration is old. The possibility of eliminating much violence and war is very recent. For this reason, it can be considered a truly revolutionary change in ideas and attitudes. Education is of vital importance in explaining that peace, as religion tells us, is at once a mysterious gift and a means to edify freedom. It is mysterious in the sense that peace is related to the deepest dimensions of human experience which religions call the spiritual or sacred sphere. It is also something constructed out of human responsibility. All individuals and all groups must be educated in the spirit of tolerance, of openness and peace. Everyone should be initiated in the ideas, the desires and the techniques and myths of peace. Education for peace must be one of the priorities of any educational system. Today there are a series of educational methodologies

Understanding and dialogue between religions to promote the spirit of peace

at the service of education for peace. In the framework of UNESCO, we can mention the Associated Schools Project and the Linguapax programme. Religions devote a large part of their energy to education. Therefore a concerted effort by all the religious traditions in the field of education would give impressive results.

Alongside educational work, I must stress the importance of non-governmental organizations. Some countries have excellent associative traditions. Other countries, especially those which suffered under long-term totalitarian political regimes, still have a weak civil society, but there is growing recognition everywhere of the importance of non-profit organizations as a driving force for peace. First of all, I must mention the peace movements themselves. Some are confessional and others are non-confessional. They are associations working in favour of disarmament or promoting mediation in conflicts, or speaking out against expressions of violence. Many followers of the great religious traditions belong to these peace associations. Even the religious authorities often make public declarations in favour of peace and against violence and are not afraid to mention specific problems such as the scandal of the arms trade. Other associations have complementary objectives. I could mention three types of non-governmental organizations which act on the causes of war and violence. These are associations for individual and collective human rights, associations for co-operation between rich countries and economically poor countries, and associations for the protection of the environment. If religions ask their followers to help bring to life the movements in favour of peace, human rights, co-operation or the environment, the strength of these non-governmental organizations can be increased.

The instruments with the strongest influence on public opinion are the mass media, which have an almost magical power inasmuch as they shape reality. They bring to life myths, interpretations, feelings and passions, and cause other myths, ideas and values to disappear. Religions have a difficult relationship with the media. They often prefer their message to be transmitted more confidentially through the techniques of initiation. They know that sensationalism is a path fraught with pitfalls. They understandably avoid trivialization, confusion or the cult of immediate sensuality. Furthermore, when religious propaganda becomes marketing, it resembles mental manipulation more than an offer of spiritual life. The message of peace is not so difficult to express through the media. It calls, above all, for the gradual replacement of ideas and myths which favour violence by concepts and myths placing a value on peace. The media can serve racism, discrimination, aggression and intolerance, or they can combat prejudice, praise diversity and pluralism, improve coexistence and build peace. The concern of believers as regards the media should not be so much to ensure that their religious tradition has access to them, as to work towards communications which are media-orientated in favour of non-violence and peace, in favour of freedom and pluralism, in favour of truth and justice.

In all human societies, artists have a very special role to play. They extend human experience beyond conventional words and the usual actions. They practise a creativity which, through its beauty, brings us pleasure in our relationship with ourselves, with others and with the world. They suggest myths and symbols to explore the meaning of life. With their generosity, they free us from imprisonment in our own interest. They invite us to develop the pleasurable rather than purely functional dimensions of the individual and collective human existence. In a world such as ours, which is so lacking in Utopias, they invite us to spread our wings, sometimes expressing our unease with others imagining a more harmonious world. Religions have always valued art and have used the boldness of art to express the ineffable. Religion has inspired artists, and artists have represented certain religious experiences. Religions are favourable to beauty in the same way that they are favourable to truth and goodness. The interest of religions in art should be better expressed, not only because the arts can be paths towards religion, but because the arts contribute to human dignity to the extent that they arouse creativity, the most profound sensibility and the noblest inspirations. The spirit of peace must find the right aesthetic forms through which to communicate. Logical discourse is not enough. It needs forms, symbols, images which will take root in the most secret interior of each individual and each community. Those religions that encourage aesthetic creativity have a contribution to make.

Since peace is a combination of fragile equilibria, the structures that guarantee peace must be strengthened. In the political field, we need a reform of the United Nations Organization to make it into a structure more capable of ensuring peace. Its present design is outdated and undemocratic and its powers are too limited. We must also try and complement the policy of territorial representation, in which all nations must be present with fair and proportioned criteria, with a second policy to allow the effective participation of non-governmental organizations. The structures of peace do not belong exclusively to the sphere of politics. There must also be strong organizations to look after specific issues in relation to peace. We could mention, for example, the world of scientists, of writers or of the young. If we think of the world of religion, more organizations should be set up along the lines of the Fellowship of Reconciliation, the World Council of Churches, the Peace Council or the World Conference on Religion and Peace, which was founded in Kyoto, Japan, in 1970 and has a fascinating history of inter-religious dialogue in favour of peace. Along similar lines, I must mention the meeting of the Council for a Parliament of the World's Religions which took place in 1993 in Chicago in commemoration of the meeting held in 1893. These structures are still few and weak. Let us hope they can grow and be consolidated.

All these thoughts point out the common responsibilities of religions towards peace. Religions must make new efforts to promote the spirit of peace and it would be meaningless for each tradition to act individually. It is time for dialogue and co-operation.

Gandhi on the moral life and plurality of religions

Mrinal Miri[*]

In this paper, I shall talk primarily about Gandhi's views about what he considered to be the proper relationship between different religions or rather between communities owing allegiance to different religions – but, before doing so, I would like (1) briefly to indicate, at the risk of being banal, our own post-Gandhian predicament, which lends an aura of enchantment to the contemplation of Gandhi; and (2) to show how a Gandhian way of looking at things might contain the beginnings of a general answer to our predicament.

Let me begin with the idea of humanism. This idea is peculiar to Western modernity and informs much of our contemporary talk about human rights. Humanism is not an easy idea to present, but perhaps one can say the following: in pre-modern civilizations, where man certainly occupied an important place in the order of things, the highest object of man's moral and spiritual attention was something other than man himself; it might have been the spiritual reality permeating the world, or the cosmic order, or God and so on. For humanism, on the other hand, man himself in his purely manly existence, in his utter ordinariness, is the only proper object of man's moral attention. What then is man in his ordinariness? Man is a biological creature with a certain life-span and with special needs and desires; he can wield reason and language, has emotions of different kinds; he is liable to suffer pain and is capable of enjoying pleasure;

---

[*] Director, Indian Institute of Advanced Study, Shimla, India.

he also has freedom and autonomy, which he does not owe to anything else in the world. For humanism, man's moral endeavour must exist in the pursuit of the welfare of man understood in this sense.

The values which are associated with the humanist moral stance are: the value of human life as such, of man's freedom, of avoidance of pain and pursuit of pleasure. Human rights include the right to life, the right to freedom, the right to pursue pleasure and to avoid pain and suffering. To these one might add the right to dignity, and nowadays also the right to one's own culture. It is interesting that the language of rights is a central feature of our contemporary moral discourse. I think that this is also, as I shall try to indicate shortly, a part of what I have called our contemporary predicament.

Humanism stands in a close but extremely uneasy relationship with another pervasive feature of modernity: modern Western epistemology, dominated by what many would now call the 'ideology' of natural science. The central feature of this epistemology is its insistence on what we might call the 'purity' of knowledge, knowledge uncontaminated by human subjectivity and mediated by disengaged scientific reason. Such reason reveals a world that is, as Weber said, 'disenchanted', denuded of spirituality, or indeed any meaning or *telos*. The disenchanted world contains man with his life of subjectivity, his desires, feelings and emotions, his freedom to do one thing rather than another. Humanism simply asserts that, if anything is to be valued in such a world, it can only be man's life, the pleasures which come from the fulfilment of his desires and his capacity for freedom. To this are added man's sense of dignity and his identification with a particular culture.

The irony, however, is that while humanist values are widely acknowledged and are to a large extent the by-product of modern epistemology, the latter cannot provide a basis for our belief in the existence of these values: statements asserting these values are outside the field of our epistemic gaze. They must, therefore, be regarded as either expressions of our subjectivity or its projections onto the objective world. Another way is to regard belief in values – humanist or other – as having served, in spite of their being erroneous, a useful purpose in man's success in the evolutionary struggle and, therefore, dispensable when they no longer serve this purpose. Still another related way is to regard our moral consciousness as inherently confused and riddled with error and, therefore, best discarded altogether.[1] There are, of course, valiant attempts to reconcile the epistemic rejection of values with their apparent ineluctability. But such attempts, from the nature of the case, cannot succeed.

Another source of tension is the very need to acknowledge the existence of the disengaged self endowed with freedom and autonomy. Since the world revealed by our rational-scientific-epistemic gaze is not a world ordered in terms of values, is not what might be called a dharmic world, the humanist values must be articulated in the language of rights and not in the language of ontological commitment. Morality has to be put into effect by man's exercise of his freedom, but freedom or autonomy also implies freedom not to exercise this freedom: a right must also be capable of not being exercised, of being waived. By contrast, an ontological order cannot be waived. Thus, while humanist values are widely acknowledged, there is as it were a seed of subversion written into the humanist agenda. The autonomy or freedom of the self, a central humanist value, renders values articulated in terms of 'human rights' dispensable.

MODERN EPISTEMOLOGY AND VALUES

There have also been attempts at giving an account of values which give them an ontological status in spite of the dictates of modern epistemology. Notable among such attempts are those of Charles Taylor and Alisdair MacIntyre. Charles Taylor argues at great length and in several places for a view which can be thus stated:[2]

---

1. Consider, for instance, the debate beginning, in Anglo-American philosophy, with G. E. Moore, *Principia Ethica*, Cambridge, Cambridge University Press, 1903; and continuing through philosophers like C. L. Stevenson, *The Language of Ethics*, New York, Columbia University Press, 1945; R. M. Hare, *Freedom and Reason*, Oxford, Oxford University Press, 1963; and, very recently, John L. Mackie, *Ethics: Inventing Right and Wrong*, Harmondsworth, Penguin, 1977; Simon Blackburn, 'Essays and the Phenomenology of Value', in T. Honderich (ed.), *Morality and Objectivity*, Routledge & Kegan Paul, 1985; John McDowell, 'Values and Secondary Qualities', in Honderich, op. cit.; Barnard Williams, *Ethics and Limits of Philosophy*, London, Fontana, 1985.
2. See, for instance, his essays in *Human Agency and Language*, Cambridge, Cambridge University Press, 1985; and *Sources of the Self*, Cambridge, Cambridge University Press, 1992.

- We have what may be called brute desires, and desires to have certain desires or desires not to have certain desires. The second kind of desires may be called second-order desires.
- Choosing between brute desires requires only 'weak' evaluation (shall I have tea or coffee?), but having a second-order desire requires 'strong' evaluation (shall I succumb to the desire to be dishonest or shall I pursue the desire not to have the desire to be dishonest?).
- It is impossible to reduce 'strong evaluations' to weak evaluations in spite of famous attempts to do so (for example, Mill, Freud, Foucault).
- Our capacity to make strong evaluations is built into the very concept of a human being: human beings would not be what we know them to be if they did not have this capacity.
- The distinction between strong evaluation and weak evaluation requires that we recognize a distinction of quality between our desires – between a life that is incomparably better than some other. And this is a distinction in reality, not just an expression of our subjectivity or its projection.
- Our modern humanist values also arise from our strong evaluations and thus have an inalienable ontological status: they cannot be divorced from the real world, modern epistemology notwithstanding.

Taylor's arguments for his view are acute, penetrating and are informed by rare historical insight. Unfortunately, this is not the place to go into them. What I wish to say here, without arguing for it, is that the arguments lose surety while dealing with the fact that strong evaluation necessarily allows for the possibility of different visions of the good life: visions which may be incompatible with one another. Thus think of the difference between a life devoted to the service of the downtrodden, a life devoted to the welfare and happiness of the family and the home, and a life devoted to the pursuit of aesthetic self-expression. When each of these has the status, for a different individual, of being incomparably better than anything else, how are moral differences between them to be resolved? The situation becomes even more tricky when we consider the possible moral *impasse* arising out of allegiance (in the strong evaluation sense) to different cultures which, in many crucial ways, may be incompatible with one another. Perhaps Taylor would say that, faced with such apparent incompatibilities, one tries to achieve a finer, deeper articulation of one's own strong evaluations in the hope that similar articulations of rival strong evaluations would eventually come to rational terms with one another. But this is only a hope, laudable undoubtedly, but none the less just a hope.

MacIntyre's rearguard defence of the reality of values consists in arguing that virtues are embedded in what he calls human practices and can be stated schematically as follows:[3]

- A practice is a form of rule-governed human activity, e.g. chess, gardening, academic research.
- The crucial thing about a practice is that there is a good, an excellence, which is internal to a practice and there is a good which is external to it; for example football has a good which is internal to it, an excellence which can be articulated only in terms of the game itself, such as that achieved by, say, a Pele. They are unintelligible except in terms of the practice itself. However, there is an external good to be gained by playing football: money, fame, etc. The same is true of a practice such as academic research.
- It is in the nature of a practice that pursuit of a good internal to it requires the exercise of virtues such as honesty, justice, courage, and so on. To cheat in football is to defeat the very purpose of the pursuit of excellence in football; one must be capable of giving others their due: recognizing and acknowledging excellence achieved by others and putting one's own achievement in perspective (justice); one must be prepared to put one's limbs, if not one's life, at risk (courage). What is true of football is true of other practices as well.
- Human life would be recognizably different if it did not have room for practice in MacIntyre's sense.
- The virtues, therefore, cannot be divorced from the fabric of human life, whatever the verdict of modern scientific epistemology.

MacIntyre's attempt at finding an objective grounding for virtues is, like Taylor's attempt at showing the reality of values, brilliant, but his account also has to take stock of the turn which human life has taken in our times. The autonomy

---

3. *After Virtue*, London, Duckworth, 1981, particularly Chapter 14.

of the pursuit of internal goods is increasingly being made subservient to the pursuit of external goods. If this process continues, and there is no indication that it will not, then the natural end product of such a process will be that all pursuit of internal goods will be at the service of the external goods, such as money, fame, power. If internal goods are no longer pursued for their own sake, then virtues will no longer be an inalienable part of the fabric of human life; for the pursuit of external goods does not require the exercise of the virtues; what it might still require is perhaps simulacra of the virtues, so that the illusion of a special aura around virtuous concepts can be put to effective use in its service.

HUMANISTIC VALUES

The point I have been labouring to make is that, if we are looking for a basis for our commitment to values, humanist values included, we shall have to look rather beyond the epistemic resources of modernity, beyond – not into – what has come to be known as post-modernity, which has certainly lent a degree of respectability to assertions of radical epistemic diversity – but beyond, as it were, into our pre-modern epistemic past. Gandhi's entire approach was pre-modern or traditional. He, of course, sharply criticized, and indeed condemned, many things in his own tradition; he also had deep respect for the achievements of modern science, although he considered much of its technological by-product a terrible catastrophe for mankind. The foundation of his thought and his practice is the unqualified conviction that our existence is spiritually grounded, that spirituality and moral purity must necessarily inform each other, that man's true fulfilment lies in moral-spiritual self-knowledge and action that necessarily flows from such self-knowledge. Let us take the following passages:

But he is no God who merely satisfies the intellect, if he ever does. God to be God must rule the heart and transform it. He must express his self in every, the smallest, act of his votary. This can only be done through a definite realization more real than the five senses can ever produce. Sense perceptions can be, often are, false and deceptive, however real they may appear. Where there is realization outside the senses, it is infallible. It is proved not by extraneous evidence but in the transformed conduct and character of those who have felt the real presence of God within. Such testimony is to be found in the experiences of an unbroken line of prophets and sages in all countries and climes. To reject this evidence is to deny oneself. (*Young India*, 11 October 1928)

True religion and true morality are inseparably bound up with each other. Religion is to morality what water is to the seed that is sown in the soil. (*Ethical Religion*, Ahmedabad, Navajiban Press, 1936, p. 29)

As soon as we lose the moral basis, we cease to be religious. There is no such thing as religion overriding morality. Man, for instance, cannot be untruthful, cruel and incontinent and claim to have God on his side. (*Young India*, 24 November 1921)

Religion which takes no account of practical affairs and does not help to solve them is no religion. (*Young India*, 7 May 1925)

I have come to feel that, like human beings, words have their evolution from stage to stage in the contents they hold. For instance, the contents of the richest word – God – are not the same to every one of us. They will vary with the experience of each. (*Young India*, 11 August 1927)

For Gandhi, as for many others, the religious vision is inseparable from spiritual experience and the authenticity of the latter is guaranteed by the moral transformation that ensues. Morality, religion and mysticism are of a piece. The crucial difference between the Gandhian vision of spiritual life and what may be called the received version of such a life is that, for Gandhi, an active, total (that is, with one's entire being) engagement with ordinary life – being 'fully there', imaginatively present to that which concerns us[4] – can be informed by the most profound spirituality; spiritual pursuit does not require disengagement from *sansarik* (worldly) life. To be spiritual and to be moral is to respond with utter *ahimsa* (non-violence) to what requires our response.

My countrymen are my nearest neighbours. They have become so helpless, so resourceless, so inert that I must concentrate myself on serving them. If I could

---

4. Janet Martin Soskice, 'Love and Attention', in Michael McGhee (ed.), *Philosophy, Religion and the Spiritual Life*, p. 67, Cambridge, Cambridge University Press, 1992.

persuade myself that I should find Him in a Himalayan cave, I would proceed there immediately. But I know that I cannot find Him apart from humanity. (*Harijan*, 29 August 1936)

I do not believe that the spiritual law works on a field of its own. On the contrary, it expresses itself only through the ordinary activities of life. It thus affects the economic, social and political fields. (*Young India*, 3 September 1925)

Working on the spinning wheel, looking after an injured calf, being engaged in *satyagraha* for a particular political end, keeping one's own home clean and tidy – each one of these activities can be touched by a joyous spirituality, a sense of being in touch with the real order of things.

It might be interesting in this connection to consider the curious Gandhian notion of 'experiments with truth'. The truth that Gandhi was concerned with was the truth ('reality' as opposed to 'illusion') of moral life. He believed that there is an 'interior route' to moral truths, just as there is an 'exterior route' to the truths of natural science. His experiments consisted in traversing this interior route until the possibility of the moral life was firmly established. Gandhi's experiment was aimed, among other things, at 'the purification of the motive', by going down to the springs of action, to root attitudes, thence to their expression in conduct which may result in 'dismantling and establishing of forms of life'.[5] Gandhi's fasts were an instrument of this experimentation; and there were several occasions in his life, in the early years, while in England, in South Africa and back in India, when dismantling a form of life and establishing another took place. The journey was far from easy. As Gandhi put it:

It may entail continuous suffering and the cultivating of endless patience. Thus, step by step we learn to make friends with all the world; we realize the greatness of God – or truth. Our peace of mind increases in spite of suffering, we become braver and more enterprising. We understand more clearly the difference between what is everlasting and what is not. Our pride melts away, and we become humble. Our worldly attachments diminish and so does the evil with us diminish from day to day. (*Yervada Mandir*, Ahmedabad, Navajiban Press, 1932, p. 105)

---

5. Michael McGhee, 'In praise of Mindfulness', *Religious Studies* (Cambridge), Vol. 24, No. 1, 1988, p. 66.

The test of the ultimate reality of values or moral truths is to be firmly established in a form of life or stage of life in which a person comes to feel 'a spirit which delights to do no evil'; or, in Gandhi's case, a spirit which delights to do justice to one's adversary in practical, political, religious matters, a spirit which delights in helping the helpless.

The use of the word 'experiment' is also suggestive of the fact that the moral search, the traversing of the interior route, is not just a psychological journey but an epistemic one – a journey which yields at once self-knowledge, as opposed to self-ignorance, and knowledge of moral truths – such as that true *ahimsa* drives out all fear, that the power of *ahimsa* is incomparably superior to that of violence, that true humility is the other side of true dignity. To achieve such self-knowledge, such quickening of awareness, is also to attain true freedom, *swaraj,* a state where one's actions flow with utter spontaneity from one's knowledge. Freedom is not the capacity to choose at random between alternative courses of action, but to act from an integrated moral epistemic stance.

To be able to appreciate Gandhi, therefore, one must be open to a radical epistemic reorientation; there must be a preparedness for a dismantling or at least a radical transformation of our epistemic stance.

INTERNATIONAL FELLOWSHIP OF ALL RELIGIONS

Now to Gandhi's views about the proper interrelationship between different religions. Gandhi's views are elaborated as a response to the question which he asks himself: how ought I, as a believing Hindu, treat other religions? The question had great practical urgency for Gandhi. India was the home of many religions: Hinduism, Buddhism, Jainism, Sikhism, Islam, Christianity and numerous tribal religions. While different religious communities generally lived in harmony with each other, conflicts – frequently violent – did arise and threatened to destroy the very possibility of a community life which is informed by justice and freedom. Why do such conflicts arise? Frequently, of course, they arise because of extraneous causes, such as economic, political, sociological disparities of one kind or another; but even in a situation where such disparities do not exist or, at least, are minimized, the possibility of conflict is not ruled out, and the reason for this, therefore, must be sought in the internal features of

religions themselves. The most important of such features is that there is a claim of superiority over all other religions built into the basic articulation of some religions. This is potentially conflict-generating in three ways:
1. When two religions claim superiority over each other, this can express itself in conduct meant to establish such claims in conflicting practical terms.
2. Even when a particular religion does not claim superiority over others, it is natural for it not to accept a position of inferiority with regard to the others.
3. There are, of course, cases where an individual or a community owing allegiance to a religion is dissatisfied with the religion and embraces another 'superior' one. This may, at least at the initial stage, cause great spiritual anxiety depending on how firmly rooted the individual or the community was in the original religion.

Gandhi's answer to the question: 'How ought I, as a believing Hindu, treat other religions?' is: 'I must treat all religions with equal respect.'

We must, of course, distinguish this answer from the same answer from a relativist or a scientific-liberal outlook about religions. The relativist position is:
1. The truth of a religion and the rightness of its various practices are an internal matter of the religion.
2. The religion cannot therefore be judged in terms of criteria which are external to it.
3. No religion, therefore, can judge another to be either inferior or superior.

The only civilized attitude therefore is one of respectful indifference.

Whether or not this conclusion follows from relativist premises is, of course, debatable. In any case, it is clear that, for Gandhi, equal respect for all religions could not have been derived from relativist premises. Of course, Gandhi would readily agree that there are many aspects of a religion which are such that questions of propriety or impropriety, rightness or wrongness in respect of them are internal to the religion, for example the use of music in certain rituals in Hinduism or Christianity and its prohibition in Islam. Such aspects of a religion, Gandhi would say, belong to the periphery rather than to the moral-spiritual core, which, unsurprisingly for Gandhi, is the same for all religions.

Nor, of course, is equal respect to be derived from a scientific liberal 'sympathy' for all religions. Such a derivation may consist in taking the following steps:

1. Truth claims made by all religions are scientifically untenable.
2. All religions are profound expressions of human creativity and help man cope with psychological and social predicaments of life; thus they all have both aesthetic and utilitarian value.
3. All religions therefore deserve our respect.

From deserving respect to deserving equal respect will, of course, be another and not so easy step. In any event, it is obvious that, for Gandhi, equal respect could not be based on considerations of this kind: to denude religion of truth (or Truth) is to take the life out of it.

As opposed to the relativist and scientific-liberal attitude, Gandhi's argument begins with the assertion that the truth of all religions is the same, although there may be diverse paths to this truth:

If a man reaches the heart of his own religion, he has reached the heart of others too. (*Hind Swaraj*, Ahmedabad, Navajiban Press, 1913, p. 25)

Religions are different roads converging to the same point. (*Young India*, 14 September 1926)

What does it matter that we take different roads so long as we reach the same goal? In reality, there are as many religions as there are individuals. (*Hind Swaraj*, Ahmedabad, Navajiban Press, 1913, p. 23)

Gandhi's assertion is not based on a scholarly, theological understanding of the scriptures of different religions, although scriptures of religions other than his own had a profound effect on him. It therefore bypasses the entire theological debate which arose in the West in the nineteenth century and continues today: the debate inspired by the discovery that there were religions other than Christianity (and perhaps Judaism and Islam) which had a basis in spirituality seemingly quite profound.[6] Gandhi's claim is based quite unashamedly on his

---

6. The debate pursued in recent times, in works such as Karl Barth, *Church Dogmatics*, Vol. I, Parts 1 and 2, Edinburgh, T. and T. Clark, 1956; Ernst Troeltsch, *The Absoluteness of Christianity and the History of Religions,* Oxford, SCM Press, 1972; Arnold Toynbee, *Christianity among the Religions of the World*, Oxford, Oxford University Press,

conviction that spirituality and morality are inseparable, that to have achieved spirituality is to be established in a form of life whose motivating force is love (*ahimsa*) and justice, that spirituality is what breathes life into our religion and, therefore, that every living religion must have a spiritual-moral core:

> I cannot conceive politics as divorced from religion. Indeed religion should pervade every one of our actions. Here, religion does not mean sectarianism. It means a belief in ordered moral government of the universe. It is not less, because it is unseen. This religion transcends Hinduism, Islam, Christianity, etc. It does not supersede them. It harmonizes them and gives them reality. (*Harijan*, 10 February 1940)

But all religions also have what may be called temporal aspects, aspects such as doctrines and dogmas (what Gandhi called 'creed'), rituals, modes of worship, use of symbols, aesthetic articulation, social organization and so on. Such aspects may differ widely from religion to religion and may sometimes even be at variance with the moral-spiritual core of a religion. Gandhi's view was that, while such aspects of a religion are most intimately – even inalienably – connected with it, they are none the less historically conditioned and are subject to change, reinterpretation, loss of meaning. Frequently, they stand in need of renewal and even abandonment. A look at the history of major religions will show that Gandhi was most probably right about this.

Gandhi's view about such aspects of a religion can be summed up as follows: since they are the means whereby a particular religion finds its specific articulation, and since frequently a man's sense of identity – sense of oneness and integrity – is profoundly linked with the particular religion to which he belongs, there could be a deep emotional bond between him and these aspects of his religion. As Gandhi says about his being a Hindu:

1957; Friedrich Schleirmacher, *On Religion: Speeches to Its Cultured Despisers*, New York, Harper, 1958; R. Otto, *The Idea of the Holy*, Oxford, Oxford University Press, 1958; Paul Tillich, *The Shaking of the Foundations*, London, Penguin, 1962, and *Dynamics of Faith*, New York, Harper, 1957; W. C. Smith, *The Meaning and End of Religion*, New York, Mentor, 1964. One of the initial impulses of this debate might have been the works of Swami Vivekananda, such as *Addresses on Vedanta Philosophy*, Vol. II, London, Simkin Marshall, 1896; *Bhakti Yoga*, London, Kent & Co., 1896; *Religion of Love*, Belur, Ramakrishna, 1927.

I can no more describe my feelings for Hinduism than for my wife. She moves me as no other woman in the world can. Not that she has no faults. I dare say she has many more than I see myself. But the feeling of indissoluble bond is there. Even so I feel about Hinduism with all its faults and limitations. Nothing elates me so much as the music of the Gita or the Ramayana of Tulsidas, the only two books of Hinduism I may be said to know. I know the vice that is going on today in all the great Hindu shrines. But I love them in spite of their unspeakable failings. (*Young India*, 29 January 1932)

It is clear from the passage that Gandhi would say about such an aspect of a religion that it may be inadequate in one way or another, may degenerate, may be criticized, reformed, revised and renewed. In Gandhi's words:

All faiths constitute a revelation of truth, but all are imperfect and liable to error. Reverence for other faiths need not blind us to their faults. We must be keenly alive to the defects of our own faiths also, yet not leave it on that account, but try to overcome those defects. (*Yervada Mandir*, p. 55)

One of Gandhi's great missions in life was to reform and renew many Hindu practices which are either intrinsically unacceptable or have become degenerate.

Gandhi also believed that the authenticity and effectiveness of criticism of such aspects of religion can be best ensured if it comes from within a religion and springs from a love of the religion.

If all religions are capable of leading to the Truth, the aim of such criticism cannot be to persuade the follower of the religion in question to abandon his religion and embrace another, but to enable him to find the way through his own religion. Gandhi believed that there is an element of *hinsa* (ill-will) in the wish that another person should give up his traditional faith and embrace another.

God has created different faiths just as he has votaries thereof. How can I, even secretly, harbour the thought that my neighbour's faith is inferior to mine and wish that he should give up his faith and embrace mine? As a true and loyal friend, I can only wish and pray that he may live and grow perfect in his own faith. In God's house, there are many mansions and they are equally holy. (*Harijan*, 20 April 1934)

About the numerous tribal faiths in India, Gandhi said: 'I would like to be able to join them in their prayers.' Putting all these thoughts together, the conclusion which we must reach, according to Gandhi, is that the ideal relationship between religions of the world is an 'international fellowship' of all religions. Such a fellowship is a community of fellows, that is of equals who are bound together in a sprit of *ahimsa* and inspired by the desire genuinely to understand one another: it does not admit of criticism of the other in order to undermine him: 'Our prayer for the other must be not "Give him the light that Thou hast given me", but "give him all the light and truth he needs for his highest development"' (*Sabarmati*, 1928). To be established in such a fellowship is once again to authenticate the life of the spirit, a life permeated by self-knowledge, love and justice.

To sum up: in this paper, I have tried to do the following:

1. Show that modern epistemology is unable to provide a basis for a belief in the reality of values; that attempts at finding such a basis within the framework of modern epistemology do not succeed.
2. Indicate that in Gandhi we have an alternative epistemology – an epistemology which can be termed the epistemology of *ahimsa* or love – one that accounts for the possibility of self-knowledge which is also, at the same time, knowledge of moral truths.
3. Show that, given the Gandhian epistemic scheme, the ideal relationship between different religions of the world is one of international fellowship.

In the end, it is important to remind oneself that Gandhi was not a scholarly philosopher – he did not articulate his philosophical insights in a systematic, rational manner. However, as this paper may have modestly shown, such a reconstruction is possible and it might yield surprisingly interesting results.

An Agenda for Peace and a culture of peace

*Nazli Moawad**

INTRODUCTION

On 26 June 1945, the Preamble to the Charter of the United Nations asserted: 'We the peoples of the United Nations determined to . . . practice tolerance and live together in peace with one another as good neighbours and to unite our strength to maintain international peace and security.'

The world has and still is undergoing local, regional and international conflicts where people die and children are deprived of their families and where resources are allocated for defence purposes and/or warfare.

Instead of peace, wars and conflicts have become widespread and develop, both in kind and in degree of fatality. People are too familiar with news and reports on racial conflicts, terrorism, ideological persecution and warfare and the proliferation of nuclear weapons to the point of risking a nuclear war and the mass destruction of mankind.[1]

For most of this century, we have been living through a culture of war. The transition from a culture of war to a culture of peace calls for a new approach to conflict. Building a culture of peace involves changing attitudes, beliefs and behaviours – from everyday life situations to high-level negotiations between

---

*   Professor of International Relations, Faculty of Economics and Political Science, Cairo University; Director, Centre for Political Research and Studies, Cairo University, Egypt.
1. Phra Debvedi, *Freedom: Individual and Social,* p. 2, Bangkok, Prayudh Payutto, 1990.

countries – so that our natural response to conflict would be non-violent and our instinctive reactions would be toward negotiations and reason, not aggression.[2]

Following the end of the Cold War, the United Nations began to realize the potential for which it was created, that is, 'to save succeeding generations from the scourge of war'.

In addition to providing a conceptual framework for reflecting on international peace and security in the post-Cold War world, *An Agenda for Peace*[3] has given rise to many concrete reforms within the United Nation system. It has provided the foundation for a systematic process of reform in the Organization, irrespective of the difficulties encountered in some peace-making and peace-enforcement operations which are, fairly or not, associated with the recommendations of the *Agenda*.[4]

PARADIGM SHIFT IN PEACE STUDIES

There has been a clear shift in approaching peace in contemporary literature and practice. The traditional approaches to peace assume that peace must be actively preserved; peace is not viewed as a natural state. The varied traditional methods for the preservation of peace all imply the moral and political acceptability of war, for each requires preparation for it. The dominant strategy is then: do not plan to wage deliberate war, but rather be in readiness of war, so as to dissuade bellicose antagonists.[5]

The new approach to peace assumes that war is humanity's most pressing problem, that peace is preferable to war, and that peace can and must include not only the absence of war but also the establishment of positive life-affirming,

---

2. *The First Consultative Meeting of the Culture of Peace Programme, UNESCO, Paris, 27–29 September 1994*, p. 2.
3. Boutros Boutros Ghali, *An Agenda for Peace*, New York, United Nations, 1992.
4. Boutros Boutros Ghali, *Building Peace and Development 1994: Annual Report on the Work of the Organization*, p. 147, New York, United Nations, 1994.
5. Edward N. Luttwak, 'The Traditional Approaches to Peace', in W. Scott Thompson et al. (eds.), *Approaches to Peace: An Intellectual Map*, p. 3, Washington, D.C., USIP, 1991.

life-enhancing values and structures.⁶ The strategy is then: agreements terminate conflicts; relationships implement agreements.⁷

The paradigm shift from negative to positive peace is currently occurring in peace education: from a technological *Weltanschauung* that reduces things to their smallest component parts in order to understand them, to a systematic ecological world-view whose primary mode of thinking is whole-brain thought.⁸

Another significant feature of this shift is the transformation from 'either/or' problem-solving into 'both/and' decision-making strategies⁹ or, put another way, from the traditional competitive process of conflict resolution to the developing process of conflict partnership.¹⁰

This changing world-view acknowledges the importance of science and technologies, but holds that they must be understood and applied within the context of a global, ecological perspective.

DEVELOPMENT OF PEACE STUDIES

Peace studies are developed in response to human problems of violence and unrest. The disaster of the First World War gave impetus to the emergence of a scientific discipline of international relations. Peace studies emerged in response to critical social problems in the immediate post-Second World War era, and surged in the wake of the Viet Nam War, when there was a need to present new perspectives on the global problematic. As such, peace studies complement international relations.¹¹ However, there are important distinctions between peace

---

6. David P. Barosh, *Introduction to Peace Studies*, pp. 5–7, Baltimore, Md., Wadsworth Publishing Company, 1991.
7. James H. Lane, 'Contributions of the Emerging Field of Conflict Resolution', in W. Scott Thompson et al., op. cit., p. 302.
8. Edward T. Clark, 'The Search for a New Educational Paradigm', *Holistic Education Review*, Vol. 1, No. 1, 1988, p. 19.
9. Ibid.
10. Abdul Aziz Said, 'Global Thinking: A Call for Reinvestment in Sacred Values', *The Acorn*, March 1987.
11. Abdul Aziz Said, 'Developing Peace and Conflict Resolution Programs', p. 1. (Paper presented to the Association of Professional Schools of International Affairs, 15 October 1992.)

studies and the more traditional security studies approach to international relations. Peace studies build upon and move beyond the traditional concept of national security studies.

For peace studies, hunger, poverty and exploitation are as much breeding grounds for violence as the need for defence against military threats to national security. Peace studies generally focus on the security of the whole international or global system.

Scholars identify three waves in the ongoing development of peace studies.[12] The first began in the aftermath of the Second World War during the 1950s and the early 1960s. It was initiated primarily at research institutions and a few graduate schools, and stressed increased international understanding. The second wave, which began in the early 1970s after the Viet Nam War and the Civil Rights Movement in the USA, focused on 'global oneness', the nuclear threat and developing undergraduate programmes in peace studies. The third wave began in the 1980s and focused on structural violence and positive peace.

The subsequent period witnessed a massive increase in both undergraduate and graduate programmes in peace studies. There has also been massive private and state funding for peace research and education. Governments have sponsored or helped support several institutions and educational initiatives. A number of professional journals have emerged which support research in peace studies.

The 1980s also witnessed several changes in the development of peace studies. Whereas previous development was led from within the field, the increase in peace studies programmes during the 1980s was supported by public concern over the nuclear arms race and superpower relations. There was also a new inquiry into alternative international security systems, conditions of peace and non-violent action.

Scholars identify seven major areas of research in this era relevant to peace studies: peace movements; cognition, war and peace; alternative security; militarism and development; language and media; feminism and militarism; and conflict resolution.

The peace studies programmes in existence today differ greatly in their scope

---

12. Said, 'Developing Peace and Conflict Resolution Programs', op. cit., pp. 3–4.

and focus. Because of their interdisciplinary nature, the academic foci of peace studies programmes vary tremendously, depending upon the interests and specialities of faculty participating in these programmes. Scholars from fields as diverse as law, sociology, religion, biology, political science and meteorology are currently teaching courses under the heading of peace studies. As a result, hundreds of curricula have been developed for peace studies programmes.[13]

FOUR DILEMMAS OF A CULTURE OF PEACE

Growing cross-cultural contact

Predictions about future day-to-day living in various parts of the world include greater amounts of face-to-face contact among people from very different cultural backgrounds. The contemporary world is characterized by a growing area of cross-cultural contact. The reason for increased face-to-face contact yields a now familiar litany. There are various reasons for this. Technological factors include increased travel both between and within nations and greater exposure to various cultural groups through the mass media. Social factors include development in civil rights and affirmative action leading to more frequent contact among groups in education, work, public housing, social services and health care. Economic factors include dependence on other countries for precious commodities. Political factors include the growing awareness that, since the world is so complex and demands so much interdependence, hegemony is no longer a realistic alternative.

A combination of these factors is present in intergovernmental organizations as well as in multinational corporations. In this context, some basic issues need to be investigated in order to deal better with the chances offered and challenges imposed by increasing cross-cultural contact. For instance, what happens to people when they engage in various forms of cross-cultural contact? Can a common language of solid, useful concepts be suggested which will facilitate communication among people? Can the advantages of cross-cultural interaction be better specified? By studying the stresses and strains of cross-cultural contact

---

13. Ibid., p. 6.

and by analysing how people overcome their problems, a greater understanding of aggressive and non-aggressive reactions to stress may occur.[14]

Poor understanding of diversity

Our world is infinitely diverse, not only in climate, geography and nature, but in human cultures as well.[15] The history of human civilization is darkened by endless wars, conflict, confrontations and enmity of one country or people for another. Prejudice against those who are considered strange or simply different is an extremely widespread phenomenon. There is nothing simpler than to arouse mass enmity and hatred toward the real or imagined enemy, though, even in quieter times, mistrust and rejection of anything 'foreign' are typical phenomena.[16]

However, conflict inherent in human nature can be positive, as a source of creativity and change. Yet it becomes destructive when it is allowed to degenerate into violence. The truth is, however, that conflict is neither positive nor negative; it is an outgrowth of the diversity which characterizes our thoughts, systems and structures. It is as much a part of our existence as is evolution. Each of us has influence and power over whether or not conflict becomes negative, and that influence and power form the way we deal with it.

Many conflicts can serve as opportunities for mutual growth if we develop and utilize positive, constructive conflict-resolution skills. Indeed, conflict can serve as one of the engines of personal developments and social evolution, generating opportunities to learn from and adapt to the diversities and differences which are natural and healthy characteristics of our society.

Conflict can bring out into the open alternative ways of thinking and behaving. It can challenge us to manage our lives in ways which utilize our differences for mutual growth and benefit.

---

14. Richard W. Brislin, *Cross-cultural Encounters: Face-to-face Interaction*, pp. 1–3, New York, Pergamon Press, 1981.
15. Vladimir S. Ageev, 'Similarity or Diversity?', in Vladimir S. Ageev et al. (eds.), *Breakthrough, Emerging New Thinking*, p. 250, New York, Walker & Company, 1988.
16. Ibid.

Need to transform thinking on conflict

One of the first steps of becoming more effective at resolving conflicts is to understand the positive potential inherent in all situations of discord. We need to transform how we think about conflicts. First, the basic perception that needs a change is that conflict is always a disruption of order, a negative experience, an error or mistake in a relationship. However, we need to understand that conflict is actually an outgrowth of diversity which can be utilized to clarify a relationship, to provide additional ways of thinking and options for action not previously considered, and to open up possibilities for improving a relationship.

Second, another basic misperception of conflict is that it usually involves a struggle between absolutes, such as right and wrong, and good and evil. Some conflicts do indeed concern differences over deeply felt values but far too often people allow themselves to attach 'good v. evil' and 'right v. wrong' labels to a conflict to convince themselves that their position is beyond question. People may also go further and consider their conflict partners as non-believers. Every group may also claim that 'God is on our side'.

Rather than jumping to the conclusion that a conflict involves absolute differences, we need to explore the possibility that a particular conflict may be over subjective preferences rather than values, and realize that there are other aspects of the relationship on which we can build positively.

Third, a common perception in need of transformation is that conflict is always a battle between competing and incompatible self-interests or desires. Thinking of conflict in this way leads us to feel that the other party is trying to prevent our getting what we want; we often try to prevent their getting what they want. Both parties become more and more stubborn as they pursue their own desires and ignore the presence of needs or goals they might actually share.

Fourth, the misperception of conflict is also common. Many people view a particular conflict as defining their entire relationship with others. People may allow one conflict to become so dominant that the overall long-term relationship is ignored. A far more effective perception of conflict is that it is but one part of a complex and useful relationship. We need to look at and benefit from the potentially positive aspects of conflicts.

The aim of a culture of peace is, therefore, not to eliminate conflicts but to find ways to deal with them non-violently. It is not correct, then, to try to end a conflict either through zero-sum management or by a call to forget or ignore the reasons for it. Rather it is much wiser to call for reconciliation through which sources of conflicts could be healed and their consequences coped with. What is needed is 'amnesty not amnesia'.[17]

Missing bioethics for peace

The human body can be harmed through the abuse of medical technology as well as in violent actions of war. One should not underestimate the negative side-effects of science on the human body, caused both deliberately by greedy multinational merchants of organ transplantation and immoral treatment of the human body.

Through scientific discoveries, man has access to knowledge about his own vital mechanisms, and has gained power to transform the development process of the living species. Unfortunately, the development of the inner core of man, the mind, has not kept pace with the rapid progress of technology.[18] Man has used and is using much of this power for destructive purposes, including his own life.

'Bioethics' is an emerging term which refers to a new understanding of the relationship between man and science. It implies new thinking on change in society, or even global equilibria, and fuels a broad public debate on the choices for the future induced by scientific developments and on ways of guaranteeing the informed participation of citizens.

Bioethics then derives from a dual need: first, to ensure that the progress resulting from this new power benefits every man and woman, and mankind as a whole, without infringement of any kind; second, to identify, rationally and responsibly, the social and cultural implications of breakthroughs in the biological sciences which concern health, agriculture and food as well as development and the environment.

---

17. *The First Consultative Meeting of the Culture of Peace Programme*, op. cit., p. 7.
18. Debvedi, op. cit., p. 18.

APPROACH TO COPE WITH THE DILEMMAS OF A CULTURE OF PEACE

The suggested approach to world peace is built upon the following set of elements:

Placing emphasis on peace education

Since the early 1960s, when T. Kuhn wrote his book *The Structure of Scientific Revolution*, much has been written on the paradigm shift which is occurring in various fields of knowledge and ways of thinking about nature, peace and society. A paradigm shift occurs as the result of a shift in the underlying assumptions upon which science is based.

This also affects research and the results of research. When evidence begins to challenge commonly accepted assumptions, anomalies appear and create conflicts which can be resolved only by acknowledging a new set of assumptions. As these new assumptions gradually gain acceptance, a dramatic shift occurs both in the nature of scientific inquiry and in our understanding of the role of science in society.[19]

This new direction of conceiving 'where to start in order to enhance world peace' is manifested in the concerns of the international community to initiate, develop and support a relevant culture of peace today. For instance, education for peace, human rights and democracy received much attention at the World Conference on Human Rights, held in Vienna in June 1993. Such a new direction had already been given by the International Congress on Education for Human Rights and Democracy, organized by UNESCO in Montreal, Canada, in March 1993, which was in fact a preparatory meeting to the aforementioned World Conference. Both these meetings were a step forward on the same road. The Montreal congress emphasized the relationship between human rights and democracy and their relation to development, cultural diversity and tolerance. It reaffirmed that education for human rights and democracy is itself a human right and is a prerequisite for the full realization of social justice, peace and sustainable development.[20] The Vienna Declaration and

---

19. Clark, op. cit., pp. 18–19.
20. *Human Rights Teaching*, Vol. VIII, p. 9, Paris, UNESCO, 1993.

Programme of Action adopted by the World Conference recognized the relationship between peace and human rights education. It stipulated that human rights education, training and public information are essential for the promotion and achievement of stable and harmonious relations among communities and for fostering mutual understanding, tolerance and peace. The World Conference called upon all states and institutions to include human rights, humanitarian law, democracy and rule of law as subjects in the curricula of all learning institutions in formal and non-formal settings. Human rights education should include peace, democracy, development and social justice, as set forth in international and regional human rights instruments, in order to achieve common understanding and awareness with a view to strengthening universal commitment to human rights.[21]

The World Conference also reaffirmed that states are duty-bound, as stipulated in the Universal Declaration of Human Rights and the International Covenant on Economic, Social and Cultural Rights, to ensure that education is aimed at strengthening respect for human rights and fundamental freedoms.

Reaffirming the respect for diversity within unity

Global thinking about peace now assumes that every culture has its particular values, religious practices, moral codes of behaviour, customs, laws, and so forth. Yet among different cultures there are common traits and complexes; for example, the need for effective organizations (social, political and economic) to promote growth, restrict excessive competition and minimize physical violence.

Viewed from this standpoint, world security depends on harnessing the co-operative practices of different cultures and modifying their competitive drives in ways which curb their divisive tendencies, in order to achieve harmony without destroying cultural diversity.[22] To do this, we need to enhance the awareness that we, despite continuing our citizenship in particular nations, are world citizens. We are bound by our economy, technology, yearning to learn and

---

21. UN Document A/CONF.157/24, Part I.
22. Walter Isard, *Understanding Conflict and the Science of Peace*, pp. 14–15, Cambridge, Blackwell Publishers, 1992.

to communicate, into a global framework which demands of us an expanded citizenship.[23]

Enhancing new trends in conflict resolution

The discipline of peace-making and conflict resolution has undergone three phases: the reform phase, the reconstructive phase and the transformative phase, currently evolving. First, the goal of the reform approach is to prevent war through the control of the arms race. Its central thesis is that, if peoples and nations behaved differently and gave more consideration to non-violent alternatives, war could be prevented.

Second, the reconstructive approach reaches beyond these behavioural objectives, seeking to reconstruct international systems, to abolish war and to achieve total disarmament. The transformational approach seeks a larger, more comprehensive goal, that is, the rejection of all violence, not just the arms race and war. Its strategy is to make violence unacceptable, not only in interactions among individuals but also interactions among nations. The changes sought are behavioural, institutional and primarily cultural, such as in thinking and in the formation of values.[24]

Third, while the first approach is known as seeking negative peace and the second seeks positive peace, the third acknowledges comprehensive peace. Only this can hold a promise for the future of peace, since it mediates and interprets the development of peace research, peace study and learning, and peace action. From this standpoint, scholars of comprehensive peace identify the shift in the literature on peace as follows:
- From the emphasis on issues of conflicts to the emphasis on identifying and effecting change in the attitudes of the conflicting parties.
- From attention to states to the acknowledgement of the rights of individuals.
- From highlighting demands formulated by one party against the other to

---

23. T. M. Thomas, 'Introduction: From a Warring World to a Peaceful Global Order', in T. M. Thomas et al. (eds.), *Global Images of Peace and Education*, p. 8, Ann Arbor, Mich., Prakken Publications, 1987.
24. Betty A. Reardon, *Comprehensive Peace Education: Education for Global Responsibility*, New York/London, Teachers College Press of Columbia University, 1988.

the emphasis on discovering and meeting the needs of the parties involved.
- From the traditional process of conflict resolution which was primarily competitive, using an adversarial strategy, to the emphasis on developing co-operative processes, searching for common grounds.[25]

Developing bioethics

Bioethics, in general, emphasizes the need to respect private life, family life, community life, and economic and social life. Only through collective actions can we maintain the harmony between man and science.

Today, the bioethics movement transcends borders, since the concerns it expresses inevitably take on an international dimension. UNESCO took an important initiative and set up the International Bioethics Committee in 1993.[26] The major concerns of the bioethics movement include:

- Enhancing a worldwide respect for the human body. Steps must be taken to fight against the trade in organs and tissue, disguised as organ transplant surgery. Legislators should firmly place organ trade under penal law.
- Protection of persons in biochemical research. Ensuring that the scientific criteria for clinical testing have been met and that ethical precautions have been taken depends on two conditions: the ability to encourage and master research, and the existence of a multidisciplinary ethics committee whose authority is recognized.
- Linking human genetics to human rights. Genetic research has advanced and has raised issues concerning human rights. Biomedical applications are growing rapidly and genetic diagnosis updates the idea about medical prevention through which one can know one's genetic predisposition and adopt behavioural patterns which could prevent the onslaught of illness.[27] But, at the same time, the legitimacy of this genetic screening is very highly debatable.

---

25. Said, 1987, op. cit.
26. UNESCO, 'Bioethics and Its Implications World-wide for Human Rights Protection'. (Background document presented to the Interparliamentary Conference, Madrid, 27 March–1 April 1995.)
27. Ibid., pp. 7–8.

Recognizing the right to humanitarian assistance

People live in various countries but belong to the same family. They have the right to solidarity. The Universal Declaration of Human Rights stipulates that 'human beings . . . should act towards one another in a spirit of brotherhood'. Humanitarian solidarity means mutual assistance of peoples, moral support and active expression of sympathy with others.[28]

The right to humanitarian assistance may be invoked in peacetime, when natural disasters occur. More significantly, it may also be claimed in the course of armed conflicts. The term has crystallized in positive international law.[29] One can theoretically distinguish between the right to demand or obtain humanitarian assistance and the right to insist on providing such assistance; both aspects of rendering and receiving humanitarian assistance are inseparable.

One peace scholar cited legal instruments which oblige states to provide humanitarian assistance to victims in their territory or under their control, for example the Geneva Convention III, Article 26 et seq.[30] As a general rule, it appears that, at the present time, there is only a right to offer such assistance, its exercise being contingent on consent by the state concerned.[31]

The UN Security Council can determine when a threat to peace occurs. It is empowered to launch or approve a veritable humanitarian intervention (for example, Operation Regaining Hope in Somalia*)*. This is a substantial change in the concept of humanitarian assistance.

Although the concept of the right to humanitarian assistance dates back at least to the nineteenth century, the United Nations and its Specialized Agencies

---

28. Y. Kolosov, 'Implementation of the Right to Humanitarian Assistance at the National, Regional and International Levels', p. 1. (Paper presented to the International Colloquium on the Right to Humanitarian Assistance, UNESCO, Paris, 25–27 January 1995.)
29. Y. Dinstein, 'The Legal Consequences of Infringing upon the Right to Humanitarian Assistance', p. 1. (Paper presented to the International Colloquium on the Right to Humanitarian Assistance, UNESCO, Paris, 25–27 January 1995.)
30. D. Schindler, 'The Right to Humanitarian Assistance: Right and/or Obligation?' (Paper presented to the International Colloquium on the Right to Humanitarian Assistance, UNESCO, Paris, 25–27 January 1995.)
31. Dinstein, op. cit., p. 1.

have contributed to the redefinition of the concept. The term essentially involved the provision by an external source of health care, food and material goods to the victims of international or internal conflicts. Now the term has undergone change, making it necessary to improve the means of implementation of humanitarian assistance programmes in order to obtain access to victims, protect relief personnel and co-ordinate relief efforts.[32] However, this change in the concept of humanitarian assistance needs to be effectively legitimized, bearing in mind the dramatic situation which relief personnel and UN peace-keeping forces have faced in many areas of conflict, such as in Somalia and Bosnia.

Relief operations must be humanitarian, impartial and non-discriminatory. The right to assistance should not lead to political interference. It is both a legal and a political error that there has been an unfortunate confusion of humanitarian and political considerations; it is even more destructive to confuse humanitarian assistance with military intervention.[33]

AN AGENDA FOR PEACE AND ITS IMPLEMENTATION

In *An Agenda for Peace*, the UN Secretary-General, Boutros Boutros Ghali outlines the challenges faced by the United Nations in the areas of preventive diplomacy, which seeks to resolve disputes before violence breaks out; peace-making and peace-keeping, which are required to halt conflicts and preserve peace once it is attained; and post-conflict peace-building to strengthen and consolidate peace in order to avoid a relapse into conflict.

The UN Secretary-General recognizes that 'the sources of conflict and war are pervasive and deep. To reach them will require our utmost efforts to enhance respect for human rights and fundamental freedoms, to promote sustainable economic and social development for wider prosperity, to alleviate distress and to curtail the existence and use of massively destructive weapons'.

An Agenda for Peace contains eighty-six paragraphs and deals with the world's

---

32. Adama Dieng, 'United Nations Action and the Right to Humanitarian Assistance', p. 1. (Paper presented to the International Colloquium on the Right to Humanitarian Assistance, UNESCO, Paris, 25–27 January 1995.)
33. Ibid., pp. 3–5.

changing context as well as with the set of new definitions manifested in the United Nations political discourse. The Agenda's *Weltanschauung* is based on four main concepts regarding the United Nations role in achieving world security, peace and development:

- First, preventive diplomacy is action to prevent disputes from arising between parties, to prevent disputes from escalating into conflicts and to limit the spread of the latter when they occur.
- Second, peace-making is action to bring hostile parties to agreement, essentially through peaceful means.
- Third, peace-keeping is the deployment of a United Nations presence in the field, hitherto with the consent of all the parties concerned, normally involving United Nations military and/or police personnel and frequently civilians as well. It is a process which expands the possibilities for both the prevention of conflict and the making of peace.
- Fourth, peace-building is action to identify and support structures which will tend to strengthen and consolidate peace in order to avoid a relapse into conflict.

These concepts should together establish a solid framework for an alternative world order and international relations: for preventive diplomacy seeks to resolve disputes before violence breaks out; peace-making and peace-keeping are required to halt conflicts and preserve peace once it is attained; if successful, they strengthen the opportunity for post-conflict peace-building, which can prevent the recurrence of violence among nations and peoples.

UNESCO'S CULTURE OF PEACE PROGRAMME

UNESCO has made many important contributions towards building the foundations of peace through education, science, culture and communication. The Culture of Peace Programme was established in February 1994 with three basic responsibilities:

- Co-ordination of the many activities of UNESCO which contribute to a culture of peace.
- Establishment of national culture of peace programmes, especially in countries where conflicts are heightened and/or potential.

- Development of a network and info-systems to link other organizations involved in similar efforts.

At the first consultative meeting of this programme, a work strategy was outlined for an intensive and comprehensive effort to enhance a culture of peace. This strategy is based on a philosophy of *glasnost* in understanding a culture of peace and assessing the roots of conflict. It also adopts a multilinear work plan for building up a peaceful culture in the contemporary world. The following conceptions and ground rules are revealed in the new approach to a culture of peace:[34]

- Peace means more than the absence of war and conflict; it is a dynamic concept and process. Maintaining peace is related to the degree of social justice and harmony and the possibility for human beings to realize their full potential and their right to dignified life.
- Economic, social and human development is closely tied to the process of building a culture of peace. Without peace, development cannot be sustained; and without endogenous, sustainable human development, peace cannot be sustained. It is necessary therefore to review the concept of development based only on economic growth. Development itself can be a source of conflict when the gap between the haves and the have-nots is widened and the cycle of rising expectations and increasing frustrations is set in motion.
- Peace-building and maintenance presupposes a solid social base on which civil society formations, especially at grassroots level, can flourish. These formations could serve as mediators between social groups and *vis-à-vis* the state, and help people participate effectively in development plans.
- Democracy is the other side of the coin of peace and development. Decentralization of decision-making and power-sharing are important. It should be made clear, however, that building a culture of peace is itself a process of strengthening democratic attitudes, behaviours and institutions. Hence elections, for example, are not enough to ensure the path to democracy; they are not a 'quick fix'. Without profound commitment and long-term planning, elections are powerless to effect real change. The dynamism of a culture of peace lies in human beings being able to realize

---

34. *The First Consultative Meeting of the Culture of Peace Programme,* op. cit., pp. 4–7.

their full potential, having the opportunity to participate meaningfully in shaping their society and feeling that they are in control of their destiny.
- The nature and ethics of war have changed. Local conflicts are becoming more severe and international conflicts more destructive. Advanced technologies are increasingly used irrationally and for violent purposes. People should immediately learn to 'wage peace; not war'.
- At the macro-economic level, we should encourage building a peaceful instead of a military industrial complex. Alternatives for the military-based economy should be developed, and the military should become more involved in civilian development.
- Conflicts need to be managed, before they are resolved and prevented. This calls for non-violent conflict management. This includes training in mediation and negotiation techniques.

Whether we like it or not, we all are negotiators. Negotiation is a fact of life. Everyone negotiates something everyday. Conflict is a growth industry. People differ, and they use negotiation to handle their differences. However, it is not easy to negotiate well. People would follow either a hard or a soft negotiation style.[35] Peace requires a third way of dealing with differences, that is, principled negotiation. One should insist that the result of a negotiation be based on fair standards independent of the will of either side.[36] Constructive conflict management employs no tricks and no posturing.

---

35. Roger Fisher and William Ury, *Getting to Yes*, pp. xvii–xviii, New York, Penguin Books, 1981.
36. Ibid.

The teaching of Martin Luther King for a culture of peace

Solomon M. Nkiwane*

> Non-violent resistance is not a method for cowards . . . Gandhi often said that if cowardice is the only alternative to violence, it is better to fight . . . While the non-violent resister is passive in the sense that he is not physically aggressive toward his opponent, his mind and emotions are always active, constantly seeking to persuade the opponent that he is wrong.
>
> Dr Martin Luther King,
> as quoted in *The Seville Statement on Violence,*
> 16 November 1989

INTRODUCTION

It does not matter where you turn today, the world seems to be in danger of being overrun by violence: all kinds of violence. The most visible examples are international conflicts and internal wars. There is nothing really new here, except that the levels of violence have increased many times. Other forms of violence manifest themselves in many forms of violation of human rights, whether against peoples, tribes, defenceless minorities, women, children or non-Whites. The

---

* Chairman, Department of Political and Administrative Studies, University of Zimbabwe, Harare.

inhumane behaviour of man to man clearly distinguishes the human race from other creatures. Such systematic and calculated violence, and the scale of its magnitude, is non-existent among God's other living creatures. During the Cold War period, the scale of violence threatened the ultimate annihilation of the human race from the face of the earth through nuclear weapons.

The sum total of all these forms of violence in terms of the world social and human organizational setting, if it is placed in a historical context, can be termed a culture of violence. The world, as we have known it from the remote past and as we have come to understand it today, seems to be one which tolerates, if not promotes, such a culture of violence.

At the same time, much of the history of humankind has also been characterized by the struggle to overcome or to eliminate violence in the world. At best, however, the highest and noblest of human achievements in this area have only been partial, temporary measures, stopping violence for the time being. The elimination of the symptoms or the manifestations of violence, and not of its root causes, is all that peaceful efforts have been able to succeed in doing up till now. Thus the quest for a culture of peace in the world is the most challenging task which has faced the human race, and will continue to face the world today and in the future. The now legendary physics teaser in which the immovable object is pitted against the irresistible force happens here to be a realistic representation of the stakes involved in the contest between a culture of violence and a culture of peace.

In this paper an attempt is made to assess the contribution made by one individual, Martin Luther King, to the continuing efforts to establish a culture of peace in the world. Martin Luther King was not the first, and will not be the last, to struggle and to sacrifice his life for the establishment of a peaceful world. However, his accomplishments in a relatively short lifetime have resulted in a large following, necessitating a much closer look at his peace message.

AMERICAN SOCIETY AND A CULTURE OF VIOLENCE

The American society in which Martin Luther was born and grew up can be said to have represented, or thrived on, a culture of violence. At least, that is the view which emerges from the experiences of Martin Luther King and others like

The teaching of Martin Luther King for a culture of peace

him. To them, the American society of the post-Second World War period was anything but peaceful. It was this culture of violence that Martin Luther King struggled against and for which he sacrificed his life. He strove for its replacement by a culture of peace.

Violence to which a fairly large proportion of American society, especially the poor and the Blacks, have been (and continue to be) subjected, has much to do with the existence and stubborn maintenance of certain cultural traits, attitudes, beliefs and values by the larger, mainstream American society. It was not only his clear awareness of this and the evil of American society, but his vision of the possibility of a better alternative in the future, which makes Martin Luther King stand out among the great teachers of the twentieth century. The breadth and depth of his teachings go beyond American society. His is a message of hope which should encompass the entire world community. Ultimately, the American society of Martin Luther King's time is a microcosm of a portion of the world community, with a similar cultural background or inclination. Thus, eliminating violence in American society alone would not be enough, although it would have a major impact all over the world. To that extent, concentrating on American society for his teaching was as much as one human being could hope to do in a lifetime.

When one talks of American society being violent, one is generally referring to certain historical and concurrent social phenomena. One example is that the United States, especially the South, was a slave-owning society. Until the Emancipation Proclamation of 1863, American Blacks in the South of the United States were not a free people but were slaves to the white population. It is generally accepted that slavery is one of the most violent forms of human relationship. The reason is that not only are slaves treated cruelly, like animals, but their overall treatment is one that dehumanizes the individual. The violence against the individual slave is directed towards his physical, psychological and spiritual self.

Although officially slavery was abolished in the United States after the American Civil War in 1865, the culture of slavery – its values, beliefs and attitudes – have lingered on until today. Although slavery was outlawed in the United States, Whites, again especially in the South, continued to view Blacks as inferior beings, whom they treated as outcasts, and whom they lynched at will, thus dehumanizing them. In short, the humanity, dignity and life of Blacks were violated and trampled upon, despite the great platitudes expressed in the American Constitution. It was into this culture that Martin Luther King was born. It was in the South, in his home state of Georgia, that he first came face to face with racism and a culture of violence. But, despite the overwhelming odds against him, and all his fellow Blacks, he broke doggedly through the barriers, and worked his way up the ladder of educational success, showing intellectual excellence.

Martin Luther King's academic achievements were just the first steps in his fight to rid American society of the evil of racism. They demonstrated that, given the opportunity, all human beings, white and black, are capable of achievement. All people are equal, irrespective of race, colour or creed. What is crucial is not just legal equality but natural equality. A culture of violence related to slavery, racism and general anti-Black oppression is inhuman. Martin Luther King worked hard to educate and to preach against such a culture in the United States.

This culture of violence was not only confined to the South of the United States. It was pervasive throughout America – North and South – and manifested itself in many forms: inferior education for Blacks and other minorities; poor housing in the so-called 'ethnic neighbourhoods'; lack of economic and business opportunities for Blacks and other minorities in urban America; the lack of political and economic representation for Blacks and other minorities in those sectors which really mattered; and, most concretely, the rise in criminal activities in the so-called ghettos as the manifestation of social deprivation and dislocation in the whole social fabric of American society. To Martin Luther King, violence in the black community, often pitting Black against Black, was a symptom of the sick American society as a whole. It would be simplistic if Americans thought that violence in the black communities in the United States could only be understood as the black man's problem, and that it would always be restricted to that community. Ultimately, the solution to such violence will only come about after the root causes in the overall American political and social establishment have been tackled.

MARTIN LUTHER KING'S TEACHINGS FOR PEACE

Martin Luther King was born in Atlanta, Georgia, on 15 January 1929. Thirty-nine years later, on 4 April 1968, he was assassinated by a white, racist ex-convict named Earl Ray. In that short span of life, Martin Luther King not only earned personal acclamations and achievements, such as being awarded the Nobel Peace Prize, but, in his untimely death, he bequeathed to mankind a rich legacy of teaching which, by and large, called for the establishment of a culture of peace in the world.

Rather than reiterate the catalogue of his achievements, we will focus on those aspects which have a bearing on a culture of peace. However, in order to place Martin Luther King's thoughts in their proper context, it is necessary to examine the historical setting and the international political environment, then and now.

The world as we know it today yearns for peace – real peace, and not a caricature of peace. The problem of today is that many people talk about peace and say it is essential. In the majority of cases, peace to most people is a matter of convenience. At the end of the First World War, at the Versailles Peace Conference, a peace treaty was signed which suited only the winning powers. The defeated powers, especially Germany, did not consider that what was signed was a peace treaty at all: to Germany, it was a peace trap.[1]

The twentieth century has witnessed the two most destructive wars in history. The interim period between the world wars, and the post-Second World War period, when only limited inter-state wars occurred, cannot be described as genuine periods of peace.[2] These were only temporary lulls before another conflagration, periods of preparation for another war or, at best, a mere absence of war. The absence of violence or war is not the same thing as a condition of peace. Even the period which one historian, S. F. Northedge, has described as 'a hundred years of peace' in modern times, was 'peaceful' only in the sense that

---

1. Many students of international history have interpreted the Versailles Peace Treaty at the end of the First World War as having sown the seeds of the Second World War, in the sense that it was an imposed 'peace', and the terms of the treaty were both unfair and humiliating to the defeated powers.
2. 1919–1939, and 1945 to the present.

the major European powers avoided conflicts among each other.[3] The smaller nations, or the 'weaker' people who were at that time involved in numerous conflicts, were not considered to pose a real threat to peace.[4] In fact, some of these localized wars were often instigated by the great powers themselves.

The Cold War period could probably be classified as a period of peace merely because a Third World War was averted. Many conflict situations erupted continuously during the Cold War era, and the so-called 'bush wars' or 'proxy wars' were accepted as normal occurrences following the Second World War. Somehow, as long as one's nation was not involved in a conflict situation, it was thought that there was peace in the world.

At the national or societal levels, again peace has tended to be defined in terms of the absence of outward violence. Such a peace could, for instance, come about as a result of imposition by a dictator, a military regime, a majority over a minority, or even a minority over a majority.[5] Just because a people are in a state of acquiescence, it does not follow that conditions for a culture of peace exist. Just because a people are being bullied, intimidated, manipulated or brainwashed into submission, it does not necessarily follow that conditions for peace exist. Peace does not just happen. In fact, peace does not come about just because some person – even a good person for that matter – says 'let there be peace'. If that were the case, the world would not have known wars after the life of Jesus Christ.

On the contrary, peace in the world, or in any society, is a condition of social behaviour and forbearance, which results from a conscious and unconscious acceptance of other people's humanity. This acceptance is necessarily based on a system of values and beliefs out of which civilized norms and attitudes of tolerance, respect and love for other human beings emerge. For one to attain this level of personal behaviour and social harmony, an opportunity to be nurtured

---

3. This refers to the 1815–1914 period, sometimes termed as the 'Balance of Power International System'.
4. That is, the peace between the great military powers of the world.
5. Here we can refer to the situations of apartheid in South Africa, in Zimbabwe before independence in 1980, and those which prevailed in Rwanda and Burundi before the outbreak of the present civil wars and massacres there.

in a culture of peace must necessarily exist. The educational system and the core values of such a society must reflect that.

The genius of Martin Luther King, as was the case with Mahatma Gandhi before him, was that he did attain that level of thinking and behaviour for promoting a culture of peace in the face of the culture of violence which surrounded him.

BREAKING THE TYRANNY OF VIOLENCE

A racist society resorts to all kinds of violence – physical, psychological, economic, social, political and even spiritual – to protect itself, and what it possesses, from the 'inferior' races. But when the smoke clears and the ashes of violence are gathered, what is left is a caricature of the human community.

Martin Luther King stood up for the noble values of human dignity, freedom and equality in order to fight against racism. He used his natural talents and intellect to break away from the tyranny of a culture of violence. His decision to study theology and religion was an important factor. Christian religion and theology enabled him to appreciate the power of love over hate, and the reality of the spiritual world as opposed to materialism. With that intellectual and spiritual strength, it is understandable that he felt pity for the white racist society in the United States. He genuinely wanted to liberate the white community in the South of the United States from the chains of its tyrannical racism and violence, inasmuch as he yearned for the liberation of the non-white races from this kind of entrapment. In fact, by the savage act of assassinating Martin Luther King, Earl Ray actually attempted to perpetuate a culture of violence in American society, but the seeds of a culture of peace had already been sown.

Martin Luther King's message of peace and love was for the whole world and not just for the United States. It crossed international borders and transcended racial, ethnic and religious differences. His teaching was understood and well received in Africa, where a Western variety of cultural violence had manifested itself in the form of colonialism, apartheid, assimilation and neo-colonialism.

The message here was loud and clear: a culture of violence is not a monopoly of the United States. A large part of the world is cursed with it. In fact, the whole post-Second World War international system, which is sometimes referred to as the Cold War, was more or less a combination of military, political and cultural violence at a global level. For Martin Luther King, it was not enough to preach against cultural violence in the United States alone. The cancer of violence was universal. Therefore, he was equally vehement in bringing his message into the world arena. Any analysis of his achievements which limits or restricts him to the United States is not only incomplete but does the great man a disservice. The whole world today is in dire need of a culture of peace, and creating such a culture may very well be one of the major legacies to mankind left by Martin Luther King.

NON-VIOLENCE AND NON-VIOLENT DIRECT ACTION

Following the lead of his mentor, Mahatma Gandhi, Martin Luther King embraced the philosophy of non-violent action. He became absolutely convinced early in his career that the non-violent response to any form of violent provocation was not only Christian and civilized but was the only practical way of demonstrating the power of love over hate. This is what makes a real difference between a culture of peace and a culture of violence. While the latter is based on confronting violence with violence, thus escalating violence indefinitely, the former tends to expose the essential evil and non-constructive nature of violence. Non-violence evokes the most noble and courageous of human qualities, while violence is the expression of man's lowest and most bestial instincts. The life of Martin Luther King shows the meaning and power of non-violence for which he was ultimately sacrificed.

For his wholehearted devotion to non-violence, Martin Luther King, like Mahatma Gandhi before him, was accused of cowardice. His own black brothers, such as Malcolm X, ridiculed him for his non-violence, and challenged him to demonstrate his methods and their intended results.

The idea behind non-violent direct action is to take the initiative out of the hands of the perpetrators of violence. Non-violent direct action carries the battle for peace and hope directly into the midst of a violent community. Because the language which the violent society understands best, and is always geared for, is that of violence, non-violent direct action by the opposing side tends to startle, confuse and sometimes disarm the violence-mongers.

The potency of the non-violent direct action method is that it is inclusive, tolerant, forgiving and constructive. Martin Luther King and his supporters demonstrated and marched directly to centres of violence, to jails and police stations, to segregated institutions such as schools, hospitals, restaurants, etc., where they conducted walk-ins, sit-ins and eat-ins. There is a limit to which even the most violence-prone person or community can continue to perpetrate violence against unarmed people.

It is ironic that the outcome of the ultimate violent acts to stop the non-violent direct action of Mahatma Gandhi and Martin Luther King – their assassination – was the opposite to that intended. In fact, it contributed to strengthening the cause they were fighting for. The assassination of Martin Luther King in 1968 led to an improvement in race relations and the social and economic conditions of African-Americans and the other non-white peoples in the United States.

CHRISTIANITY AND A CULTURE OF PEACE

Martin Luther King was brought up as a Christian and he became a theologian and priest. It was in these capacities that he made the most direct contribution to a culture of peace. He was convinced that only by following the Christian way and its principles, and, in particular, following in the footsteps of Jesus Christ, could society put an end to the evil of violence. As a pastor, Martin Luther King delivered sermons that reiterated the teaching of Jesus Christ about love. The problem with most Christians in the world today is that their espousal of their religion is restricted to one day per week, that is, Sundays or Saturdays (if they happen to be Seventh Day Adventists). Although Martin Luther King was a pastor responsible for a parish and conducted the traditional weekly services for his congregations, it must be remembered that his style and orientation were reminiscent of that of the Messiah himself in the sense that he took Christianity to the people, rather than bringing people to Christianity.

The problem with modern-day Christians is that the way Christianity is conducted in the world today makes it possible for this religious community to qualify as one of the thousands of private clubs which are found in all human societies. Everything that is contained in the New Testament about the life and work of Jesus Christ reveals a different picture of what Christianity should be, at least as understood from the life of its founder, Jesus Christ Himself. To that extent, Martin Luther King's understanding and work as a Christian was closer to that which Jesus Christ stood for.

Martin Luther King will always be remembered for his civil rights campaigns in the South of the United States; for his leading role in the fight to desegregate schools, workplaces, hospitals, transportation, social services of all kinds; his political campaigns and marches against the political establishments at local, state and federal levels. In his sermons, he always exhorted his followers to go out and confront evil wherever it was, and not to hide behind the comfort and exclusiveness of church buildings. That is to say, a culture of peace will not be created within the churches, but in the world outside.

A CULTURE OF PEACE ON A GLOBAL SCALE

The entire world has increasingly become a global village. For instance, the fear of the spread of the Ebola virus to all corners of the earth gets medical experts rushing to Zaire almost instantly from all over the world. The AIDS epidemic has become a salutary lesson in the globalization of a culture of medical consciousness. Terrorism of all kinds, including nuclear terrorism, has literally placed all mankind in the same boat. It no longer makes any sense in this day and age to argue glibly about some calamities of violence as being restricted to certain societies, states or regions. The whole world is now witnessing a growing number of international conflicts. What happens anywhere has its effects everywhere.

It was the genius of Martin Luther King which allowed him to foresee the perils of the globalization of a culture of violence. His messages and exhortations to the American people were equally aimed at all peoples all over the world. To merely provide a cure for a disease in one part of the body, without taking immediate measures to prevent it from spreading to the rest of the body, is of no avail. Working simultaneously to rid American society of violence, with equal concern for the global manifestation of the same problem, was the essence of Martin Luther King's approach.

In Africa, Martin Luther King saw that European colonialism had subjected

African people to the same fate of suffering, poverty and dehumanization that the American Blacks had also suffered. What was even more painful about the African situation, however, was that many of these African nations had become sovereign independent states immediately following the end of the Second World War in 1945, and yet the suffering of the people went on unabated. Under these circumstances, it was no longer valid continuously to point a finger at the European colonizers. African leaders were now also to blame for the misery and violence which gripped the African continent. According to Martin Luther King, evil was evil, and violence was violence, whether it was promoted by Whites or Blacks. It is a truism that all peoples and societies, irrespective of colour of skin or level of civilization, are capable of wallowing in a culture of violence.

Martin Luther King saw remarkable parallels between apartheid in South Africa and the American segregationist practices in the South. The only difference, if any, was that the American Civil War and the American Constitution had made racist practices illegal. On the contrary, in South Africa, at least from 1948,[6] apartheid and all that it entailed, was legal according to the law of the land. In South Africa, Blacks were not only considered naturally and biologically an inferior species but the state actually legislated to ensure that this inferiority remained a permanent feature of the South African political, economic and social landscape. That situation was totally unacceptable to Martin Luther King who lashed out at the South African authorities and the white supporters of the apartheid regime within South Africa, as well as the American and other Western governments and their peoples who sustained the apartheid regime. His harsh words were also pointed towards the white Rhodesians after their Unilateral Declaration of Independence (UDI) on 11 November 1965.[7]

---

6. The South African election of 1948 was won, for the first time in the history of South Africa, by the Afrikaaner-led Nationalist party of Dr D. F. Malan on the platform of apartheid. As soon as this party formed the government, it immediately implemented its campaign promise of wholesale legislation on separate development for Blacks and Whites.
7. Ian Smith, Prime Minister of former Rhodesia, declared white Rhodesia independent (UDI) on 11 November 1965 in defiance of the British Government and the international community. That immediately led to the fifteen-year war of liberation which ended in 1979. It was immediately followed by the independence of Zimbabwe in 1980.

For Martin Luther King, it was impossible to create and maintain peace under circumstances of racial domination and oppression, economic deprivation, military dictatorships, tribalism and underdevelopment. All these were manifestations of evil, whose ultimate outcome would be unending violence and suffering for people everywhere. Thus, the liberation of the African continent was good in so far as it unlocked the chains of African servitude to the European world. However, when practically the whole continent of Africa is now engulfed by internal wars, border conflicts and tribal massacres, with millions of destitute refugees and displaced persons and the maiming of thousands of women and children by landmines planted all over their land, we cannot say that we are on the road to a culture of peace.

Finally, Martin Luther King turned his attention to the Viet Nam War. Here was a superpower, the United States, engaged in the exportation of violence to a small underdeveloped country at the other end of the world. Young Americans were used as cannon fodder in a far-off land for dubious reasons and obscure objectives, in a war whose national interest to the United States in is even now unclear. Martin Luther castigated the US administration for its unnecessary involvement in Viet Nam and, in particular, for brutalizing and terrorizing the people of that land with napalm bombs. It appears that the single most serious sin which the people of Viet Nam had committed against America was that they had defeated their former colonial power, France, at the battle of Dien Bien Phu in 1956. What the world should know, however, is that the Vietnamese people had no quarrel with the Government and people of the United States. The war in Indo-China, including Viet Nam, was a war between the Vietnamese people and the French. The Vietnamese people fought against the French in self-defence, in order to liberate themselves from the yoke of French colonialism.

Why and how Americans allowed themselves to be sucked into that Vietnamese quagmire will ever remain one of the worst intrigues in American foreign policy ventures abroad. It took the likes of Martin Luther King vehemently to castigate the overbearing and bullying international behaviour of the superpowers. It was apparent to Martin Luther King that the whole post-Second World War period, especially the Cold War era, was characterized by a sham peace. While the superpowers did everything to avoid wars between themselves and within their regions, they did not hesitate to promote destructive wars in the Third World, the so-called 'bush wars' or 'proxy wars'. There may have been peace in America, in the Soviet Union and in the whole of the Western world, but in the Third World there was anything but peace.

Martin Luther King's 'dream' of a future peaceful America, of a prosperous Africa, and indeed of a peaceful world, still remains far from being realized. Reality on the ground is cluttered by numerous Rwandas, Bosnias, Somalias, Oklahoma-type bombings, etc. However, that the relentless struggle for peace must go on was Martin Luther King's teaching. He died trying to realize his dream to make the world a better place to live in. All of us owe it to him to do our utmost to make the world a better place to live in for present and future generations, and to make the dream of a culture of peace come true.

BIBLIOGRAPHY

ANSBRO, J. J. 1982. *Martin Luther King Jr.: The Making of a Mind*. New York, Orbis Books.
BONDURANT, J. 1971. *Conquest of Violence, The Gandhian Philosophy of Conflict*. Berkeley, Calif., University of California Press.
DEWOLF, L. H. 1960. *A Theology of the Living Church*. New York, Harper & Row.
HASKINS, J. 1977. *The Life and Death of Martin Luther King Jr*. New York, Lothroplee & Sheperd.
JOHNSON, C., et al. 1968. *The Wisdom of Martin Luther King in His Own Words*. New York, Lancer Books.
PUCKREIN, G. A. 1993. *The Civil Rights Movement and the Legacy of Martin Luther King Jr*. New York, Smithsonian Institution.
SHARP, G. 1973. *The Politics of Non-Violent Action*. Boston, Porter Sargent.
UNESCO. 1991. *The Seville Statement on Violence*. Paris, UNESCO.

The role of education for a culture of peace

Keith D. Suter*

INTRODUCTION

Peace is everyone's concern – but no one's business. In other words, everyone likes the idea of peace but few people are making it the priority item of their work.

However, UNESCO is taking the lead in creating a culture of peace. A culture of violence is so embedded in many societies that a culture of peace cannot be created easily or quickly. Additionally, to create a new culture of peace will require tackling many matters simultaneously. There is no one single, simple formula that can transform a society based on a culture of violence into one based on a culture of peace. Therefore 'education' for a culture of peace has to be defined very broadly. The overall aim should be to create a culture of peace – think it, talk it, work it.

THE END OF THE COLD WAR AND PEACE PERSPECTIVES

The Cold War is over. But peace has not broken out. Indeed, there are probably as many conflicts under way today as there were during the more intense periods of the Cold War (1945–90), which was the central defining event in international politics. Many foreign policy issues were examined in the higher political context of the Cold War, namely that a country had to avoid alienating its Cold War allies, while losing no opportunity to continue to put pressure on the Cold War

---

*   President, Centre for Peace and Conflict Studies, University of Sydney, Australia.

opponents. During the Cold War, governments planned for war but not for peace; thus, the rapid end of this era took them by surprise and they had few plans to cope with the end of tensions. There was a culture of war – and not a culture of peace. 'Culture' was identified in one study published by UNESCO: 'The core of any culture consists of traditionally accepted ideas and their attached values, in so far as these determine patterns of behaviour. Culture is society's way of life and the content of its social relations. A culture contains the basic values important to that society, and its ordering principles.'[1]

The authors said later: 'The arms race is accompanied by the cultivation of enemy images, by fear, and by an obsession with the use or threat of use of violence.'[2] They again subsequently commented: 'Disarmament, development and human rights are probably the most important issues of our time.'[3] But this assessment was not reflected in governmental priorities.

The culture of war meant that priority was given to preparing for war rather than to preparing for peace. For example, in 1981, the US Commission on Proposals for the National Academy of Peace and Conflict Resolution reported that in the US: 'There are approximately 200 scholars studying conflict resolution, compared with 200,000 scientists who do military research.'[4] Ironically, the people who were doing the research on today's (post-Cold War) agenda included peace researchers, with research topics such as racism, unemployment, gang violence and drugs. Peace researchers were doing the work which is now receiving the recognition it deserves but which, during the Cold War, did not get the funding or encouragement needed. There was no equal opportunity for peace.

In short, when the Cold War ended, governments were not in a good position to exploit the new opportunities provided by the end of tensions. They had contingency for wars but no contingency plans for peace. There is a difference between winning a war and winning the peace.

---

1. Asbjørn Eide et al., 'The Impact of the Arms Race on Education, Science and Technology, and Culture and Communication', in *UNESCO Yearbook on Peace and Conflict Studies 1987*, p. 77, Paris/Westport, Conn., UNESCO/Greenwood Press, Inc., 1989.
2. Ibid., p. 82.
3. Ibid., p. 103.
4. *Report of the Commission on Proposals for the National Academy of Peace and Conflict Resolution*, p. 36, Washington, D.C., US Government Printing Office, 1981.

UNESCO'S PIONEERING WORK

Governments during the Cold War did not pay enough attention to UNESCO's pioneering work on peace. UNESCO has always had an interest in peace and was conceived during the Second World War, when in 1942 the Allied Ministers for Education met to discuss the creation of an international organization to co-ordinate educational co-operation in the post-war world.

When the war ended, governments met in London in November 1945 to finalize the arrangements for UNESCO's creation. The British Prime Minister, Clement Attlee, in his opening speech said: 'Is it not, after all, in men's minds that wars begin?' The poet Archibald MacLeish, who was in the US delegation, took up that phrase and used it in the Preamble to the UNESCO Constitution: 'Since wars begin in the minds of men, it is in the minds of men that the defences of peace must be constructed.'

UNESCO, from the outset, has pioneered a sophisticated understanding of peace which meant that 'peace' was more than just the absence of fighting. As early as 1950, UNESCO publications pointed out that textbooks tended to describe wars and conflicts in a prejudiced way by attributing blame to the enemy and virtue to one's own country. Second, it was recognized that too much attention to the dividing military and political aspects of conflicts tends to under-communicate uniting factors such as the history of civilization. Moreover, there is a tendency to glorify one's own national heroes compared with heroes of other nations.[5]

In 1986, an international meeting of scientists, convened in Seville by the Spanish National Commission for UNESCO, adopted a Statement on Violence refuting the notion that organized human violence is biologically determined.[6]

---

5. Eide, op. cit., p. 116.
6. The core of the Statement contains five propositions. They all set out what does *not* cause war: (1) War is not acquired from animals (they do not kill each other as humans do); (2) war is not inherited from our forebears; (3) war is not necessary to ensure a better standard of living (humans can gain more from co-operation); (4) war is not due to the biological composition of the brain (humans need to be trained for war); (5) war is not due to some basic 'instinct'.

Humans are not genetically programmed to be violent towards one another. UNESCO continues to gain international acceptance of the Statement.

At the end of the Second World War, UNESCO produced a statement on race, challenging the then fashionable notion that white people were somehow genetically superior to black people. That statement, by receiving international endorsement and publicity, helped reshape attitudes to race. People may still be racist, but there are no scientific arguments to support their opinions. The intention is to build a similar momentum in favour of the Seville Statement. People may still say that war is inevitable because it is somehow part of human nature, but they will not have scientific arguments to support their opinions. Educational associations and other organizations are being invited to join the list of bodies which have endorsed the Statement. They are also being invited to distribute the Statement and publicize it. It is now beginning to be printed in textbooks.[7] UNESCO has produced a booklet on the Seville Statement, giving both the text and a commentary on it.[8]

LESSONS FROM A CULTURE OF VIOLENCE

To understand how we can create a culture of peace, it is useful to look at how humans created a culture of violence. There are many explanations why this is so. The purpose of this section is to identify two factors which have been present in many conflicts since 1945.

Ignorance of history

It seems that the lesson of history is that people do not learn from history. There is a tendency for human affairs to go in cycles, as each generation is obliged to learn afresh from its experiences. There is little cumulative learning experience. It seems that just as a generation learns the lessons of history, it goes to the grave, taking the lessons with it. As stated in the *Final Report* of the 1989 UNESCO

---

7. For example, David Barash, *Introduction to Peace Studies*, pp. 139–41, Belmont, Calif., Wadsworth, 1991.
8. David Adams (ed.), *The Seville Statement on Violence: Preparing the Ground for the Constructing of Peace*, Paris, UNESCO, 1991.

International Congress on Peace in the Minds of Men, there is a 'powerful inertia which leads individuals and people to reproduce the same models of behaviour generation after generation. . . .'[9]

In 1980, Captain G. F. Liardet of the British Royal Navy made a detailed survey of war aims and actual achievements between 1854 and 1973. He compared the original reason why a country started a war with the eventual outcome: in short, does war pay? Among his findings were: 'the war aim is very unlikely to be achieved' and 'the lessons of previous conflicts will be misread'.[10] Thus the chances of a government getting what it wants by starting a war are very small but, because governments ignore history, they are unaware of this lesson. In 1982, American writer William Greider commented upon the lack of a sense of history among mass media commentators which permitted the generation of periodic hysteria in the United States.[11]

A decade and a half later, it is clear that the fears aroused in the United States and its allies were, in fact, an overestimation of the power of the USSR and its allies. But in the period leading up to the end of the Cold War, there was a considerable increase in military expenditure which hurt all the economies in the world.

The military-industrial complex

The institutions working for a culture of violence have been better organized than the institutions working for a culture of peace. There has been, for example, more money to be made out of war than peace. Additionally, governments regard war as their monopoly, but are willing to share peace education with the private sector (such as private educational institutions with peace courses and non-governmental organizations), as if to suggest that peace is not nearly as important as war.

---

9. *Final Report of the International Congress on Peace in the Minds of Men*, Paris, UNESCO, 1989, p. 34.
10. G. F. Liardet, 'War Aims and Achievements 1854–1973', *Seaford House Papers*, p. 89, London, 1980.
11. William Greider, 'Hysteria is Coming! Hysteria is Coming!', in Jim Wallis (ed.), *Waging Peace*, p. 52, San Francisco, Calif., Harper & Row, 1982.

In 1961 President Eisenhower, in his farewell address to Congress, popularized the phrase 'the military-industrial complex'. This was a warning, not least to his incoming successor John Kennedy, who had promised in the election campaign to expand US military expenditure, to beware of the implications flowing from the pressure to increase the size of the US defence forces.

Prior to the Second World War, a large army was not part of the United States heritage. In 1970, the United States political scientist Bruce Russett said that the first American President, George Washington (1789–97), 'neither led nor left a standing army' and:

> During the first 170 years of our history, only in actual wartime or in the year or two immediately afterwards did our armed forces ever employ as many as one per cent of the working-age male population. It is since the Second World War that the nation's living style has changed. We have at no point since 1941 had fewer than 1,400,000 men under arms nor as little as three per cent of working age males in the armed forces. . . . The same pattern appears when we look at military expenditures. Before 1939 the peacetime military budget was barely higher than one per cent of the gross national product. The post-Second World War floor was three per cent in 1947 and since Korea (1950–1953) has fluctuated between 7.3 and 11.3 per cent.[12]

The US defence forces were then transformed in the Second World War. They acquired extensive responsibilities and so did not reduce fully back to their pre-war levels. President Eisenhower was a career soldier who had seen how much the military had changed in his lifetime and was worried about the post-war growth of the military and its industrial interests. For example, bases and factories were spread around the United States, so that any attempt to reduce them would result in the local people complaining to their members of Congress and Senators. Russett also pointed out: 'The long-standing practice of allowing congressman of the President's party to announce the award of defense contracts to their districts, does nothing to diminish the image of military spending as contributing

---

12. Bruce Russett, *What Price Vigilance? The Burdens of National Defence*, p. 2, New Haven, Conn., Yale University Press, 1970.

to legislators' political well-being.'¹³ The United States had created a permanent war economy. A similar development was under way in the USSR.

As US political scientist Richard Barnet pointed out in 1977, the military establishments in the United States and the USSR are no doubt each other's best allies. A military bureaucracy, like any other, has a professional interest in keeping what it has, in enjoying the power and prestige of being at the frontiers of technology, and in projecting a threat which justifies bigger budgets.[14]

The Cold War is over. But this is not obvious from the continued high level of military expenditure. Many countries still have a military-industrial complex, even if there are now no clear enemies. Indeed, the complex has become even larger. It is now a military-industrial-scientific-media-trade-union complex. Scientists, the media and trade unions have all recognized the gain to them from having high military expenditure (be it for employment, news stories or advertising). Thus, the creation of a culture of peace will need to involve these people as partners in the process, otherwise they will undermine any attempt to create such a culture of peace.

THE TRIANGLE OF PEACE

'Peace' is more than the absence of war. 'Peace' means harmony, wholeness and well-being in all human relationships. One way of setting this out is via the Triangle of Peace:[15] disarmament, conflict resolution and justice.

One side of the Triangle is the removal of existing weapon systems: hence arms control and disarmament. Arms-control measures are designed to slow down the arms race (such as the South Pacific Nuclear Free Zone Treaty). Disarmament measures (which are much rarer) require governments to destroy existing weapon systems.

But governments are not going to disarm in a security vacuum and so there have to be alternative ways of settling disputes: hence conflict resolution. Such

---

13. Ibid., p. 27.
14. Richard Barnet, *The Giants: Russia and America*, p. 106, New York, Simon & Schuster, 1977.
15 See Keith Suter, *The Triangle of Peace*, Perth, Trinity Peace Research Institute, 1990.

techniques include diplomacy (with one government talking directly with another government), arbitration (where governments have their disputes settled by recourse to international law and international courts) and mediation (where a third party tries to find a way of settling a dispute though negotiation).

The third side of the Triangle is justice. It is necessary to look for the underlying causes of violence. This work requires attention to such matters as the protection of the environment and respect for human rights. There may be some employment opportunities here for members of the military-industrial complex in that, through a process of 'conversion', defence facilities can be used for peaceful purposes, such as an army corps of engineers building bridges and irrigation systems in developing countries.

THEMES FOR A CULTURE OF PEACE

Inclusiveness

People working for a culture must become part of the change they want to create. In other words, people working for a culture of peace must themselves manifest the values which they wish to create in a wider society.

For those of us who have been involved in peace research for many years, it is very easy to assume that peace education is a self-evidently valuable activity. But that may not be how 'peace' is perceived in the wider community. Half a century of the Cold War and being suspicious of other countries has taken deep roots in all societies. What may be clear to peace researchers may not be so clear to the ordinary person who, among other things, receives a daily diet of violence in the mass media. Therefore, it is important that written and oral material for a culture of peace should be presented in a way which makes sense to the ordinary person.

Second, there is a need to be careful about the language used. The language should be 'inclusive', for example, 'chairperson' rather than 'chairman'. Additionally, the language should itself be 'peaceful', with an avoidance of militaristic language (such as calling people 'warriors' for peace).

Third, creating a culture of peace means bringing together a diverse range of organizations which would include not only the more obvious education and peace groups, but also gun-control groups and groups concerned with domestic violence.

Fourth, peace education and peace research centres should also have diverse roots. Those created in universities should not just be derived from the disciplines of political science, psychology and law. Instead, other disciplines should also be encouraged to see how they can become involved in this work. A faculty of architecture and town planning, for example, could create such a centre whose work would enhance the faculty's efforts in its more traditional fields. Additionally, such centres should not be regarded as the sole preserve of educational institutions.[16]

Additionally, it is important to avoid the fragmentation of peace. Peace and conflicts have diverse causes and consequences, so there needs to be an all-embracing approach. This means being careful to avoid, for example, people studying economics looking only at the economic consequences of the arms race or international law students being taught only the laws of war. Students should be encouraged to look beyond the boundaries of their academic disciplines and take a holistic view of humankind.

Finally, national defence forces need to be involved as partners in the creation of a new culture of peace. This may, as expressed by the UN Secretary-General,[17] mean greater training for peace-keeping operations.

Inspiration

History books, monuments and museums are usually based on war rather than peace. History books are too often about generals and battles. There is much glorification of war and the brave deeds of men and women. The sacrifices of one generation inspire later generations to follow their example. A culture of violence is propagated partly by inspiration.

---

16. For example, the Trinity Peace Research Institute, Perth, Western Australia (of which I was the director, from 1986 to 1990), was the first privately funded peace research institute in Australia. It received no government assistance. It was financed by a parish church, which had great financial resources and which wanted to make its own contribution to 1986: International Year of Peace.
17. Boutros Boutros Ghali, *An Agenda for Peace,* 2nd ed., New York, United Nations, 1995.

Peace too has its heroes. But these men and women receive far less attention in history books, monuments and museums. Another theme in the creation of a culture of peace is therefore the need to ensure that a culture of peace itself is of an inspirational nature.

This problem was recognized in 1901 by William James, the Harvard philosopher, who wrote about the need to create 'the moral equivalent of war'.[18] War is a great mobilizer: people are willing to make self-sacrifices and confront dangers in ways that they would rarely do in peacetime. War builds up personal character and creates a national sense of purpose. James had in mind the creation of a common campaign by countries against such general problems as disease and famine, with young people being conscripted in new national forces to tackle these problems rather than being trained for war.

Over ninety years later, James's idea is still relevant. This may be seen at two levels. At the national level, war is still publicized and seen as a virtuous, inspiring activity, with considerable attention to commemorating military events.

At the personal level, boredom is a great problem among young people in developed countries. As the material standard of living has gone up, so young people have more time on their hands, more money to spend, less parental supervision (because both parents are often in the paid workforce to earn money for the increased standard of living), more time to watch violent programmes on television – and there are few challenges. For example, in Sydney in April 1994, a teenager admitted to stealing thirty-seven cars in twenty-two days because he was 'bored'.[19] War, violence and crime are exciting alternatives to boredom. In other developing countries, there is not so much boredom as a lack of purpose and a loss of confidence in the future. A South African study of the problems of educating young people about AIDS noted: 'In order to practise safe behaviour, [street kids] have to be persuaded that their lives are worth preserving.'[20]

Much remains to be done, then, in portraying peace itself as an inspiring

---

18. William James, *The Varieties of Religious Experience: A Study in Human Nature*, pp. 355–7, London, Collins, 1975 [1901].
19. 'Boy Stole 37 Cars in 22 Days', *Daily Telegraph Mirror*, Sydney, 13 April 1994, p. 1.
20. Quoted in Sue Armstrong, 'Women Hit Hardest by HIV in Divided South Africa', *New Scientist* (London), 3 July 1993, p. 10.

and exciting activity. Publicity needs to be given to positive stories of the quest for peace. For example, Rodrigo Carazo, then President of Costa Rica, explained at the 1990 UNESCO World Congress on Disarmament Education how his country had decided to scrap its defence forces three decades earlier:

> We, in Costa Rica, wished to undertake a unique experiment. We asked ourselves if, in the end, it would be worth while, in terms of security or conquest, to maintain an army, or if, instead, and owing to man's rationality, it were possible to have greater trust in reason and the world than in weapons. The question seems naive, but the answer has given us excellent results. Weapons do not offer security, and the most substantial and delightful victory is that which is attained without violence.[21]

The experiment is still under way but it does not get enough attention by the international mass media. Good news is often not news – wars sell newspapers, not peace. Consequently, some ideas are given below on the need for a more critical approach towards the mass media and how the mass media can become partners in creating a culture of peace.

People examine the present from the perspective of the past. The British historian Sir Michael Howard recalled in 1961 how his study of history challenged the myths with which he had grown up:

> I remember my own bitter disillusion of learning that the great English victory over the Armada in 1588 was followed, not by a glorious peace but, after 16 years, by as dishonourable a compromise settlement as England ever made, and by 20 years during which we were little more than a satellite of the great Spanish Empire. After this it came as less of a shock, on studying the Napoleonic wars from continental sources, to learn how incidental was the part Britain played in the climactic campaigns of 1812, 1813 and 1814 which finally smashed the Napoleonic hegemony of Europe, great though our indirect contribution to that overthrow undoubtedly was. Such disillusion is a necessary part of growing up in and belonging to an adult society.[22]

---

21. Rodrigo Carazo, 'To Learn to Live Peacefully', in Marek Thee (ed.), *Armaments, Arms Control and Disarmament: A UNESCO Reader for Disarmament Education*, p. 322, Paris, UNESCO, 1981.
22. Michael Howard, 'The Use and Abuse of Military History', *Journal of the Royal United Services Institute* (London), February 1993 [1961], p. 27.

By implication, though Howard did not state this, most people never do become 'adults'.[23] The myths of childhood remain with them throughout their lives because, unlike Howard, they do not get the opportunity to study history at undergraduate level. Their knowledge of history remains based on what they learnt from school textbooks, which reproduce the views of that country. British and German textbooks, for example, provide different descriptions on which force was responsible for defeating Napoleon at the Battle of Waterloo in June 1815.

Thus history books play an important role in creating a culture of peace. UNESCO itself has made a fine contribution to this work by its *History of Humanity* (first published about two decades ago and now in the process of updating)[24] and its regional histories such as *The General History of Africa* (in eight volumes).

In regard to monuments, an obvious task is to create more monuments celebrating peace. The Stockholm Peace Research Institute (SIPRI), one of the world's most important peace research institutes, is a living monument created by Sweden in 1966 to commemorate its 150 continuous years of peace. 1986 was the International Year of Peace (IYP), and the Australian Government's IYP Committee, of which I was a member, recommended that, as one of its activities for the year, Australia should create a peace monument in its national capital, Canberra, which the Governor-General unveiled on 24 October (UN Day) 1990.

Similarly, there is a need to create more peace museums. Terence Duffy, of the Peace and Conflict Studies Programme at the University of Ulster, United Kingdom, has commented:

---

23. Much the same could be said about what people retain from their science classes. Here they are not the subject of national myth-making; they simply forget what they are taught. A conference in the United States discussed the way that '20 per cent of Americans still believe that the Sun orbits the Earth, and 17 per cent of the rest believe that the Earth circles the Sun once a day. . .'. See Rosie Mestel, 'Education: The Final Frontier', *New Scientist*, 26 February 1994, p. 11.
24. S. J. De Laet et al. (eds.), *History of Humanity*, Vol. I: *Prehistory and the Beginnings of Civilization*, Paris, UNESCO, 1994 (with the other six volumes to appear by 1997).

Peace museums are now emerging as a global trend in museum development. The product of state, group, or individual efforts, these museums explore the relationship between conflict and the visual arts. They act as vehicles of peace education by preserving the heritage of peace-making and peace culture and by promoting an informed understanding of the origins of conflict. Peace museums often approach their subject by juxtaposing peace with the tragic consequences of war.[25]

Duffy went on to identify the four strands within the peace museum trend:

> . . . distinct peace museums, which specifically, use the term 'peace museum' to describe themselves and that are dedicated to peace themes; museums that are devoted to particular events (such as Hiroshima's Memorial Peace Museum); museums that celebrate peace as exemplified through international humanitarian law (such as the International Red Cross and Red Crescent Museum); and gallery projects that, while not currently full-blown explorations of peace issues, have the potential to evolve as functional peace museums.[26]

To sum up, a culture of violence became embedded in so many societies, partly though its inspirational nature. It is necessary for a culture of peace to be seen as equally inspirational.

THE MASS MEDIA AND A CULTURE OF PEACE

The mass media have a crucial role to play in the development of a culture of peace. For example, television has become a major factor in modern life. What began sixty years ago as a small system for the conveying of news and entertainment has itself become a major news item.

This section deals with the way in which the mass media report on wars, the rise of 'info-tainment' (a mixture of information and entertainment), some ideas for improving the quality of mass media reporting, the way that there are some signs of a community reaction against violence on television, and some ideas on how television can be 'tamed'.

---

25. Terence Duffy, 'Exhibiting Peace', *Peace Review* (San Francisco), Winter 1993, p. 488.
26. Ibid.

Reporting war

Television is of little help in the search for truth. This does not mean that television journalists set out deliberately to lie. The problem is that television is a superficial medium; it engages the emotions rather than the intellect. The World Association of Christian Communication, based in London, pays particular attention to two main centres of mass media: the United Kingdom and the United States. The World Association has set out some of the detailed shortcomings of the media during the 1990–91 Gulf War.[27]

The truth often does come out eventually, but the interests of the mass media and the general public have by then moved on. The *Guardian* newspaper in the United Kingdom, over a year after the Gulf War ended, reported that 'Allied ground forces in the Gulf War outnumbered the Iraqis by more than three-to-one at the start of the hostilities and the Bush Administration vastly overestimated the Iraqi military's fighting strength.'[28] This revelation was preceded by the Pentagon's admission 'that its so-called "smart" bombs and Tomahawk cruise missiles were not nearly as successful at hitting their intended targets as previously stated. The ground-launched Patriot missile, used against Iraqi Scud missiles, also turned out to be less effective than advertised.' Three months later, the same newspaper reported: 'The US Congress yesterday released Pentagon documents showing that as early as 1985 it had warned that Iraq was diverting American technology imports to a nuclear weapons programme. This directly contradicts President Bush's latest insistence that the US Government had no knowledge of the uses to which US imports were put.'[29]

Unfortunately, by the time that the truth does emerge, the attention of the media consumers has often moved on. Additionally, the truth appears in only small stories in newspapers, since television and the front pages of newspapers are now devoted to what is the latest interesting issue. 'Smart' bombs, for example, retain their favourable image since that is what people remember, rather than the later, more balanced assessments of their (limited) effectiveness.

---

27. World Association of Christian Communication, *Recent Activities and Future Plans 1992-3*, p. 9, London, 1993.
28. 'Pentagon Got its Iraqi Sums Wrong', *The Guardian* (London), 24 April 1992.
29. 'Pentagon Warned US to Shun Iraq', *The Guardian* (London), 3 July 1992.

Info-tainment

One problem, then, with television is the superficial nature of its reporting. It blurs the distinction between news and entertainment. Ann Sanson of the University of Melbourne was worried about the impact of Gulf War television coverage on children:

> We know that some children got taken in by this new action-packed soap opera – 'the television' war – and said to each other 'Did you watch the Gulf War last night?' as if it were just another soapie. The death and destruction seemed to become as irrelevant and distant as in any other 'show'. This was facilitated by the 'linguistic detoxification' that was used to cover the true human costs of war. . . . So we saw the bombing of Baghdad referred to as a great fireworks display, and civilian deaths became 'collateral damage' – a term which would be incomprehensible to most children anyway.[30]

Tragedies are presented in an entertaining way. The Rome-based Society for International Development has reported on the way that the media have turned human suffering into a circus.[31] Somalia has become Showmalia. In an editorial, the French newspaper *Libération* warned that the line between presenting information and putting on a show was extremely thin: 'In Mogadishu . . . this line was not only crossed; military and media alike have trampled upon it savagely.'

The world witnessed the first military landing broadcast by satellite, and a United States source has admitted that this was planned by the military command and the technicians of the North American news channel Cable News Network.

The UN Secretary-General, speaking, ironically, in a CNN televised conference, in May 1993, set out his concerns about the media's capacity to focus attention on one problem while ignoring another:

---

30. Ann Sanson, 'The Impact of Television on Children', *Chain Reaction* (Melbourne), No. 65.
31. 'Media Attacked for Turning Human Suffering into a Circus', *Development Hotline* (Rome), December 1992, p. 6.

The [UN] Member States never take action on a problem unless the media take up the case. When the media get involved, public opinion is aroused. When public pressure builds up, the UN is asked to get involved. This is why we see UN operations in Bosnia and Somalia. The world will act when the media arouse the public. Public emotion becomes so intense that UN work is undermined. On television, the problem may become simplified and exaggerated. Constructive statesmanship, which takes time and must have nuance, is almost impossible. When one crisis is in the spotlight, other equally serious situations are left in the dark. There are problems in Afghanistan, Angola, Armenia and Azerbaijan, Myanmar and Tajikistan. Very few people are interested. More people were killed in one day in Luanda or in Huambo in Angola, than in months in Sarajevo. Why is the UN deeply involved in one crisis and not in another? One of the reasons is media attention.[32]

To sum up, the global media revolution has enabled us to see more about events occurring around the world. But are we really learning more about those events? Is the coverage based on entertaining us rather than informing us?

Improving the quality of reporting

Johan Galtung (see this volume, pp. 75–92), one of the founders of peace research, has offered some ideas on how the 1990–91 Gulf War could have been reported better.[33] First, tell the story from all sides. A conflict has many parties and many issues; trying to reduce the complexity down to the classical simplistic formula of two parties and one issue may be only marginally better than presenting one side only.

Second, get access to events, people, issues. This means getting to where the action is, not where some of the action is reported or distorted, such as at a press conference.

Third, do not overuse élites as sources. Avoid the incessant parade of experts, mostly in uniform, with overheads and maps. This type of presentation

---

32. 'Media Sets UN Agenda, Says Boutros-Ghali', *Unity* (Canberra), June 1993.
33. Johan Galtung, 'Reporting on a War: The Gulf War', *Social Alternatives* (Brisbane), Vol. 11, No. 1, 1992, pp. 8–11.

is a mixture of university lecture, combined with management seminar and 'salespersonship' for some new product.

Fourth, do not glorify technology. This can easily become advertising for new weapons, done glibly with insensitivity to the victims of all these weapons.

Finally, stress and promote peace initiatives. Of course, nobody would argue that the media should turn themselves into instruments of peace education, even of peace propaganda. But they should also be tuned to that angle of the story.

A successful example of this final point is the Australian Media Peace Prize. My colleague, Sydney businesswoman and peace philanthropist Mrs Stella Cornelius, received the endorsement of the United Nations Association of Australia in creating, over a decade ago, that peace prize. It is not sufficient just to criticize the media. They should be rewarded when they do well; they should be encouraged to do better. This peace prize project is now copied in over twenty countries around the world.

This media peace prize work could be taken much further at both at the national and local levels. National Commissions for UNESCO could create media peace awards, using UNESCO's culture of peace programme as the basis for the criteria for winning. Locally based non-governmental organizations could create their own awards for local media outlets. Service clubs, such as Rotary, Soroptimists and the Scout Movement, could also introduce media awards for reporting which meets the principles of those organizations. Another possibility is that teaching bodies could also follow this example. Local schools could encourage students to become 'media monitors' and at some appropriate time each year the students could vote on their own programmes and newspaper articles which they think have done the most to create a culture of peace. The students could also organize the prize and the prize-award ceremony. The mass media will publicize these events because they love to report events concerning the media.

Television and violence

Parents would not let a stranger into their homes to have unrestricted access to their children. But this is what is happening with television, as explained by Dr Victor Strasburger, Chief of the Division of Adolescent Medicine at the University of New Mexico's School of Medicine:

Imagine inviting a stranger into your home for two or three hours every day to tell your children all about a perverse world where violence solves problems, and all anyone needs [in order] to be happy is the right beer, a fast car, good looks and lots of sex. . . . The stranger could do a lot of damage during that long daily visit, planting misperceptions no one could ever change and causing problems no one could solve.[34]

Television drama creates an appetite for violence that spills over into other television programmes and even into other mass media. News programmes are more dramatic, gory and fast-paced. So-called human interest television documentaries are also excessively violent. There is a blurring between television news and drama. There is also a blurring between violence in the news and in sport. Australian academic Helen Yates has complained about the portrayal of football violence.[35] There is also a blurring between television crime and newspaper crime.

There has been a considerable campaign against violence on television. For example, Terry Rakolta of Americans for Responsible Television has claimed that the level of violence has passed the point guaranteed by civil rights and she has argued that television executives should exercise greater control over programming. In one year the average 16-year-old sees 1,500 sexual acts, 16,000 murders, and 200,000 acts of violence on prime-time television. Terry Rakolta has decided that such violence is shaping our future society and needs to be controlled.[36]

All of this type of campaigning by churches and non-governmental organizations is beginning to bear fruit. In July 1993, the American media industry itself said that there was too much violence. In short, all the campaigning done by non-governmental organizations against violence on television and in the movies has started to be successful. There is a still a long way to go but there

---

34. 'Unsupervised TV Equal to Inviting a Stranger to Influence Your Children', *The Australian,* 3 April 1993.
35. Helen Yates, 'Women, the Media and Football Violence', *Social Alternatives,* Vol. 11, No. 1, 1992, p. 17.
36. 'Sex and Violence on TV', *TRANET Newsletter,* March 1993, p. 6.

may at last be some progress made, and a foundation upon which UNESCO can build a culture of peace.

We need to create discerning television viewers, who can peer beneath the gloss and glitter of so much of contemporary television and demand higher standards. Everyone can play a part in improving the quality of the mass media. Thus, creating a culture of peace is a broadly based activity which gives everyone the opportunity for participation – and a sense of 'ownership' of the progress being made.

FROM CONFLICT TO CO-OPERATION

A culture of peace is necessary because a culture of fear has not deterred people from going to war. The late Bert Roling[37] recalled the hope that Nobel had in 1890 that the invention of his explosive would deter people from going to war: 'Perhaps my factories will put an end to war. . . . On the day when two army corps may mutually annihilate each other in a second, probably all civilized nations will recoil with horror and disband their troops.' Humans are slow learners. Since that prediction, there have been two world wars and the invention of nuclear weapons – and countries are still going to war.

A better way to avoid war is not so much to make war unattractive – because that is not a deterrent – but to make peace as attractive as possible. Thus countries need to see that they can gain far more from peace than from war. This links the development of a culture of peace into other UN work on international economic and social co-operation.

Additionally, countries which have simmering disputes, for example over boundaries, should be encouraged to have their own bilateral arrangements, such as developing projects for mutual gain in response to natural disasters like floods or famines. They could also have student exchange schemes and joint research projects. In other words, rather than attempt to deal with their disputes directly, the disputes should be put to one side and instead there should be co-operation on common threats. This united focus on a common problem will create a climate

---

37. Bert Roling, 'The Historical Perspective', in Thee, op. cit., p. 69.

of trust so that simmering disputes can be tackled later in a more tranquil environment.

To conclude, UNESCO's work on creating a culture of peace is a massive undertaking. It will result in the eventual replacement of one dominant culture, that of violence, with another. A good omen for UNESCO's work is that community groups and even parts of the mass media are questioning the current culture of violence and are looking for alternatives. Thus UNESCO is able to set a lead in this work. In due course, its work on creating a culture of peace will no doubt be seen as having been as important as its pioneering work against racism.

Towards a culture of peace based on human rights

*Marek Thee**

THE CONCEPT OF A CULTURE OF PEACE

A 'culture of peace' is a value-loaded, highly demanding concept. The amalgam of the notion of culture with the idea of peace, with equal emphasis on both, confers on the concept particular import and intensity. Indeed, it induces a sense of conscientious virtue and rightfulness. Given today's international environment, marked as it is by insecurity, conflict, socio-economic turbulence and militarization, the vision of a culture of peace presents a challenge, calling for redress and innovation in human affairs. There is a need to infuse into society and international relations higher standards of ethical/moral behaviour, human understanding and empathy, all aiming at peaceful co-operation and the improvement of the human condition.

In the context of the acute 'peacelessness' which surrounds us and the striving for amiable peaceful relations among nations, the achieving of a culture of peace acquires singular urgency. Inherent in this goal is a human-oriented

---

* Marek Thee is Senior Research Fellow of the Norwegian Institute of Human Rights. He was previously Senior Research Fellow of the International Peace Research Institute, Oslo (PRIO), as well as founder and editor of the quarterly peace research journal, *Bulletin of Peace Proposals* (1969–1988), published by PRIO.

The author would like to thank Asbjørn Eide, Donna Gomien, Tore Lindholm and Bård-Anders Andreassen of the Norwegian Institute of Human Rights for helpful comments on the draft; the final version of the paper remains his own responsibility.

ethos of freedom, non-violence and mutual respect. A culture of peace should be capable of mobilizing people and serving as a material force for progressive change.

The quest for a sound culture of peace requires, then, that we repudiate those power relation structures, national and international, which rest on the use of violence and, as such, are pregnant with conflict and war. We must aim at the abolition of war and of power relations based on violence, and strive instead for a peaceful settlement of conflicts and an environment of mutual understanding and common security.

A culture of peace requires an expanded conceptualization of peace, above and beyond the 'negative' meaning of absence of war and armed conflict. It needs to encompass the 'positive' values of non-violence and social justice, striving to meet basic human needs. In this perspective peace appears as the proviso for life itself.

The concomitant of culture embodies the sum total of human civilizational achievements in all creative fields of art and science integrated with human values, institutions, attitudes, customs, ways of life and behaviour, joined with a civic consciousness disposed to co-operation, and placed in the service of human advancement.

Culture is historically and situationally conditioned. It reflects a multidirectional process, nationally and internationally, with components liable to produce divergent results, both constructive and destructive. Each culture tends to develop its own ethical norms. By a culture of peace, we envisage the blossoming of all that is good in the human being, all that cares for human life and upholds the ethos of human fulfilment. Of paramount importance within these values are the ethical dimension and a sense of moral judgement.

At the opposite pole, we find a sombre culture, sociopolitically infiltrated by violence, by a *Realpolitik*-militaristic and hegemonic way of thinking which treats peace in an expedient, instrumental way, with war, in the Clausewitzian mode, envisaged as a continuation of politics by other means. This orientation gives rise to a state of mind which professes the virtue of armaments, fighting and soldiering, as well as all sorts of military deterrence strategies (preparation for war), as a prudent implementation of security postures, with no cognition that throughout history arms races have in fact generated conflict and war.

There exists, then, in international relations today a tension between an enlightened and altruistic culture of peace on the one hand, and on the other, a 'peaceless culture' which begets human estrangement, hatred and enmity among peoples and nations: a destructive penchant to pathologies of domination, militarism, ethnocentrism and xenophobia.

The result is a morality gap which is utterly harmful and calls for the activation of 'defences of peace in the minds of men', as envisaged in the UNESCO Constitution. A persistent educational effort is required to bring about change, to make a culture of peace work for global humane transformation. For such a commitment, human rights may serve as a norm-setting guide, a pointer for the progression of a global culture of peace providing a framework for a new, just and peaceful world order.

A CULTURE OF PEACE AND HUMAN RIGHTS

No international charter or political-philosophical tenets can mirror the spirit of a culture of peace and serve its purpose better than the juridical foundation of human rights. Particularly relevant here are three dimensions of human rights:

1. Instruments, such as conventions, declarations, UN General Assembly resolutions, principles, guidelines, rules and recommendations defining civil and political freedoms, setting norms of civilized human behaviour; asserting generic standards of non-discrimination and making it illegal to practise degrading treatment on fellow human beings or to discriminate on grounds of race, colour, ethnicity, sex, language, religion, political opinion or social origin. Essentially, these provisions boil down to the civil freedom tenets of democracy with their general outlines inscribed in human rights instruments.
2. The socio-economic provisions enumerated in human rights instruments concerned with welfare and freedom from want, which are a precondition for the full enjoyment of a life in dignity and for the harmonious and non-violent development of society, nationally and internationally.
3. Solidarity rights concerned with freedom from want and from fear. On the one hand, they proclaim the right to development aimed at overcoming acute socio-economic global disparities between developed and developing nations, with the human being as the central subject of development. On the other

hand is the crucial assertion of the basic human right to peace, calling for demilitarization of international relations, and striving for a world free from the scourge of war and caring for human security.

All of these human rights are closely interrelated, indivisible and interdependent. As a whole, human rights offer a comprehensive legal framework for the establishment of a cultural climate favourable to the creation of a stable peace, the democratization of national and international relations and human well-being. Essentially, human rights are about human dignity, integrity and emancipation, and a conscientious and desirable future in freedom, justice and peace.

Rooted in the enlightenment and modernization of recent centuries, human rights emerged after the Second World War as a result of revulsion against the barbarity of war. Their basis was the tenet that, as stated in the Preamble to the Universal Declaration of Human Rights, 'recognition of the inherent dignity and of the equal and inalienable rights of all members of the human family is the foundation of freedom, justice and peace in the world'.[1]

Violations of human rights are still frequent in all corners of the globe. Also, many provisions inscribed in human rights instruments lack tangible substantial formulation and are often vague and diffuse. This is particularly true of economic, social and cultural rights. A basic deficiency of most of the instruments is the

---

1. The United Nations Charter of Human Rights comprises the International Bill of Human Rights encompassing the 1948 Universal Declaration of Human Rights and the 1966 International Covenant on Civil and Political Rights and the 1966 International Covenant on Economic, Social and Cultural Rights, complemented later by a number of United Nations Conventions, Declarations and Recommendations. They cover the right to self-determination; the prevention of racial discrimination; the rights of persons belonging to national or ethnic, religious and linguistic minorities; the rights of women; the rights of the child; human rights in the administration of justice; the right to freedom of information, to social welfare; and humanitarian law, etc. These international human rights instruments are complemented by regional instruments of the Council of Europe, the Organization of American States, the Organization of African Unity and the Organization of Security and Co-operation in Europe. For texts of human rights instruments, see *Human Rights: A Compilation of International Instruments*, New York, United Nations, 1993.

lack of mechanisms providing for complaints by victims of violations of their rights and for appropriate redress. In addition, many human rights provisions are not inscribed in state legislation. Full institutionalization of human rights would seem to be a protracted process. Vague political commitments need to be transformed into legal obligations. Thus, as much as human rights are visionary and norm-setting, they still remain in the domain of aspiration. Much effort is required to make them truly universally respected and to establish a statutorily binding culture of peace.

A CULTURE OF PEACE AND ITS INTERFACE WITH DEMOCRACY

There is a close affinity between human rights and democracy. Indeed, respect for and observance of human rights lie at the core of a democratic system. They are the litmus tests of democracy. Likewise, genuine democracy must strive to enact and implement the provisions inscribed in human rights instruments. This refers to civil, political, economic, social and cultural rights, with particular emphasis on the rule of law and regard for the four basic freedoms: freedom of speech and belief as well as freedom from want and fear.

Adherence to the above rights, in theory and practice, forms the legal infrastructure of a culture of peace. Historical experience tells us that stable democracies, as opposed to non-democratic systems, have been the least inclined to go to war against each other.

Freedom of speech is central for a peaceful democratic course and the fruition of a culture of peace. Article 19(1) of the International Covenant on Civil and Political Rights emphasizes that 'everyone shall have the right to hold opinions without interference', including 'the right to freedom of expression' (Article 19(2)). This is then qualified in Article 20: '(1) Any propaganda for war shall be prohibited by law. (2) Any advocacy of national, racial or religious hatred that constitutes incitement to discrimination, hostility or violence shall be prohibited by law.'

It is the general climate of a democratic society which promotes the values of a culture of peace, internally and externally. Democracy means popular sovereignty, with the government accountable to the people through regular elections. As laid down in Article 21(3) of the Universal Declaration of Human Rights: 'The will of the people shall be the basis of the authority of government; this will shall be expressed in periodic and genuine elections which shall be by universal and equal suffrage and shall be held by secret vote or by equivalent free voting procedures.' This assumes majority rule whether the electoral system is based on majoritarian plurality or proportional representation. On the other hand, the stress on individual freedom and on protection of minorities rules out arbitrary and authoritarian majority governance. It presupposes consent and willingness to tolerance and compromise.

Concerning individual rights, Article 3 of the Universal Declaration of Human Rights stipulates that 'everyone has the right to life, liberty and security of person'. Consequently, 'All persons are equal before the law and are entitled without any discrimination to the equal protection of law. . . .' (Article 26 of the International Covenant on Civil and Political Rights). Furthermore, 'Everyone is entitled in full equality to a fair and public hearing by an independent and impartial tribunal, in the determination of his rights and obligations and of any criminal charge against him' (Article 10 of the Universal Declaration).

The gist of these provisions is the paramountcy of the rule of law, as indicated by the 1993 World Conference on Human Rights.[2] This means that the law is above politics and that the administration has strictly to abide by existing laws with an inbuilt system of checks and balances based on impartial and independent courts. A precondition for such a system is a clear division of power between the legislature, the executive and the judiciary.

However, comprehensive democracy is more than freedom of thought and conscience, freedom of peaceful assembly and freedom of association, or all the other civil and political rights dominated by the primacy of the rule of law. Human rights are equally concerned with the material socio-economic conditions of humanity as a crucial composite part of loving and peaceful behaviour. Thus, the Universal Declaration also provides for social security (Article 22), the right to work (Article 23), the right to rest and leisure (Article 24), the right to an

---

2. See pp. 27, 34 and 67 of the *Vienna Declaration and Programme of Action, World Conference on Human Rights, June 1993,* New York, UN Department of Public Information, 1993.

adequate standard of living and well-being (Article 25), the right to education (Article 26), the right to participate freely in the cultural life of the community (Article 27) and the right to a social and international order in which all freedoms set forth in the Universal Declaration can be fully realized (Article 28).

Today, these socio-economic conditions of human rights remain aspirational and promotional. For lack of resources and follow-up, they are rarely fully adhered to, even in democratic societies. All the same, they remain objectives which are vital for a life in dignity based on freedom from want. Concern about satisfaction of basic human needs is also a prerequisite for effectively shaping a culture of peace.

The founders of human rights were well aware of the difficulties in early and universal implementation of their provisions. They foresaw therefore contingencies which could allow derogation from certain human rights obligations, with the qualification of 'meeting the just requirements of morality, public order and the general welfare in a democratic society' (Article 29(2) of the Universal Declaration). Thus, as indicated by Torkel Opsahl, 'the universality of human rights yields to national standards'.[3]

Thus, in perusing human rights instruments we may, on the one hand, feel comfortable in many instances about their moral and constitutional legal force but, on the other, we may also be aware of the rather visionary aspect of other provisions, far from being practised in today's international society. Both the binding legal provisions and those still awaiting material embodiment serve intrinsically as a beacon for democratic transformation and for the achievement of a human-rights-based culture of peace.

HUMAN RIGHTS AND POSITIVE PEACE

Seen from the perspective of the vision of a culture of peace, prominent in human rights thought are elements of a positive peace theory focused on social development, social justice and human advancement. The positive conception

---

3. Torkel Opsahl, 'Articles 29 and 30: The Other Side of the Coin', in Asbjørn Eide et al. (ed.), *The Universal Declaration of Human Rights. A Commentary,* p. 460, Oslo, Scandinavian University Press, 1992.

of peace perceives an organic linkage between intranational and international violence, and seeks to eliminate the seeds of 'peacelessness' and tension pregnant with conflict. Central in this respect is the International Covenant on Economic, Social and Cultural Rights.

In human rights theory, civil and political rights on the one hand, and economic, social and cultural rights on the other, are equally important: they are indivisible, closely interrelated and interdependent. The International Covenant on Economic, Social and Cultural Rights is an integral part of human rights law, dealing specifically with the promotion of welfare in society. Following the Universal Declaration of Human Rights, this Covenant recognizes the right of everyone to work (Article 6), the right of everyone to the enjoyment of just and favourable conditions of work (Article 7), the right to form and join trade unions, including the right to strike (Article 8), the right of everyone to social security, including social insurance (Article 9), the right to 'the widest possible protection and assistance' to the family, with special protection for mothers and children (Article 10), the right of everyone to an adequate standard of living for himself and his family, including adequate food, clothing, housing, and the continuous improving of living conditions (Article 11), the right of everyone to the enjoyment of the highest attainable standard of physical and mental health (Article 12), the right of everyone to education (Articles 13 and 14) and, finally, the right of everyone to take part in cultural life and enjoy the benefits of scientific progress (Article 15).

Although the above rights are laid down in terms of individual freedoms, they pertain to the collectivity of the human family. In this sense, almost all human rights which denote the individual as the ultimate bearer of the rights actually hold good for the society as a whole.

A specific feature of the International Covenant on Economic, Social and Cultural Rights is its idealistic and imaginative wording, without concrete modalities of implementation. The term 'right' is generally interpreted not as an immediate material obligation of the state but rather as creating opportunities for making use of these rights: a diffused hope. As opposed to the International Covenant on Civil and Political Rights, the International Covenant on Economic, Social and Cultural Rights does not provide for procedures for legal complaints against the violation of its provisions and for appropriate remedies.[4] The wording of the International Covenant on Economic, Social and Cultural Rights is weak and ambivalent. It reflects a penchant for 'negative' rather than 'positive' peace. Too often the obligations of this Covenant are largely ignored.[5]

Human rights advocates are concerned with infusing greater vigour and intelligibility into the International Covenant on Economic, Social and Cultural Rights provisions, and with empowering the victims of their violation. This problem has two aspects: on the one hand, many countries, especially developing nations, lack resources to set up a welfare system as foreseen by the Covenant; on the other hand, conservative forces, even in developed democratic states, resist the full implementation of the provisions of the Covenant for ideological reasons. Although, by June 1994, the Covenant had been ratified by 117 states, neither China nor the United States[6] have ratified it. It remains a reality that the Covenant is one of the least honoured instruments in the field of human rights.

The difficulties in implementing the International Covenant on Economic, Social and Cultural Rights were evident when it was formulated. Thus Article 2 provides that:

Each State Party to the present Covenant undertakes to take steps, individually and through international assistance and co-operation, especially economic and technical, to the maximum of its available resources, with a view to achieving progressively the full realization of the rights recognized in the present Covenant by all appropriate means, including particularly the adoption of legislative measures.

Emphasis here is on the expressions 'to the maximum of its available resources' and 'to take steps individually and through international assistance and

---

4. See Philip Alston, 'No Right to Complain about Being Poor: The Need for an Optional Protocol to the Economic Rights Covenant', in Asbjørn Eide and Jan Helgesen (eds.), *The Future of Human Rights Protection in a Changing World, Essays in Honour of Torkel Opsahl,* pp. 79–100, Oslo, Norwegian University Press, 1991.
5. See Rolf Künnemann, 'A Coherent Approach to Human Rights', *Human Rights Quarterly,* Vol. 17, 1995, pp. 323–42.
6. See United Nations, *Human Rights: International Instruments, Chart of Ratifications as of 30 June 1994,* New York/Geneva, United Nations, 1994.

co-operation'. This wording acquires special meaning in a world where more than a quarter of the population does not get enough food, and nearly one billion go hungry and suffer from absolute poverty.[7] Individual steps in these circumstances, especially in developing countries, can only be very modest, while resources from international assistance and co-operation are far from meeting even the most minimal needs.

In this context, the concerned voices of human rights lawyers can be heard saying that, in the meantime, until a start can be made in the effective realization of the International Covenant on Economic, Social and Cultural Rights, 'particular attention should be given to measures to improve the standard of living of the poor and the disadvantaged groups'.[8] Others have suggested country-specific 'minimum threshold approaches' to narrow the problem of distributive justice to socially guaranteed minimum levels of goods and benefits such as food, shelter and education.[9]

The state of affairs regarding the implementation of the International Covenant on Economic, Social and Cultural Rights indicates the essential limitations and inadequacy of human rights legislation in covering rights related to the positive conception of peace. It also points to the daunting tasks to be accomplished and the distances to be covered in the human rights domain, if we are to arrive at a genuine, humane culture of peace. Human welfare, as posited by the Covenant, is clearly an essential component of such a culture.

---

7. See *Human Development Report 1994*, New York/Oxford, United Nations Development Programme, 1994.
8. See *The Limburg Principles on the Implementation of the International Covenant on Economic, Social and Cultural Rights*. (UN Economic and Social Council Document, E/CN.4/1987/17 of 8 January 1987.)
9. See Bård-Anders Andreassen, 'Compliance with Economic and Social Human Rights: Realistic Evaluations and Monitoring in the Light of Immediate Obligations', in Asbjørn Eide and Bernt Hagtvet (eds.), *Human Rights in Perspective: A Global Assessment*, pp. 252–67, Oxford, Blackwell, 1992.

THE RIGHT TO DEVELOPMENT

Akin to the International Covenant on Economic, Social and Cultural Rights is the 1986 UN General Assembly Declaration on the Right to Development. This declaration *par excellence* addresses the predicaments of developing countries and specifies remedies needed to overcome them. It denotes a solidarity right, essentially foreseeing strategies for implementing positive peace, applied internationally with particular consideration of the plight of peoples in developing countries. It marks a plea for sustainable development.

In its Preamble, the Declaration envisages development as 'a comprehensive economic, social, cultural and political process, which aims at the constant improvement of the well-being of the entire population and of all individuals on the basis of their active, free and meaningful participation in development and in the fair distribution of benefits resulting therefrom'.

The Preamble further recalls 'the right of peoples to self-determination, by virtue of which they have the right freely to determine their political status and to pursue their economic, social and cultural development'. This is a reminder that the right to self-determination has both external and internal aspects, meaning also the right democratically to shape in freedom their internal economic-political system.

There is emphasis on the interrelationship between development and peace among nations. The Preamble notes: 'International peace and security are essential elements for the realization of the right to development.' Hence the need for disarmament, meaning 'general and complete disarmament under effective international control' (Article 6), with resources released through disarmament measures to be devoted 'to the economic and social development and well-being of all peoples and, in particular, those of the developing countries' (Preamble). A definite goal is the establishment of a new international economic order, 'based on sovereign equality, interdependence, mutual interest and co-operation among all States' (Article 3(3)).

Here we may recall efforts to make the disarmament/development linkage work, in accordance with the above provisions of the right to development. Sadly, the first initiative in this domain was wrecked.

In 1982 a Group of Governmental Experts appointed by the UN Secretary-

General, in its report entitled *The Relationship between Disarmament and Development*, concluded that 'an effective relationship between disarmament and development can and must be established',[10] recommending that 'further considerations be given to establishing an international disarmament fund for development (IDFD)'.[11] The 1982 UN General Assembly then mandated the United Nations Institute for Disarmament Research (UNIDIR) to elaborate modalities for the operation of an IDFD. In its detailed report to the UN General Assembly in 1984, UNIDIR took a most positive stand, concluding that 'the establishment of a disarmament fund for development is desirable as a means of giving tangible expression to the recognized link between disarmament and development and starting the process of transferring to development the resources that are allocated to armaments'.[12] However, in the climate of the Cold War and North-South stratification, the 1987 UN International Conference on the Relationship between Disarmament and Development dropped the idea of an IDFD from its agenda. Finally the whole project was aborted.[13]

Of even greater importance were the efforts of concerned scholars, like those participating in the Pugwash Conferences, to bring about the redeployment of substantial parts of research and development (R&D) resources from military to civilian purposes. Available data estimated that, by early 1990, out of 5.7 million persons engaged globally in R&D, some 1.5 million were working for military R&D, including at least 1 million scientists and engineers with full academic degrees.[14] Obviously, the redeployment of thousands of the best qualified scientists and engineers from armaments to serve human needs could mean a decisive

---

10. United Nations Centre for Disarmament, *The Relationship between Disarmament and Development*, p. 154, para. 391, United Nations, New York, 1982.
11. Ibid., p. 169, para. 426(7).
12. *Establishment of an International Disarmament Fund for Development*, p. 32, para. 47(a), Geneva, United Nations Institute for Disarmament Research, 1984.
13. See Marek Thee, 'The Quest for the Reallocation of Resources from Disarmament to Development: In Pursuit of Tangible Peace Dividends', *The Journal of East and West Studies*, Vol. 22, No. 1, 1993, pp. 45–52.
14. See Marek Thee, *Science and Technology: Between Civilian and Military Research and Development. Armaments and Development at Variance*, United Nations, New York, 1990. (United Nations Institute for Disarmament Research, Research Paper No. 7.)

contribution to solving many urgent problems of development. It could act to increase productivity in industry and agriculture, to advance health care and biosciences, to improve the quality of the environment, to generate alternative sources of energy, to reduce the developmental disparities between rich and poor countries. It could perceptibly and substantially improve human development. Unfortunately, as pointed out in the following section on the exercise of the right to peace, no visible progress has been made in this domain.

Repeatedly, the Declaration on the Right to Development stresses the requirement of international economic assistance for developing countries. Article 4(2) states: 'Sustained action is required to promote more rapid development of developing countries. As a complement to the efforts of developing countries, effective international co-operation is essential in providing these countries with appropriate means and facilities to foster the comprehensive development.'

International aid must go hand in hand with efforts on the national level, adhering to principles of social justice and non-discrimination. As indicated in Article 8:

States should undertake, at the national level, all necessary measures for the realization of the right to development and shall ensure, *inter alia*, equality of opportunity for all in their access to basic resources, education, health services, food, housing, employment and the fair distribution of income. Effective measures should be undertaken to ensure that women have an active role in the development process. Appropriate economic and social reforms should be carried out with a view to eradicating all social injustices.

Beyond the call for overcoming the socio-economic global divide, the right to development, as a solidarity right, also has normative importance in human rights theory. It pertains to the conceptualization and comprehension of human rights themselves. Basically, as reflected in the wording of the Universal Declaration of Human Rights and other human rights instruments inspired by the Western world-view, human rights are perceived as individually centred, pertaining inherently to the freedoms and dignity of the individual. Yet the right to development, while stressing that 'the human person is the central subject of the development process' (Preamble) also has, following the perception of Third

World countries, a clear collective tone. It stresses the need for the constant improvement of the well-being of the entire population and of all peoples. The beneficiaries of this right are meant to be all nations of the world, particularly the developing countries. Also the call for disarmament, with resources thereby released devoted to the economic and social development of all peoples, has national and international resonance.

Problems of the right to development, with demands for equitable international economic relations and the immediate alleviation of extreme poverty in developing countries, were prominent in the June 1993 World Conference on Human Rights.[15] The Vienna Declaration and Programme of Action, adopted by the Conference, attaches particular importance to implementation of the right to development. It calls on the thematic Working Group on the right to development appointed by the UN Commission on Human Rights to 'promptly formulate for early consideration by the United Nations General Assembly, comprehensive and effective measures to eliminate obstacles to the implementation and realization of the Declaration on the Right to Development and recommending ways and means towards the realization of the right to development by all States'.[16]

Although the Declaration on the Right to Development has no legally binding force, its message concerning moral solidarity is compelling. It underlines the awareness of dangers to the whole world community inherent in the global socio-economic divide. It embodies the urge for freedom from fear, and reflects in an exemplary way the role of human rights as a promotional force for peace and for a culture of peace.

THE RIGHT TO PEACE

The right to peace was proclaimed by the 1984 UN General Assembly Declaration on the Right of Peoples to Peace. This is perhaps one of the briefest human rights instruments, but nevertheless one of the most notable, as it pertains

---

15. See *World Conference on Human Rights: The Vienna Declaration and Programme of Action, June 1993*, pp. 25–71, New York, UN Department of Public Information, 1993.
16. Ibid., Part II, p. 72.

to the crux of freedom from fear and of human survival in an overarmed world. It is a solidarity right, voicing alarm on the dangers to humanity caused by armament, the spread of weapons of mass destruction, perennial armed conflicts and constant preparation for large-scale war.

In its Preamble the Declaration expresses 'the will and the aspiration of all peoples to eradicate war from the life of mankind and, above all, to avert a worldwide nuclear catastrophe'. Further, that 'in the nuclear age the establishment of a lasting peace on Earth represents the primary condition for the preservation of human civilization and the survival of mankind'.

In Article 1 the Declaration 'solemnly proclaims that the peoples of our planet have a sacred right to peace'; and further 'emphasizes that ensuring the exercise of the right of peoples to peace demands that the policies of the states be directed towards the elimination of the threat of war, particularly nuclear war, the renunciation of the use of force in international relations and the settlement of international disputes by peaceful means on the basis of the Charter of the United Nations' (Article 3).

Intimately linked with the right to peace is the 'inherent right to life', as inscribed in Article 6 of the International Covenant on Civil and Political Rights. Commenting on the right to life, the Human Rights Committee mandated to critically consider the observation of the International Covenant on Civil and Political Rights noted:

It is a right which should not be interpreted narrowly. . . . The Committee observes that war and other acts of mass violence continue to be a scourge of humanity and take the lives of thousands of innocent human beings every year. . . . The Committee considers that States have the supreme duty to prevent wars, acts of genocide and other acts of mass violation causing arbitrary loss of life. Every effort they make to avert the danger of war, especially thermo-nuclear war, and to strengthen international peace and security would constitute the most important condition and guarantee of the right to life.[17]

---

17. Manfred Nowak, *UN Covenant on Civil and Political Rights: CCPR Commentary*, p. 851, Strasbourg, N. P. Engel, 1993.

These reflect supreme concern about the fate of mankind. Bearing in mind this declaration, the Human Rights Committee draws particular attention to the peril of the stockpiling and development of nuclear weapons which could lead to nuclear catastrophe.

We all need to be reminded of this sword of Damocles hanging over mankind. With the end of the Cold War, our general awareness of the global vulnerability regarding nuclear weapons has diminished. Yet the doomsday legacy of the nuclear arms race, the stockpiling of nuclear weapons, their proliferation and further modernization, are still with us.

Here we should note the efforts to arrive at a comprehensive nuclear test ban (CTB), specifically meaning the cessation of underground nuclear testing. A CTB would be a step in the right direction and would create some barriers to further nuclear weapon development and modernization, including the increase in the number of new nuclear-weapon states. Yet, with nuclear weapon technology now reaching out beyond underground testing, it would not mean a standstill in nuclear modernization or global denuclearization.

As the major nuclear-weapon states have repeatedly stressed, they do not intend to relinquish their nuclear stockpiles, accepting to eliminate only those surplus obsolete classes agreed under the Strategic Arms Limitations Talks (SALT).[18] Thus, in the military mind, nuclear weapons are still perceived as useful and required for defence-offence purposes, under the name of legitimate nuclear deterrence.[19]

As long as the major powers see nuclear weapons as necessary and useful for defence and war, weaker states will strive to follow suit and acquire nuclear capability as a shield against stronger neighbours or pressures from great

---

18. As of the end of 1994 it has been estimated that the USA and Russia have each an active arsenal of 7,000 to 9,500 nuclear weapons. See R. Jeffrey Smith, 'U.S. and Russia to Trade Nuclear Arms Secrets', *International Herald Tribune*, 23 December 1994, p. 3.
19. One example of the nuclear deterrence mentality and the continued reliance on nuclear weapons by the major powers is the prolongation in 1994 until the year 2004 of the US–United Kingdom agreement on 'Co-operation on the Uses of Atomic Energy for Mutual Defense Purposes', *Trust and Verify*, No. 52, November 1994, p. 1.

powers. Nuclear proliferation remains a compelling *raison d'être* for a militarized world.[20]

Moreover, a CTB would not be able to halt nuclear development and modernization, as technologies are developing which enable one to bypass underground testing and to continue nuclear military advances through laboratory testing.[21]

New nuclear testing technology is in line with the general trend in nuclear weapon modernization to replace the unwieldy nuclear Behemoth of the Cold War by new generations of compact, highly accurate and deliverable mini- and micro-nuclear arms which cause lesser collateral damage but are more flexible, together with a trend towards 'conventional' use even in local low-intensity engagements.

Here we should also note that the nuclear danger is only the most conspicuous element of current armaments. Despite the end of the Cold War, the production and trade in conventional weapons has not ceased. Cutthroat competition has developed between the major powers and weapon producers to deliver these arms to almost all corners of the world.

As never before, solidarity rights, the right to peace, as linked with the right to development calling for general and complete disarmament (GCD), have acquired an importance which is critical to ensuring a transition from a war system to a peace system, from military to political solutions in human affairs. It promises authentic freedom from fear.

Denuclearization, the implementation of GCD and demilitarization of international relations remain the supreme goals in the quest to exercise the solidarity right to peace.[22] Embracing the whole of mankind, they call into

---

20. The case of Iraq is a striking example of the possibility of evading control and trying in secrecy to develop nuclear arms.
21. A comparison can be made with the circumstances which led to the Partial Test Ban Treaty (PTBT) in 1963. Under the pressure of public opinion, which protested against pollution injurious to health caused by nuclear testing in the atmosphere, the PTBT prohibited such tests. But the major powers consented to the PTBT only after mastering the technology of underground nuclear testing. Testing simply moved underground, becoming even more intense.
22. See Robert S. McNamara, 'A Long-Range Policy for Nuclear Forces of the Nuclear

play the whole array of human rights and are essential to a functional human rights regime.[23] This is synonymous with a civilized, law-based culture of peace.[24]

CULTURE OF PEACE: DIVERSITY AND UNIVERSALITY

In the above, we focused on the exercise of solidarity rights, the right to development and the right to peace. In the post-Cold War era, their realization becomes crucial to a civilized, tolerant and just new world order based on respect for human rights and organically linked to a global culture of peace.

Globalization of a culture of peace thus presumes the universality of the human rights canons. As outlined in the Preamble to the Universal Declaration of Human Rights, human rights norms have been proclaimed 'as the common standard of achievements for all peoples and for all nations'. The Universal Declaration further mandates that every individual and every organ of society 'shall strive by teaching and education to promote respect for these rights and freedoms . . . to secure their universal and effective recognition and observance'.

While accepting in good faith the universality of human rights as a point of departure, we must also remain attentive to the diversity of civilizational/cultural world-views and behaviours – regional, ethnic, national and religious – within the family of peoples and nations. The heterogeneity in beliefs and conduct can be understood, beginning with simple temperamental bearing to more complex conceptions of rights and duties towards family, society and the realms of work and labour. This world of ideas and mental images is rooted in dissimilarities of life experience, languages, traditions and habits. The political deployment of

---

Powers', *Pugwash Newsletter,* October 1994/January 1995, pp. 138–43, with the call 'to move back to a non-nuclear world'.
23. See Marek Thee, 'Demilitarizing International Relations and the Quest for a Human Rights Regime', *Proceedings of the Forty-Second Pugwash Conferences on Science and World Affairs,* Vol. II, Singapore/New Jersey/London/Hong Kong, pp. 572–8, World Scientific, 1994.
24. See Marek Thee, 'Arms Reduction and Global Reconstruction: A Blueprint for the Year 2000', *Journal of East and West Studies,* Vol. 23, No. 1, 1994, pp. 123–8.

cultural differences has too often led to conflict and war. Cultural diversity is a historical reality of our world.

The universalization and transnationalization of human rights, intertwined with a culture of peace, makes it imperative to recognize and appreciate cultural plurality. This should be seen as a source of spiritual and civilizational enrichment with a unity of purpose, brought about by mutual understanding and a will to achieve the good of all peoples and nations. In the process, greater convergence towards a culture of peace may unfold.

This process will be enriched by the adoption of new ideas and ways of thinking, and stimulated by the globalization of the economy, the interdependence of new civilizational adventures, the ongoing worldwide technological revolution, the explosion of informatics and the thrust of high-speed intercontinental transport. Historically, there is a close linkage between changes in economic and existential conditions of life and superstructural, spiritual, intellectual and emotional values. However, we must be alert lest new technological demons prevail over humane aspirations. We must heed carefully the Universal Declaration of Human Rights command to pay prime attention to teaching and education for human rights, thereby promoting a global culture of peace.

National and international peace becomes in this endeavour a unifying force. It corresponds to the ethical and moral creeds and commands of almost all world religions and humane values. It also meets the essentials of the solidarity rights which perceive lasting peace on Earth, in the words of the Declaration on the Rights of Peoples to Peace, as 'the primary condition for the preservation of civilization' and a 'primary international prerequisite for the material well-being, development and progress of mankind'. Genuine peace is thus a beneficial force for human development and positive societal transformation.

To all this, one may rightly object that a global culture of peace seems Utopian, a tall order indeed. In the end, the decisive factor may well be the commitment and perseverance of the peoples and nations on our Earth to make the dream come true.

BIBLIOGRAPHY

1. Documents and studies

BROWNLIE, I. (ed.). 1992. *Basic Documents on Human Rights.* 3rd ed. London, Clarendon Press.

CENTRE FOR HUMAN RIGHTS, GENEVA. 1993. *Human Rights: A Compilation of International Instruments,* Vol. 1 (1-2): *Universal Instruments.* New York, United Nations.

COUNCIL OF EUROPE. 1992. *Human Rights in International Law.* Strasbourg, Council of Europe Press.

UNITED NATIONS. Reports from the preparatory regional meetings in Tunis, San José (Costa Rica) and Bangkok, prior to the 1933 World Conference on Human Rights. (A/Conf/PC/57 of 24 November 1992; A/Conf/PC/58 of 11 February 1993; and A/Conf/PC/59 of 7 April 1993.)

UNITED NATIONS DEPARTMENT OF PUBLIC INFORMATION. 1993. *World Conference on Human Rights: The Vienna Declaration and Programme of Action, June 1993.* New York, United Nations.

2. Books and papers

ALGER, C.; STOHL, M. (eds.). 1988. *A Just Peace through Transformation: Cultural, Economic and Political Foundations for Change.* Boulder, Colo., Westview.

ALSTON, P. (ed.). 1992. *The United Nations and Human Rights: A Critical Appraisal.* London, Clarendon.

BERTING, J., et al. (eds.). 1990. *Human Rights in a Pluralist World.* London, Meckler.

BOULDING, K. E. 1978. *Stable Peace.* Austin, University of Texas Press.

BRANDT, W. 1987. *Arms and Hunger.* Cambridge, Mass., MIT Press.

BRUNDTLAND, G. H. 1993. Peace, Democracy, Environment and Development. In: G. Lundestad and O. A. Westad (eds.), *Beyond the Cold War: New Dimensions in International Relations.* Stockholm, Scandinavian University Press, pp. 189–94.

CLAPHAM, A. 1991. *Human Rights and the European Community: A Critical Overview.* Baden-Baden, Nomos.

CLAUDE, R. P.; WESTON, B., H. (eds.). 1992. *Human Rights in the World Community: Issues and Action.* Philadelphia, Pa., University of Pennsylvania Press.

COUNCIL OF EUROPE AND THE INTERNATIONAL INSTITUTE OF HUMAN RIGHTS. 1990. *Universality of Human Rights in a Pluralistic World.* Strasbourg, N. P. Engel.

COUSINS, N. 1987. *The Pathology of Power.* New York, Norton.
DUMAS, L. J.; THEE, M. (eds.). 1989. *Making Peace Possible: The Promise of Economic Conversion.* Oxford, Pergamon.
EIDE, A., et al. (eds.). 1992. *The Universal Declaration of Human Rights: A Commentary.* Stockholm, Scandinavian University Press.
EIDE, A.; HAGTVET, B. (eds.). 1992. *Human Rights in Perspective: A Global Assessment.* London, Blackwell.
EIDE, A.; HELGESEN, J. (eds.). 1991. *The Future of Human Rights Protection in a Changing World.* Oslo, Norwegian University Press. (Essays in Honour of Torkel Opsahl.)
EIDE, A.; KRAUSE, C.; ROSAS, A. (eds.). 1995. *Economic, Social and Cultural Rights.* Dordrecht, Martinus Nijhoff.
EIDE, A.; THEE, M. (eds.). 1983. *Frontiers of Human Rights Education.* Oslo, Norwegian University Press.
FALH, R. A.; MENDLOWITZ, S. H. (eds.). 1966. *The Strategy of World Order, Disarmament and Economic Development.* New York, World Law Fund.
FISHER, G. (ed.). 1985. *Armement – développement – droits de l'homme – désarmement.* Paris, Faculté de Droit de l'Université René Descartes.
GALTUNG, J. 1969. Violence, Peace and Peace Research. *Journal of Peace Research,* Vol. 6, No. 3, pp. 167–91.
GLEDITSCH, N. P.; NJØLSTAD, O. (eds.). 1990. *Arms Races: Technological and Political Dynamics.* London, Sage.
GOMIEN, D. (ed.). 1993. *Broadening the Frontiers of Human Rights. Essays in Honour of Asbjørn Eide.* Stockholm, Scandinavian University Press.
INTERNATIONAL INSTITUTE OF PHILOSOPHY, PARIS. 1986. *Philosophical Foundations of Human Rights.* Paris, UNESCO.
KRIPPENDORF, E. (ed.). 1968. *Friedensforschung.* Cologne, Kiepenheuer & Witsch.
KUTUKDJIAN, G. B.; PAPISCA, A. (eds.). 1991. *Rights of Peoples.* Padua, CEDAM.
LERNER, N. 1991. *Group Rights and Discrimination in International Law.* Dordrecht, Martinus Nijhoff.
MAHONEY, K. E.; MAHONEY, P. (eds.). 1993. *Human Rights in the Twenty-first Century: A Global Challenge.* Dordrecht, Martinus Nijhoff.
MALLMANN, C. A.; NUDLER, O. (eds.). 1986. *Human Development in Its Social Context.* London, Hodder & Stoughton, United Nations University.
MELMAN, S. 1988. *The Demilitarized Society: Disarmament and Conversion.* Montreal, Harvest House.

ROTBLAT, J. (ed.). 1994. *Feasibility of a Nuclear-weapon-free World. Proceedings of the Forty-second Pugwash Conference on Science and World Affairs*, Vol. 1, pp. 349–59. London, World Scientific.

SAKAMOTO, Y. (ed.). 1987. *Strategic Doctrines and Their Alternatives.* New York/London, Breach Science Publications.

STOCKHOLM INITIATIVE ON GLOBAL SECURITY AND GOVERNANCE. 1991. *Common Responsibility in the 1990s.* Stockholm, Prime Minister's Office.

SUBRAHMANYAM, K. 1993. Nuclear Proliferation and Non-proliferation. In: G. Lundestad and O. A. Westad (eds.), *Beyond the Cold War: New Dimensions in International Relations*, pp. 57–70. Stockholm, Scandinavian University Press.

THEE, M. 1981. The Establishment of an International Disarmament Fund for Development: A Feasibility Study. *Bulletin of Peace Proposals*, Vol. 11, No. 1, pp. 53–100.

——. (ed.). 1981. *Armaments, Arms Control and Disarmament: A UNESCO Reader for Disarmament Education.* Paris, UNESCO.

——. 1986. *Military Technology, Military Strategy and the Arms Race.* London, Croom Helm in association with the United Nations University, Tokyo, the International Peace Research Institute, Oslo, and St Martin's Press, New York.

——. (ed.). 1987. *Preparation of Societies for Life in Peace.* Tokyo/Oslo, United Nations University/Norwegian University Press.

——. 1991. *Whatever Happened to the Peace Dividend? The Post-Cold War Armaments Momentum.* Nottingham, Spokesman for European Labour Forum.

——. 1993. The Philosophical-Existential Issues of the Human Rights Project: Challenges for the 21st Century. In: B.-A. Andreassen and T. Swinehart (eds.), *Human Rights in Developing Countries, Yearbook 1993*, pp. 1–19. Oslo, Nordic Human Rights Publications.

TOMASEVSKI, K. 1989. *Development Aid and Human Rights.* London, Pinter.

Towards a Nuclear Weapon Free and Non-Violent World. 1990. (Foreword by P. V. Narasimha Rao.) Delhi, Vikas Publications. 2 vols.

VÄYRINEN, R. (ed.). 1987. *The Quest for Peace: Transcending Collective Violence and War among Societies, Cultures and States.* London, Sage/International Social Science Council. (In collaboration with C. Schmidt.)

WESTON, B. H. (ed.). 1984. *Toward Nuclear Disarmament and Global Security: A Search for Alternatives.* Boulder, Colo., Westview.

YORK, H. F. 1987. *Making Weapons – Talking Peace.* New York, Basic Books.

UNESCO and a culture of peace: promoting a global movement

UNESCO's Culture of Peace Programme

INTRODUCTION

As we enter the twenty-first century, humanity faces unprecedented threats to its very existence. We first became aware of this through the nuclear confrontation and, today, we realize that this threat to our security is even broader, including the degradation of the earth's environment and its linkage to poverty, overpopulation, massive migrations, intolerance and the unequal distribution of resources in the world.

In the face of this challenge, people are responding by joining together in mobilizations of unprecedented size. We are familiar with them as global movements for disarmament, equitable and sustainable development, the environment, and the rights of women and indigenous peoples. They have been recognized by world conferences convened by the United Nations in Rio, Cairo, Vienna, Copenhagen and Beijing. A common theme runs through these movements – that all people are interdependent and that the right to a peaceful and fruitful existence, not only of all people, including future generations, but of all life on our planet, must be respected.

This is the historical context in which UNESCO launched its Culture of Peace Programme (CPP) in February 1994. After a little more than two years, we find that the theme of a culture of peace is being taken up by organizations around the world, as it becomes a global movement which links together all other movements for a peaceful future.

First, we will briefly consider UNESCO's Culture of Peace Programme.

This programme has been given the highest priority in UNESCO's strategy for the coming years. Its role is that of a catalyst, serving as an inspiration and initiator of key programmes and a centre for the exchange of information and ideas both within and beyond UNESCO.

Second, we will look at UNESCO and its related institutions. The Organization was founded in 1946 to build peace in the minds of men and women and was given responsibility in the United Nations family for education, science, culture and communication, the essential tools with which a culture of peace may be created. UNESCO works with partners at all levels throughout the world.

Third, we will consider the national culture of peace programmes in which UNESCO co-operates with the government and civil society in El Salvador, Mozambique and Burundi to put the theoretical concepts of a culture of peace into practice on a national scale.

In conclusion, we will consider the emergence of a global movement and vision of a culture of peace which unites the people working in the various social movements for peace and justice. Through its information and networking system the UNESCO Culture of Peace Programme invites everyone to join in contributing to this movement and providing the elements for its conception.

THE EVOLVING CONCEPT OF A CULTURE OF PEACE

The concept of a culture of peace is founded on the recognition of the values of peace and non-violence and the fundamental rights and freedoms of every person, as recognized in the Universal Declaration of Human Rights.

A culture of peace is not the absence of conflict. Given a world of rich diversity, conflict will continue to be part of life itself. Instead of fearing conflict we must learn to appreciate its non-violent aspects: courage, heroism, creativity, the redress of injustice.

A culture of peace is both a process and a vision for the future. It transforms and ultimately replaces a culture of war which has pervaded civilization since the beginning of history. Therefore a culture of peace is necessarily linked to a broad movement which replaces both war and its culture.

A culture of war has also served another function, a function 'in the minds of men', uniting people in solidarity against an enemy and inspiring acts of courage and heroism. A century ago the philosopher and psychologist William James argued that war would not be abolished until a substitute could be found for the psychological needs it fulfils, such as solidarity, audacity, comradeship, loyalty, courage, those qualities traditionally associated with the warrior. In his treatise, *The Moral Equivalent of War*, he argued for international sporting events such as the modern Olympics as a possible substitute.

It is UNESCO, charged with building 'the intellectual and moral solidarity of mankind', which plays the key role in intellectual leadership and the promotion of global solidarity for a culture of peace within the United Nations system. It is responsible for the modalities appropriate to this task: education, the media, cultural institutions, social sciences.

Power, in a culture of peace, grows not from the barrel of a gun but from participation, dialogue and co-operation. And in such a culture, its youth, both men and women, are not prepared to be military warriors but to be active participants in a world in which the differences among people are seen as a challenge for peace and a cause for celebration. Training in non-violence is a key to a culture of peace. Although a culture of peace is characterized by non-violence, it is not a passive but an active non-violence, as described by Mahatma Gandhi, Martin Luther King Jr. and Nelson Mandela. As they learned and taught, active non-violence requires great courage and strength to harness anger into struggle against injustice.

As women have been excluded from the power associated with a culture of war, their full participation and empowerment is essential to the development of a culture of peace. Women have a special stake in peace, because it was the monopolization of warfare by men from the beginning of history which reinforced their exclusion from the inner circles of power. Hence it is to be expected that women will play an ever-increasing role in the struggle for a culture of peace.

The elucidation of the concept of a culture of peace is one of the key tasks of UNESCO's Culture of Peace Programme. This development evolves as a result of practice and consultation, including a continuous dialogue within UNESCO and with its various partners. Of particular importance are the experiences of National Culture of Peace Programmes, those initiated both by UNESCO and by national governments themselves.

A number of forums have been organized by the UNESCO Culture of

Peace Programme for the elaboration of an operational concept of a culture of peace. These have included the Roundtable of Eminent Persons on 'An Agenda for Peace: A Challenge for UNESCO' in Paris in July 1993, the First International Forum on a Culture of Peace in February 1994 in El Salvador, and the First Consultative Meeting of the Culture of Peace Programme in Paris in September 1994. A Second International Forum was held in November 1995 in the Philippines, where an expert group meeting on women's contribution to a culture of peace had also been hosted in April 1995. The results of these forums have contributed greatly to the evolving concept of a culture of peace.

UNESCO'S CULTURE OF PEACE PROGRAMME

UNESCO has engaged in activities to promote a culture of peace from its beginning, when it was founded in the aftermath of the Second World War to construct the defences of peace in the minds of men and women.

As early as the fifth session of its General Conference, it was noted that 'all UNESCO's work in every field is directed to securing improved international understanding'. However, with the end of the Cold War and the renewed capacity of the UN Security Council to make decisions by consensus, it became evident that a new approach was needed which would review institutions and functions long serving a culture of war and to transform them into instruments for peace.

1989: Meeting in Yamoussoukro, Côte d'Ivoire, in July, the International Congress on Peace in the Minds of Men called for UNESCO to help construct a new vision of peace by developing a peace culture.

1992: An operational programme for promotion of a culture of peace was presented to the 140th session of UNESCO's Executive Board (document 140 EX/28). Placed in the framework of *An Agenda for Peace,* which had recently been published by United Nations Secretary-General Boutros Boutros-Ghali, it proposed local activities of reconciliation and co-operation in countries where peace-keeping operations had been implemented or could be anticipated.

1993: At the twenty-seventh session of UNESCO's General Conference, Member States enthusiastically supported the proposal for an Action Programme to Promote a Culture of Peace, emphasizing the need for concrete action as well as theory. They stressed the linkage between a culture of peace and a culture of democracy and human rights. As a result, provisions for the Culture of Peace Programme were included in UNESCO's Programme and Budget for 1994–95.

1994: On 1 February the Director-General established a unit for a Culture of Peace Programme under his direct authority. In establishing this, he allocated to it a number of functions in addition to the elucidation of the concept, as described above. These functions include:
- provision of an integrated approach to activities in the various units and field offices of UNESCO which contribute to the promotion of a culture of peace;
- development of national and subregional programmes of a culture of peace;
- coordination of these activities with those of the United Nations system and of intergovernmental and non-governmental organizations.

In order to provide an integrated approach to UNESCO's activities for a culture of peace, an intersectoral committee was established in April 1994, chaired by the Director-General and comprising high-level sectoral representatives. In addition, consultations concerning joint activities are held regularly between the staff of the Culture of Peace Programme and other units at Headquarters and in the field. Some of these activities are initiated by the Culture of Peace Programme.

National programmes of a culture of peace are under way in El Salvador, Mozambique and Burundi. These will be described in the following section along with a number of other related national initiatives.

Finally, in order to co-ordinate these activities with those of other institutions, the Culture of Peace Programme is developing an information and networking system to link up the many organizations promoting a culture of peace. The hope is that this movement will take on a life of its own and become a self-sustaining irreversible transformation process from a culture of war to a culture of peace. This is why the programme emphasizes education, training and deployment of individual 'peace promoters' and the transformation and development of institutions and organizations to promote a culture of peace.

UNESCO'S SECTORAL ACTIVITIES PROMOTING A CULTURE OF PEACE

The Culture of Peace Programme aims at stimulating and co-ordinating the many activities in UNESCO's different sectors which are making significant contributions to a culture of peace. The programme works closely with them, making recommendations to avoid obvious overlap, signalling gaps which could be covered, and helping to develop new initiatives which can play a catalytic role in the development of a culture of peace.

The number of UNESCO activities promoting a culture of peace is very large; therefore, rather than trying to list all of them here, only a few are given as illustrations from each sector of the Organization.

In its work in the Education Sector, UNESCO works directly with the educational systems of its Member States through the International Conference on Education (ICE) and through the International Institute for Educational Planning (IIEP). In its role as the lead agency for the global programme of *Education for All*, UNESCO promotes the goal of universal basic education which is of good quality and relevant to the tasks of our time.

At the 44th session of the ICE, held in Geneva in October 1994, over 800 people, including some 100 ministers and deputy ministers of education, devoted their energies to improving education for international understanding, including a culture of peace. In the Declaration on Education for Peace, Human Rights and Democracy subsequently adopted by the ICE, ministers agreed 'to base education on principles and methods that contribute to the development of the personality of pupils, students and adults who are respectful of their fellow human beings and determined to promote peace, human rights and democracy' and pledged to take steps to ensure that educational institutions become 'ideal places' to practice tolerance.

Teachers play a key role in creating a culture of peace because of their direct involvement with the training of the next generation, as well as their contacts with parents and the surrounding community. Curricula will be updated to ensure an approach to ethnic, racial and cultural differences among peoples which emphasize their unique contributions to the enrichment of a common heritage. History will be taught in a way that gives as much emphasis to non-violent social change as to military conquests. Human rights teaching will lead to the development of a sense of loyalty to the family, the community, the cultural group, the nation and the planet.

A pillar of UNESCO's educational activities aimed at promoting a culture of peace is the Associated Schools Project (ASP), which promotes the teaching of peace, justice, solidarity and international co-operation, through links with some 3,200 schools, at pre-primary, primary and secondary level, in over 120 countries. In celebrating in 1995 the fiftieth Anniversary of the United Nations and of UNESCO, as well as the United Nations Year for Tolerance, UNESCO has organized a series of subregional children's culture of peace festivals, sponsored jointly by the Culture of Peace Programme and the ASP. At the festivals, children from different countries between the ages of 11 and 13 gather for activities, discussion and drafting of an appeal to world leaders. It is expected that the festivals will launch an educational process which will allow the children to undertake specific actions to promote a culture of peace in their environment.

To directly address the rising problem of violence in major urban centres, a new project is being launched within the framework of the ASP and the Culture of Peace Programme. The Interregional Project of Schools to Promote Community Conflict Management in Violence-Prone Urban Areas will link up a network of schools located in cities plagued by violence, by which programmes are developed to train students, teachers and other staff, parents and the surrounding community in methods of mediation and non-violent conflict resolution. In these schools, training in mediation and conflict-management will be an integral part of the curriculum and of the activities of the surrounding communities.

For the coming years, UNESCO's Communication and Informatics Sector has defined a new strategy aimed at strengthening freedom of expression and the press, by achieving more balanced dissemination of information and increasing the communication capacities of developing countries. Only pluralistic and independent media providing access to all can ensure the free flow of ideas needed for the development of a global culture of peace. In pursuing this goal, UNESCO maintains close relations with professional press and journalists' organizations, and provides technical advisers to assist Member States in preparing media legislation and to propose structures for editorially independent public service broadcasting.

Specific projects in a number of countries, including Rwanda and Burundi, contribute directly to a culture of peace. In former Yugoslavia, UNESCO has supported independent media who bridge the ethnic divisions encouraged by other partisan media and which have contributed to a culture of violence in recent years. For example, newsprint and equipment were flown into Sarajevo to keep alive the independent newspaper *Oslobodenje,* which came to symbolize the multi-ethnic harmony of that city surrounded by intolerance and war. Also with the help of UNESCO, NTV 99, the only independent television station in Sarajevo, began broadcasting in early 1995, providing daily information and education programmes reflecting the multi-ethnic character of the city.

In the future, UNESCO will place a new emphasis on the educational and cultural dimensions of the media and on the problem of violence on the screen and its impact, especially on the young. With the 125th anniversary of the birth of Mahatma Gandhi as a fitting backdrop, an international roundtable on non-violence, tolerance and television was organized jointly in New Delhi in April 1994 by UNESCO's International Programme for the Development of Communication and the Indian Government. In emphasizing self-regulation, the round table singled out the guidelines used by the BBC for its television programming. These guidelines recognize that the need to provide programmes which reflect the diversity of life and which unavoidably include violence, must be 'kept in proportion along with the humour, celebration, warmth and kindliness which will also be depicted'. In the future one may hope that media guidelines emphasize non-violent solutions to conflict.

UNESCO's Sector of Social and Human Sciences, recognizing that a scientific approach to a culture of peace requires a process of research, development and evaluation of appropriate methodologies, as well as the dissemination of relevant findings, supports the collaboration of social scientists from around the world. For example, the International Peace Research Association (IPRA) was founded with support from UNESCO and has always maintained close ties to the Organization.

Of particular importance for a culture of peace are a series of scientific studies and declarations which address the various myths of race and violence which have led some to believe that inequality and war are natural states of humanity and therefore inevitable.

UNESCO and a culture of peace: promoting a global movement

Beginning in 1950, UNESCO supported a process in which scientists addressed the pseudo-scientific theories of the inequality of humanity and races which had been used to justify the doctrines leading to the Second World War. They asserted the fundamental unity of humanity and declared that we all belong to the same species. Scientists emphasized that the concept of race reflects a social image bound up with the physical appearance of individuals rather than a scientific fact based on specific biological data.

The Seville Statement on Violence was drafted for the United Nations International Year of Peace (1986) by an international team of scientists. They concluded that 'biology does not condemn humanity to war, and that humanity can be freed from the bondage of biological pessimism and empowered with the confidence to undertake the transformative tasks needed in this International Year of Peace and in the years to come'. UNESCO has publicized and disseminated the Statement as part of its programme of education for peace, human rights and democracy.

UNESCO also has a long tradition in adopting international instruments aimed at upholding human rights and the preparation and dissemination of teaching materials to make their provisions known to the widest possible audience. The International Congress on Education for Human Rights and Democracy, held in Montreal in March 1993, adopted a World Plan of Action based on the body of international human rights and humanitarian law and conceiving of human rights in their broadest sense to include learning about tolerance and acceptance of others, solidarity, participatory citizenship and the importance of building mutual respect and understanding.

Among the many recent initiatives for a culture of peace within the social sciences, one should mention the meetings on the contribution of religions to a culture of peace, organized with the UNESCO Catalunya Centre in Barcelona. At the 1994 meeting participants from all major religious traditions issued the Declaration on the Role of Religion in the Promotion of a Culture of Peace, calling upon all religious and cultural traditions to unite their efforts to spread the message of peace.

Since the foundation of the Organization, UNESCO's Culture Sector has worked to develop dialogue between cultures as an essential element of building a culture of peace. To cite one example, UNESCO's Silk Roads Project epitomizes the recognition of the important role that cultural tourism can play in increasing understanding between peoples. Since the project began in 1990, four international expeditions – the Desert Route, the Steppe Route, the Maritime Route and the Nomad's Route – have been undertaken and a fifth, retracing the Buddhist Route through Nepal, India, Pakistan and Central Asia to China, is now being prepared. Activities such as research programmes, exhibitions, publications and the setting up of research centres and institutions (for example, the International Institute for Central Asian Studies in Samarkand) have been stimulated by the expeditions.

The Silk Roads Project has inspired a number of related projects. One of them, the Slave Route, launched in the framework of the International Year of Tolerance, seeks to ensure that the slave trade is the subject of an international, multidisciplinary study, leading to a 'climate conducive to a revival of co-operation'. Another, the Roads of Faith, focuses on Jerusalem's 'eternal mission . . . to promote peace and understanding among people' (in the words of the resolution that created it). By concentrating on the roads of pilgrimage leading to the Holy City which have been travelled over the centuries, the project hopes to promote knowledge about the city's 'unique role in the world and its essential contribution to human dignity', so that 'a future more in keeping with the nature of Jerusalem can be realized'.

Through its Field Offices, UNESCO is able to promote a culture of peace at national and local levels in every corner of the globe. The UNESCO Office in Costa Rica, with the help of other offices in the region, has played a key role in the initiation of national culture of peace programmes in Central America. Their management is being handled by new Field Offices in El Salvador and Mozambique. To cite a few examples, the UNESCO Liaison Office in New York provides a constant source of dialogue between the programme and the various institutions of the United Nations system. In Asia, the Beijing Office has organized meetings on a culture of peace to which diplomats in that city were invited and which addressed issues such as 'How a culture of peace programme can be implemented in a multiracial, multicultural, multi-language country'.

In Africa, the Regional Office for Education (BREDA) has organized, in conjunction with the National Commission for UNESCO of Côte d'Ivoire, an interregional colloquium on 'Present-day Conflicts and the Culture of Peace'. In the Caribbean, the UNESCO Office in Kingston, Jamaica, has undertaken a series of symposia in the framework of a culture of peace to address the rising problems of alienation, crime and violence.

NATIONAL CULTURE OF PEACE PROGRAMMES

From its inception, the Culture of Peace Programme was called upon by the Executive Board and the Director-General to be an action programme. Therefore, in addition to its co-ordinating and information/networking functions, it has helped to initiate several national culture of peace programmes which put the concept of a culture of peace into daily practice on a national scale.

National culture of peace programmes provide a setting in which all sides of a conflict sit around the same table, to design and implement human development projects from which all the people in the country and the region can benefit. These programmes are based on building trust between all parties, often requiring reconciliation following conflict. This approach reflects the basic finding in social psychology that the most effective method of resolving conflict between two groups is to promote their co-operation toward a goal of mutual benefit.

Workers in the various development projects are trained to facilitate the process of participation, dialogue and co-operation using both traditional and universal principles and methods of conflict-management. In this way, they come to function as 'peace promoters', assuring that all sides of the conflict continue to participate and benefit from the development process.

Since a basic premise of the programme is that a culture of peace cannot be imposed, the training of peace promoters is based upon the study and use of traditional practices of conflict management. At the same time, training also stresses universal values such as those of the Universal Declaration of Human Rights and other related United Nations standard-setting instruments.

Recognizing that the work of the peace promoters is both difficult and essential to the success of a national programme, a network and support system is provided for peace-promoters which ensures the regular exchange of information, periodic updates of training curricula and mutual encouragement.

The evaluation of culture of peace projects is also a participatory process.

Whereas traditional methods of evaluation for development projects have emphasized the product of a project exclusively, a culture of peace ensures that evaluation also considers the process by which it was planned and implemented.

The Culture of Peace Programme is working with donor countries to develop an expanded methodology of project evaluation by which the analysis of the results achieved is combined with a qualitative and quantitative analysis of the participation of the various parties in planning and implementation of the project concerned. This analysis places a priority on teaching people from all sides of a conflict to work together in achieving goals which would be impossible working alone or in competition with each other.

In the first year of the Culture of Peace Programme, national programmes were launched in three countries: El Salvador in 1993 (that is prior to the formal establishment of CPP), Mozambique and Burundi. El Salvador and Mozambique were chosen because they were each engaged in a United-Nations-sponsored peace process, which included a formal peace accord and an extensive UN peace-keeping mission. Burundi was chosen because of the danger that it would undergo another period of extreme violence similar to that which had recently devastated its neighbour, Rwanda. Thus, from the beginning, UNESCO national culture of peace programmes have been closely linked to the full process of United Nations actions for peace

The pioneer national programme was launched in El Salvador in 1993. The people of El Salvador, at that time, were carrying out a process of national reconciliation based on the agreements in the 1992 Chapultepec Peace Accords. The accords had ended a bitter civil war between the government and the guerrilla movements united in the Farabundo Marti National Liberation Front (FMLN). UNESCO's initiatives were in the framework of a broad and extensive post-conflict peace-building programme of the United Nations, which had helped to broker the Peace Accords and which also included an extensive military peace-keeping operation.

From its beginning, UNESCO's culture of peace programme in El Salvador has been a process of consensus-building for co-operation in human development. The process was formalized in a Memorandum of Understanding following the Forum for Education and Culture of Peace held in San Salvador in April 1993. The forum was sponsored by the El Salvador Ministry of Education and

UNESCO, with the presence of the Director-General of UNESCO and broad participation of organizations from civil society, including representatives from the FMLN. Following the forum, UNESCO helped to mediate in a process wherein the former enemies worked together in the design of the programme and the planning and implementation of a series of human development projects for the benefit of all Salvadorian society. Each project was conceived through a participatory process and, once an expression of interest was obtained from donor countries, the detailed project document was elaborated in workshops involving all parties. A total of twenty-three projects have been proposed; by early 1995 seven had been elaborated as detailed project documents through joint governmental/non-governmental sessions. These include support to Salvadorian indigenous communities, programmes for disabled children and children affected by the armed conflict, support to Salvadorian youth, and literacy for a culture of peace, as well as a general information project for the programme.

One of the first projects to be implemented provides for national women's radio programmes and corresponds to the strategic guidelines which emphasize a national, co-ordinated approach and which gives priority to those who suffered most from the previous conflict. Women were especially affected, not only by violence but also by the economic crisis which followed. Mothers often lack adequate social support as regards legal resources, education, health, nutrition and other basic needs.

Radio, with its largely female audience, has been found to be an effective means of reaching the poorest women, very often illiterate, who are most in need of orientation, information and support. The project, with daily half-hour broadcasts, provides information about the services and activities available to women, seeking to increase their awareness of their basic rights and enable them to improve their lives. It should also serve to break down gender stereotypes which have been perpetuated in the past through the media.

A series of institutional structures have been created in order to ensure the participation process by which the radio project has been developed. The UNESCO CPP representative plays an essential role in the functioning as well as the establishment of each institution.

Bearing in mind that the aim of a culture of peace is to reconcile people and consolidate peace, the radio project must maintain a constant process of participation, dialogue and consensus. This naturally takes considerable time and many meetings to resolve the various conflicts which arise among the project actors in the course of their work. Although progress on many aspects of the project is necessarily slow, the decisions, once they are made, are 'owned' and hence supported by all of the participants.

During the course of the work on the radio project, the role of the UNESCO representative has developed from that of an arbitrator (between conflicting groups) to that of mediator and, finally, to that of facilitator, making possible the joint accomplishment of the common goal.

The progression – arbitration to mediation to facilitation – illustrates concretely what might be called a 'culture of peace process'. In its long-term development the CPP in El Salvador plans to train peace-promoters, including actors in the various projects, who are able to play the role of arbitrator/mediator/facilitator, involving all parties to conflicts in the planning and implementation process.

In response to the Rome Peace Accords of October 1992, the people of Mozambique responded spontaneously to build a culture of peace. The Peace Accords put an end to more than twenty-five years of armed struggle, first for liberation from the Portuguese colonial power and, second, in an armed conflict supported by foreign powers. The United Nations assisted in the demobilization of the two conflicting armies, the preparation of the national elections of October 1994 and the administration of humanitarian aid.

Within the context of these events, UNESCO's Culture of Peace Programme is designed to support the grassroots initiatives for peace of the Mozambican people, in a multi-stage process beginning with support for Mozambican non-governmental organizations (NGOs) working in this area. The programme was organized in its initial phase by the Mozambican National Commission for UNESCO. This phase was surveyed by a steering committee representing a broad range of interests ranging from government ministries to independent NGOs at times in opposition to the government.

In the first stage of the programme in 1994, a number of NGOs received support for projects of national and community mobilization and the gathering and dissemination of materials concerning the Mozambican experience with peace-making.

The second phase of the programme was designed in 1995. In this phase, eight projects have been identified for implementation on a national scale, aimed at elected and community leaders, demobilized soldiers, schoolchildren, rural women, culture and sports, the media and the development of science as a contribution to rural sustainable development.

The training of peace-promoters is based on traditional Mozambican peace-making practices as well as on universal principles of conflict management. For example, use is made of the tradition of the *milando,* which is a variant of the palaver found in many traditional African cultures. Among the Makua people of Mozambique the *milando* is a kind of judicial process in the form of a public debate presided over by the chief and involving the parties in conflict and their families and neighbours. The *milando* employs a patient question-and-answer procedure which proceeds through the telling of traditional stories and proverbs by the two parties. Indirectly, in this manner, they approach the causes of the conflict, weaving around it a web of traditional wisdom, to the point that the resolution of the conflict becomes self-evident.

The first project to be implemented in the second phase of the Mozambique programme provides for the newly-elected Mozambican parliament – the Assembly of the Republic – to reflect on democracy, human rights and peace-building. This project is of special significance because the FRELIMO government has had an uneasy relationship with the opposition RENAMO party, which received 45 per cent of the vote in the October 1994 elections. A group of twelve parliamentarians, representing a cross-section of all the parties and all provinces, travelled to South Africa and Malawi to meet with parliamentarians there and to closely examine the ways they have found to co-operate in the creation of social legislation. The study visit and ensuing process is being recorded and publicized broadly by the media as a form of popular education in peace and democracy.

In December 1994, a national culture of peace programme was launched in Burundi, with the opening of a House of a Culture of Peace, staffed by a multi-ethnic team. A House of a Culture of Peace, such as the one in Burundi, is the symbolic expression of the national desire for peace and, at the same time, the material structure with the means and institutional power to put it into practice.

The first event in the Burundi programme, after the opening of the House of a Culture of Peace, was a national forum involving 160 leading political, religious and academic figures of the country from both ethnic groups and all strata of society. In addition to the Prime Minister, the forum was presided over by the Ministers of Secondary and Higher Education, Primary Education and Alphabetization, and Culture, Youth and Sports. The forum made a series of recommendations in education and communication, upon which further development of the programme is being based.

The training of peace promoters in Burundi is patterned after the tradition of *bashingantahe,* men known for their integrity in their daily life who were formerly chosen by the community to mediate conflicts and to guarantee moral values. This tradition has to be revived. Because they represented a counterforce to colonialism, they were suppressed by colonial administrations and by the governments which succeeded them after independence.

The House of the Culture of Peace in Bujumbura, in the few months since it was opened, has already become a centre for many individuals and groups who wish to join in working for peace. Despite the violence which presently afflicts the city, work continues on seminars for a culture of peace with journalists, government administrators, educators and representatives from other agencies, from the United Nations system, as well as governmental and non-governmental organizations.

The search for funding for national programmes has proved to be the most difficult part of the process. Faced with limited funds and increased demands for development assistance, major donors complain of 'donor fatigue'. The Culture of Peace Programme finds itself in competition for the attention and priority of donors.

However, if ex-combatants are to lay aside their mistrust and commit themselves to building a new society, we have an obligation to support this process. If not, there is a risk of disillusionment and a return to violence, and we may lose the opportunity to set out on a new path to peace, with benefits for every country in the world, in industrialized and developing countries alike. If we are to achieve peace, we must pay the price. A culture of peace will not be achieved until the present emphasis on military peace-keeping is matched by a commitment at least as great to non-violent peace-building.

Where can these funds be found? Despite the end of the Cold War, the majority of funds, within countries and worldwide, is still directed towards military solutions. The resources devoted by nations to the military are the equivalent of the total income of half of the world's population. While the United Nations devotes 80 per cent of its resources to peace-keeping and emergency assistance, it provides relatively little to conflict prevention and peace-building. For these reasons, the success of national culture of peace programmes ultimately depends upon a global reallocation of priorities in which international organizations and their Member States place a much greater emphasis on peace-building and a culture of peace.

OTHER NATIONAL PROGRAMMES AND INITIATIVES

The UNESCO Culture of Peace Programme has provided support to other national initiatives which unite parties to long-standing conflict in a process of reconciliation and peace-building. These include national culture of peace programmes in Nicaragua, Honduras and the Philippines, a national forum of reconciliation in the Congo, and forums for a culture of peace in Sudan and with Somali intellectuals. In all of these cases the basic principles remain similar to those listed above for national culture of peace programmes.

THE EMERGING MOVEMENT AND VISION OF A CULTURE OF PEACE

The United Nations and its Specialized Agencies, and especially UNESCO, are taking the lead in the building of a culture of peace. *An Agenda for Development*, presented by the Secretary-General to the General Assembly in May 1994, begins from the standpoint that peace and development are inseparable; at the same time that 'Development is the most secure basis for peace', peace is seen as the foundation for development.

Pulling up the roots of conflict goes beyond immediate post-conflict requirements and the repair of war-torn societies. The underlying conditions that led to conflict must be addressed. As the causes of conflict are varied, so must be the means of addressing them. Peace-building means fostering a culture of peace.

Increasingly, regional and other intergovernmental organizations are also shifting their priorities to conflict resolution, long-term peace-building and the building of democratic institutions, all of which are essential for a culture of peace.

In addition to the national initiatives linked directly to UNESCO's Culture of Peace Programme that have been mentioned here, there are many similar initiatives by other countries.

Nevertheless, the most extensive work for a culture of peace is perhaps being accomplished by non-governmental organizations throughout the world. Every day the Culture of Peace Programme is contacted by individuals and organizations taking actions to promote a culture of peace and seeking to link up with others from around the world with similar goals and experiences. In many cases the UNESCO programme is requested to provide advice and support to these efforts, which gives the programme a multiplier effect throughout the world. The extent of spontaneous activities for a culture of peace by non-governmental organizations confirms the expectation that a culture of peace is becoming a global movement in which every person has an important role to play.

In order to facilitate and inform this global movement, the Culture of Peace Programme is developing an information and networking system. Data about the activities of various organizations are entered into a computerized system and will be used in periodic publications, including a newsletter which is expected to be sent out two or three times a year. The programme also disseminates information on its own activities, including a brochure and occasional publications and reports.

The information and networking task is seen as essential because, in the final analysis, the task of constructing a culture of peace is accomplished by the work of thousands of individuals, operating on their own or through some institutional structure, and acting on the basis of their own consciousness. For this consciousness to develop, information, vision and a sense of purpose and optimism are crucial. A vision is beginning to emerge from the combined efforts of all those working together in this common task. It is a vision which can give purpose to the coming generation, which has both a responsibility and an opportunity greater than any that has gone before – the transition from a culture of war to a culture of peace.

Annex I. Declaration on the Role of Religion in the Promotion of a Culture of Peace

We, participants in the meeting 'The Contribution by Religions to the Culture of Peace', organized by UNESCO and the Centre UNESCO de Catalunya, which took place in Barcelona from 12 to 18 December 1994,
Deeply concerned with the present situation of the world, such as increasing armed conflicts and violence, poverty, social injustice and structures of oppression,
Recognizing that religion is important in human life,
Declare:

OUR WORLD

1. We live in a world in which isolation is no longer possible. We live in a time of unprecedented mobility of peoples and intermingling of cultures. We are all interdependent and share an inescapable responsibility for the well-being of the entire world.

2. We face a crisis which could bring about the suicide of the human species or bring us a new awakening and a new hope. We believe that peace is possible. We know that religion is not the sole remedy for all the ills of humanity, but it has an indispensable role to play in this most critical time.

3. We are aware of the world's cultural and religious diversity. Each culture represents a universe in itself and yet it is not closed. Culture gives religions their language, and religions offer ultimate meaning to each culture. Unless we recognize pluralism and respect diversity, no peace is possible. We strive for the harmony which is at the very core of peace.

4. We understand that culture is a way of seeing the world and living in it. It also means the cultivation of those values and forms of life which reflect the world-views of each culture. Therefore neither the meaning of peace nor of religion can be reduced to a single and rigid concept, just as the range of human experience cannot be conveyed by a single language.

5. For some cultures, religion is a way of life, permeating every human activity. For others its represents the highest aspirations of human existence. In still others, religions are institutions that claim to carry a message of salvation.

6. Religions have contributed to the peace of the world, but they have also led to division, hatred and war. Religious people have too often betrayed the high ideals they themselves have preached. We feel obliged to call for sincere acts of repentance and mutual forgiveness, both personally and collectively, to one another, to humanity in general, and to Earth and all living beings.

PEACE

7. Peace implies that love, compassion, human dignity and justice are fully preserved.

8. Peace entails that we understand that we are all interdependent and related to one another. We are all individually and collectively responsible for the common good, including the well-being of future generations.

9. Peace demands that we respect Earth and all forms of life, especially human life. Our ethical awareness requires setting limits to technology. We should direct our efforts towards eliminating consumerism and improving the quality of life.

10. Peace is a journey – a never-ending process.

COMMITMENT

11. We must be at peace with ourselves; we strive to achieve inner peace through personal reflection and spiritual growth, and to cultivate a spirituality which manifests itself in action.

12. We commit ourselves to support and strengthen the home and family as the nursery of peace.

Annex 1. Declaration on the Role of Religion in the Promotion of a Culture of Peace

IN HOMES AND FAMILIES, COMMUNITIES, NATIONS AND THE WORLD

13. We commit ourselves to resolve or transform conflicts without using violence, and to prevent them through education and the pursuit of justice.

14. We commit ourselves to work towards a reduction in the scandalous economic differences between human groups and other forms of violence and threats to peace, such as waste of resources, extreme poverty, racism, all types of terrorism, lack of caring, corruption and crime.

15. We commit ourselves to overcome all forms of discrimination, colonialism, exploitation and domination and to promote institutions based on shared responsibility and participation. Human rights, including religious freedom and the rights of minorities, must be respected.

16. We commit ourselves to assure a truly humane education for all. We emphasize education for peace, freedom and human rights, and religious education to promote openness and tolerance.

17. We commit ourselves to a civil society which respects environmental and social justice. This process begins locally and continues to national and transnational levels.

18. We commit ourselves to work towards a world without weapons and to dismantle the industry of war.

RELIGIOUS RESPONSIBILITY

19. Our communities of faith have a responsibility to encourage conduct imbued with wisdom, compassion, sharing, charity, solidarity and love, inspiring one and all to choose the path of freedom and responsibility. Religions must be a source of helpful energy.

20. We will remain mindful that our religions must not identify themselves with political, economic or social powers, so as to remain free to work for justice and peace. We will not forget that confessional political regimes may do serious harm to religious values as well as to society. We should distinguish fanaticism from religious zeal.

21. We will favour peace by countering the tendencies of individuals and

communities to assume or even to teach that they are inherently superior to others. We recognize and praise the non-violent peacemakers. We disown killing in the name of religion.

22. We will promote dialogue and harmony between and within religions, recognizing and respecting the search for truth and wisdom that is outside our religion. We will establish dialogue with all, striving for a sincere fellowship on our earthly pilgrimage.

APPEAL

23. Grounded in our faith, we will build a culture of peace based on non-violence, tolerance, dialogue, mutual understanding and justice. We call upon the institutions of our civil society, the United Nations System, governments, governmental and non-governmental organizations, corporations and the mass media, to strengthen their commitment to peace and to listen to the cries of the victims and the dispossessed. We call upon the different religious and cultural traditions to join hands together in this effort, and to co-operate with us in spreading the message of peace.

Annex II. Advisory Board for UNESCO's series on Peace and Conflict Issues

Francisco BARAHONA
Rector a.i.
University for Peace
Apartado 138
Ciudad Colón
Costa Rica

Mohamed BENNOUNA
Director-General
Institut du Monde Arabe
1, rue des Fossés St Bernard
75005 Paris
France

Hans Günter BRAUCH
Chairman, AFES-PRESS
Alte Bergsteige 47
74821 Mosbach
Germany

Kevin P. CLEMENTS
Director
Institute for Conflict Analysis and Resolution
Georges Mason University
Fairfax, VA 22030
United States

René-Jean DUPUY
6, rue Le Goff
75005 Paris
France

Vasu GOUNDEN
Director
African Centre for the Constructive Resolution of Disputes
c/o University of Durban Westville
Private Bag X54001
Durban 4000
South Africa

Heitor GURGULINO DE SOUZA
Rector
The United Nations University
53-70, Jingumae, 5-chome
Shibuya-ku
Tokyo-170
Japan

Guido LENZI
Director
Western European Union
Institute for Security Studies
43, avenue du Président Wilson
75775 Paris Cedex 16
France

Félix MARTI
Director
Centre UNESCO de Catalunya
Mallorca, 285
08037 Barcelona
Spain

Annex II. Advisory Board for UNESCO's series on Peace and Conflict Issues

Sanāa W. Osseiran
Vice-President
International Peace Research Association (IPRA)
Farah Bldg, Makhoul Street
Ras-Beirut
Beirut
Lebanon

Adam Daniel Rotfeld
Director
Stockholm International Peace Research Institute (SIPRI)
Frösunda
S-171 53 Solna
Sweden

Kumar Rupesinghe
Secretary-General
International Alert
1, Glyn Street
London
United Kingdom

Yoshikazu Sakamoto
International Peace Research Institute Meigaku (PRIME)
1518 Kamikurata
Totsukaku-Yokohama 244
Japan

Dan Smith
Director
International Peace Research Institute (PRIO)
Fuglenauggata, 11
N-0260 Oslo 2
Norway

Juan SOMAVIA
Ambassador
Permanent Mission of Chile to the United Nations
305 East 47th Street, 10th Floor
New York, NY 10017
United States

Janusz SYMONIDES
Director
Division of Human Rights, Democracy and Peace
UNESCO
Paris
France

Anatoly TORKOUNOV
Rector
Moscow State Institute of International Relations of Foreign Affairs
Ministry of the Russian Federation
76, Vernadskovo Avenue
117854 Moscow
Russian Federation

Lev VORONKOV
Director
International Institute for Peace
Möllwaldplatz 5
A-1040 Vienna
Austria

Secretary:
Kishore SINGH
Division of Human Rights, Democracy and Peace
UNESCO
Paris
France